WEALTH

Unlock the secrets to creating and protecting black family prosperity!

James L. Marshall, Jr.

///trimarkpress

The FAQ's portion of this book
was written by Hillel L. Presser, Esq.

This book is intended for general information purposes only. While the publisher and authors have utilized their best efforts in preparing this book, they make no claims or warranties with respect to the accuracy or completeness of the contents. The information may not be applicable to you and is intended for general demonstration purposes only. There are many exceptions to the general principles stated herein. Before you apply or act on this or any other legal, investment, funding, tax, insurance or other financial information you should consult with a financial planner who can evaluate the facts of your specific situation and advise you on the proper course of action based on that evaluation.

***Note to readers:** Personal situations are uniquely different. Investments, taxes and estate planning concepts addressed in this book are complex subjects. With this in mind, please be sure to consult with a qualified tax, estate and/or investment advisor(s). In addition some of the information included within this book might be outdated.*

ISBN: 978-0-9886145-3-6
Library of Congress Control Number: 2013933157

Printed and bound in the United States of America

Marshall Wealth Management, LLC
7322 Southwest Freeway, Suite #1940
Houston, TX 77074
832-740-4148
marshallcapitalmgmt.com

Published by TriMark Press, Inc.
368 South Military Trail · Deerfield Beach, FL 33442
800-889-0693
www.TriMarkPress.com

About the Author

James L. Marshall, Jr. has been in the investment management industry for over 20 years. He started his career with Merrill Lynch in 1988 as a stockbroker trainee and then moved to Washington, DC to work for New York Life, where he began to realize the importance of educating the black community about comprehensive wealth building.

James converted these early years of training into a successful 9 year career with American Express Financial Advisors before starting Marshall Capital Management Group, a wholly owned Registered Investment Advisory Firm in April 2001. During this period he has reached great heights in the industry by qualifying for the last 7 years straight into the Million Dollar Round Table, which consist of the top 5 percent of all producing insurance agents. The last three of those seven years he has qualified for the Top of the Table designation, which is the top 1 percent of producing insurance agents. James says that he has been able to accomplish this level of success by staying committed to educating the black community about the wealth building process.

After graduating from Western Kentucky University and the Kentucky Military Academy, James realizes the importance of continuing his formal education.

James continues his involvement with Western Kentucky University by serving on the WKU Foundation Board and the Board of Advisors to the President. His commitment to encouraging more African Americans to choose a career in financial planning has led him to establish the J.L Marshall Living and Learning Community at Western Kentucky University, Gordon School of Business.

Of all the blessing's God has bestowed on James Marshall, Jr., the greatest is his family. He is married to Donna Lacy Marshall, and together they have two beautiful girls, Zoë and Ava.

Table of Contents

Introduction 7

Financial Needs Assesment 57

Section One: *Investing* 69

Section Two: *Taxes* 135

Section Three: *Estate Planning* 177

Section Four: *Retirement Planning and Social Security* 215

Section Five: *Insurance and Risk Management* 271

Section Six: *Choosing Your Advisor* 307

Glossary 315

Index 331

I dedicate this book to

the women of my life: Donna, Zoë and Ava

Introduction

Over the last 25 years, I have helped hundreds of families in their attempt to build, protect and transfer wealth. Along the way I have developed the ability to predict with some certainty which family will fail and which one will succeed.

The successful family is the family that approaches wealth building as a partnership, a team; with each member doing his/her part; but one member taking the lead. As the saying goes, "The family that plans together, stays together".

This book is based on some of the knowledge I have accumulated from advising diverse families in wealth building strategies over the past 25 years. It is meant to provide you with a basic foundation for understanding the concepts of building and protecting wealth.

Once you complete this book you will be ready to construct your own personalized family wealth book, by utilizing our comprehensive family wealth planning system. This system is a very effective tool that will give your immediate and extended family the guidance, encouragement and resources you need to build wealth. Wealth not only for you and your family today, but for generations to come! Go to *www.blackfamilywealth.com* for more information on the family wealth planning system.

We start with my basic rules of wealth building:

- Build wealth instead of living wealthy
- If you can't afford it, you don't need it
- A dollar earned is a dime saved
- Dig your well before you're thirsty

- Insurance is your friend
- Minimize taxes, maximize wealth
- Pigs get fat and hogs get slaughtered
- Diversify, diversify, diversify
- Ownership, ownership, ownership
- Pass it on

I am convinced that most anyone can build wealth. The question is what is your definition of wealth? What is wealth to you?

Wealth is relative. It is personal and unique to the person or family trying to accumulate it. The most common mistake and source of frustration for people trying to build wealth, is buying into other peoples definitions of wealth.

Some people consider themselves wealthy because they live in a very expensive house, drive an expensive car and travel around the globe. Others believe they are wealthy simply because they are able to pay their bills on time. And there are those that believe wealth is about spirituality, good health or family and friend relationships.

I believe wealth is a combination of these things, and I call it wellness.

Wellness is the holistic approach to wealth, which includes a supportive and loving family, good health and a healthy lifestyle. Personal growth through education, self improvement and financial stability. Most of all, it is having a strong spiritual foundation.

In the following pages I will educate you about the basic concepts of building wealth, and encourage you to take action now! But, first things first; our prayer.

We have written a prayer as a part of our "Faith, Family & Finances" workshop series; and it may help you in your journey to achieve wellness.

My Lord and Savior,

Help me to remember, God, that my money, my possessions, my riches belong to You. May I use it for Your glory. Keep me from making it the center of my life. Lord, please help me to use the fruits of the spirit in my walk with You. Wisdom, discernment and understanding are what You gave Solomon and we are asking for the same. Lord keep us and guide us, because You said if we put You in everything we do, You would direct our paths the right way. We believe and have faith in Your promises. Assist us in keeping a balance in our lives through our faith, family and finances. We ask these things in the precious name of Jesus...Amen

Now let's get started!

What is wealth and how do you get it for yourself, your family, and your community?

The statistics about the economics of the African American community are recited often:

- Average net worth = approximately $6,000 to $12,000

- Average household income = approximately $29,000 to $33,000

- Average consumer debt = approximately $ 18,000

We appear to be way behind and losing ground! Doom and gloom, doom and gloom! As singing legend Marvin Gaye sang in the 1970's, "It makes you want to holla and throw up both your hands!"

According to the media, African Americans are sliding down a slippery slope into a pool of despair.

And they appear to be right. And if they are right, how did we get to this point?

Picture a heated saucepan of water on a stovetop, hot to the touch. Now imagine placing a live, healthy frog in the heated water. No surprise! The frog leaps out of the pan, recognizing the immediate danger and the threat to its survival.

Now, imagine placing the same frog into a pan of room-temperature water. Let the frog settle in. Then, very gradually, start turning up the heat, starting at very low temperature settings. Feeling complacent and comfortable, the frog won't realize that the temperature is gradually getting hotter. It gets more and more groggy, less and less conscious, until it eventually succumbs after being virtually "boiled to death."

We became too preoccupied with living wealthy instead of building wealth; we sought the *ideal* of wealth instead of the process of attaining it. We got caught up in Madison Avenue's vision of wealth for us, instead of our own vision of wealth for us, all along not realizing we were being boiled to death – boiled to death by high interest credit card debt, buying stuff we didn't need...boiled to death by purchasing high ticket depreciating items meant to *symbolize* wealth, as opposed to adding to our wealth. (Big hat; no cattle!)

So now here we are being squeezed out by a global economy and a government that appears to be focused only on making the rich richer.

I say this realizing that a lot of you are rich, but what about your children? A lot of you are secure, but what about your siblings? A lot of you have wealth, but what about your community?

- Have your kids seen your family wealth plan?

- Do they understand your business plan?

- Is your succession plan in sync with your will?

- Have you established a family bank to help advance the wealth of your extended family?

- Does your church have a 10 or 20-year endowment fund or a financial literacy program?

Are you building wealth or are you living wealthy?

Booker T. Washington said:

"At the bottom of education, at the bottom of politics, even at the bottom of religion... there must be for our race economic independence."

Economic independence is wealth. Wealth = Success and Poverty = Failure!

I am not talking about individual wealth or poverty; I am talking about community wealth or poverty (collective economics).

So how do you define wealth? I define it as wellness, health, and spirituality. In a word: Stewardship! Wealth is the proper care and management of God's blessings to you – happiness!

Happiness is a state of mind, not a destination, and wealth is an important part of the foundation upon which it is built. I call it wellness: wealth, health and spirituality, and it is attainable through diligent, disciplined and focused planning.

Every plan must start with a vision – a mental snapshot of the future as you would have it. The good news is that it is your vision, your future and you are free to make it a reality. The world you want to live in starts with you!

"Where there is no vision, the people perish…" *Proverbs 29:18*

The book of Proverbs in the Bible represents one of the most ancient forms of instruction that is commonly called the "Wisdom Literature." It provides vision, goals, and direction on how to live a good life. Read it!

This book among other things, is about the financial aspect of wealth building and the foundation of basic knowledge needed to create and protect your family's wealth.

And just like building a house, the foundation on which it is built is critical. You cannot effectively build the foundation however, without a clear vision of the finished product. What will it look like? How big will it be? How will it be positioned on the plot? How will the uncontrollable forces of nature like wind, sun, and water drainage, be considered in the house construction?

You must begin with the end in mind.

In wealth building, you must also begin with the end in mind. **What Do You Want For Yourself (and for your family)? What is your WDYWFY?**

Goal-oriented people have a much better chance of success than those flying by the seat of their pants. I have identified five simple concepts that can further increase your chances for financial success:

- Set short-term, intermediate, and long-term goals

- Be realistic

- Establish time frames

- Devise a plan

- Be flexible: Goals can change.

The best defined goal however, means nothing without structure. And structure in wealth building means adhering to the four cornerstones of wealth building.

WEALTH-BUILDING CORNERSTONES

1. Cash Reserves

2. Protection

3. Fixed Assets

4. Equity Assets

Built upon these cornerstones is the concept of financial planning.

This book will help you to begin and sustain your Family Wealth Building Campaign. But before we begin, there are ten things that must be done:

1. Pray for clarity and good judgment. We make a lot of decisions every day, and Lord knows that a lot of them are the wrong decisions. So just remember you cannot make it alone. Prayer works!

2. Never start the day without a plan! The more you control your time, energy, and resources, the greater your chances of accomplishing your goals.

3. Establish clear, well-defined and measurable goals! If you don't know where you are going, any road will get you there and you will not know if you're lost.

4. Build and maintain a strong financial foundation! Have you ever seen a house built upside down? You have to start with the foundation, and your financial foundation is insurance, cash reserves and good spending habits.

    *   **Insurance:** We could totally change our economic landscape with the proper amount of life insurance. Stop worrying about some other brother or sister sliding in chumming up with your family and spending what you left behind; or the possibility that the kids might squander the money. There are ways to guard against all of that. Just do the right thing and advance the baton with a lead! Get properly insured.

    *   **Cash reserves:** You must maintain three to six months living and business expenses in liquid accounts for emergencies and/ or opportunities. This keeps you from negating the effects of compounded interest on your wealth accumulation accounts, as well as helps to minimize your use of consumer debt.

    *   **The ultimate good spending habit:** Spend less than what you make! The Marshall Wealth Management Cash Flow Model is: Tithe 10 percent, save 10 percent, invest 5 percent and debt reduction 25 percent (as debt is reduced, redirect debt reduction dollars to investments). Live off of the rest!

5. Establish a family wealth plan with action steps that can be reviewed quarterly. This includes cash flow management, debt reduction, protection planning, tax reduction strategies, college savings, retirement savings, and estate planning. Hold an annual meeting with the family to review this plan. Make a **big deal** of it; perhaps in conjunction with a family vacation.

6. If you own a business, create and update a working business plan quarterly; with valuation, balance sheet and cash flow statements. Your business must be treated like all other equity holdings in your family wealth plan. It must be analyzed at least quarterly and adjusted as needed. You must know the value of your business!

7. Adapt, modernize and improve. As the saying goes, if you always do what you've always done, you will always get what you've always gotten! Take classes, go to conferences, and read as much about business management and wealth building as you can.

8. Talk to your parents, aunties, uncles, siblings, and cousins about establishing a family bank, holding company or trust to help progress family wealth. Imagine the benefit of a family holding company that could step in and purchase the home of a cousin that has fallen on hard times. Perhaps the company could then rent it back to the cousin and allow him time to bounce back from the setback and repurchase his home, thereby avoiding foreclosure.

9. Get involved with the business of your church! Most churches stopped holding business meetings because they could not get enough people to meet the quorum. Help the leadership be more forward thinking by establishing 10, 20, or 30-year endowment funds to assure the financial viability of the church for years to come. Help them to free the church from its dependence on loans and federal grants that often come with hidden agendas.

10. Thank God each and every day for another day's journey, and another opportunity to be a good steward of whatever blessings he has given you!

THE HIVE
BLACK FAMILY WEALTH BUILDING SYSTEM™

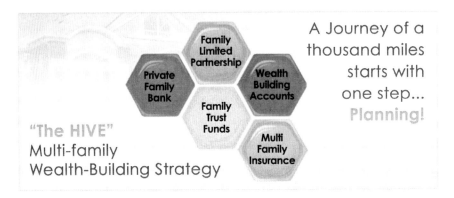

This is a multi-family wealth building concept that uses family cooperatives, family banks, Trust owned life insurance and accumulation accounts to advance family wealth through multiple generations—helping yourself and your family, while you strengthen the Community.

Before we get into the case study, let's learn a little about these concepts.

Family Cooperative: A family business or entity owned jointly by all its members or workers, who share all profits equally. In this case all the separate family units combining under one organized cooperative

Family Bank: A special account that keeps pooled family money for individual family members, family units or family run companies. It makes loans, and offers other financial services.

Family Trust: A trust into which the trustor places assets to be distributed to family members or units following his/her death. Specifically, a family trust does not name the trustor's spouse as a beneficiary. The benefit is to control family assets beyond the death of the original trustor's.

Life Insurance: A plan under which regular payments are made to a company during somebody's lifetime, and in return the company pays a specific sum to the person's beneficiaries after the person's death. In this case the beneficiary will be the family trust.

Accumulation accounts: Savings and/or investment accounts that are designed to grow family assets over time by investing in stocks, bonds, exchanged traded funds, money market savings account, CD's, etc.

Founders: Elder family members that currently benefit from the family wealth building system by way of income, healthcare assistance and long term care. The Elders also fund the trust with life insurance proceeds.

Directors: Are the brain trust of the Colony. They are responsible for the overall direction and growth of the Colony.

Managing Director: This is the family member that is responsible for the day to day management of the family trust, cooperative or limited partnership. They work directly with the financial advisor and other professional advisors.

Managers: The managers are the working bees of The Colony, they are very stable and usually have the highest income. This income is needed to finance the wealth building and protection expenses of The Colony.

Shareholders: The youngest members of The Colony, They are the benefactors of The Family Wealth System. They bring a lot of technical knowledge to The Colony, and are expected to repay The Colony for financing their future by growing the Families Wealth.

CASE STUDY FAMILY (CELL)

James & Gwen Williams (Founders)

James Williams is William Williams's brother. James & Gwen are the parents of Sharon Williams

- Age: James (80) Betty (79)
- Household income: $80,000/yr
- Household expenses: $40,000/yr
- Net worth: $2500 (assets have been moved to family trust)
- Monthly Trust contribution: $2,000

Profile: James died shortly after setting up the family wealth plan. He left a $1,000,000 insurance death benefit to the family trust. Gwen has transferred $800,000 in assets to the trust, including the house she is currently living in.

William & Doris Williams (Director)

William Williams, Sr. and Doris Williams are the parents of William, Jr. (Bill)

- Age: William (70) Doris (68)
- Household income: 40,000/yr
- Household expenses: $38,000/yr
- Net worth: $875,000
- Monthly Trust income: $500

Profile: Strong net worth with no debt, concerned about cash flow. William and Doris want to leave a strong family legacy for multiple generations. The Williams are in the process of transferring a $250,000 annuity policy to the trust. The trust owns a $500,000 life insurance policy on each of their lives.

William, Jr. (Bill) & Yvette Williams (Managing Director)

Bill is the son of William & Doris Williams. Bill & Yvette are the parents of Carole Williams-Smith

- Age: Bill (52) Yvette (51)
- Household income: $200,000/yr
- Household expenses: $125,000/yr
- Net worth: $600,000
- Monthly Trust contribution: $1000

Profile: Great cash flow and cash reserves; however, currently behind on retirement savings. They are concerned about taking care of their parents and healthcare cost. The trust owns $1,000,000 in life insurance on each of them. Bill and Yvette have the opportunity to supplement their retirement income with up to $25,000 per year from the trust when they reach age 65.

Mike & Carole Smith (Manager)

Mike is married to the daughter of William & Doris William, and the sister of Bill Williams. Yvette introduced the Smith name to the Colony

- Age: Mike (46) Carole (47)
- Household income: $150,000/yr
- Household expenses: $130,000/yr
- Net worth: $260,000
- Monthly Trust contribution: $750

Profile: Struggling middle class family, one paycheck away from financial ruin. Cash reserves are weak, and they have no health insurance. The trust owns $500,000 life insurance policies on each. Because of some recent financial hardship, the trust is currently paying their monthly mortgage payment for a year to allow them to build up a comfortable level of cash reserves and retirement savings. They have the opportunity to supplement their retirement income with up to $25,000 per year from the trust.

Sharon Williams (Manager)

Sharon Williams is the daughter of James & Gwen Williams, and the cousin of Bill Williams

- Age: 40
- Household income: $60,000/yr
- Household Expenses: $51,000/yr
- Net worth: $100,000
- Monthly Trust contribution: $500

Profile: Commission income (not steady). Single mother of a special needs child; and has a lot of healthcare related debt. The trust has a $1,000,000 life insurance policy on Sharon's life, and purchased her home to avoid foreclosure. She will buy it back for the loan amount when she is financially able. Also the trust paid off her daughter's medical bills.

Malik & Toni Smith (Shareholder)

Toni Williams-Smith is the Granddaughter of William & Doris Williams, and the daughter of Mike & Carole Smith

- Age: Malik (23) Toni (22)
- Household income: 58,000/yr
- Household expenses: $60,000/yr
- Net worth: -$25,000

Profile: Newlyweds, short on everything. They need help getting their first house, so the trust loaned them the money to put a 50% down payment on a starter home. The trust has a $1,000,000 on each of them.

Lesa Smith (shareholder)

Lesa is William & Doris granddaughter, and Mike & Carole's daughter. Lesa and Toni are sisters

- Age: 25
- Household income: $75,000/yr
- Household expenses: $48,000/yr
- Net worth: $37,000
- Monthly Trust contribution: $500

Profile: Young attorney, with excellent money management skills. She is very ambitious and family oriented. She is next in line to move into the Managing Director position in about 13 years. The trust has a $1,000,000 on Lesa.

Notes:

- Each member family should contribute at least 2% of their household income to the Colony

Potential Colony or Cooperative Family Trust activities:

- Supplement member family expenses as needed when approved by board of directors

- Make loans to members for home purchase, education, business start-ups, etc.
- Purchase troubled member family assets i.e home, investment property, business, etc.

Family Cooperative Trust kit:

- Legal documents: trust forms, account applications, corporate resolution and loan agreements.
- Sample letters and agreement templates
- Member assistance guidelines and request forms.

Meetings:

- Annual meeting for all member families (this should be in conjunction with family reunion)
- Quarterly board of directors meetings for updates and Executive Directors report
- Emergency meetings called by board members or Executive Director as needed

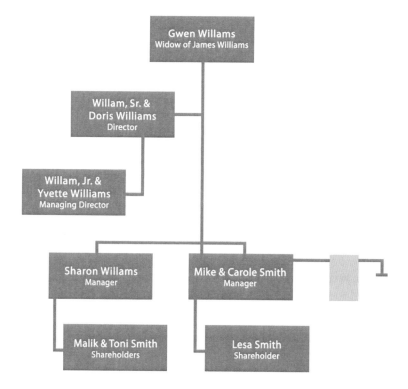

WILLIAMS – SMITH FAMILY TRUST
FINANCIAL PROFILE

Assets

Apartment Building	$700,000
Annuities	$500,000
Stock Portfolio	$250,000
Family Bank Cash-Management Account	$250,000
Houses	$250,000
Total	$1,950,000

Monthly Income ... $12,000.00

- Family Contributions ... $4,750.00
- Rental Income ... $6,250.00
- Investment Income ... $1,000.00

Monthly Expenses ... $12,000.00

- Life insurance premium ... $2,525.00
- Group health insurance premium ... $2,000.00
- Mortgages ... $3,275.00
- Family support ... $2,000.00
- Colony support ... $1,200.00
- Savings and Investments ... $1,000.00

HOW THE HIVE WORKS

The Hive contributes through the community cooperative trust to:

- **Credit Unions**
- **Small Business Investment Corporations**
- **Health Insurance Cooperatives**
- **Endowments**

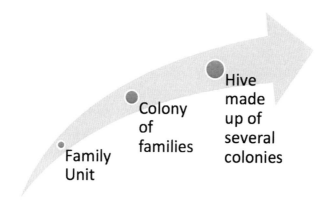

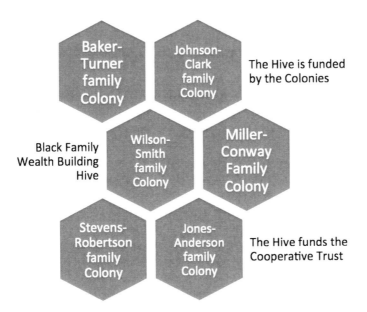

Example

This Colony contributes:

- $10,000 per month to "The Hive"
- $6,000,000 in life insurance proceeds to "The Hive"

Each adult in the Cell or family leaves at least $1,000,000 in life insurance proceeds to the next generation.

- Each Cell or family leaves at least $1,000,000 in life insurance proceeds to The Colony.
- Each Colony leaves at least $1,000,000 in life insurance proceeds to the Hive.
- Each generation is expected to double the families assets at a minimum.
- Family wealth is guaranteed and perpetual. The key is ongoing financial education and advice for the Cells, the Colony and the Hive.
- BlackFamilyWealth.com provides financial education through its Financial Planning Institute.
- Financial advice and Wealth management is provided by Marshall Wealth Management, LLC a registered investment advisory firm.

PROPOSAL AND INVESTMENT POLICY STATEMENT

Prepared for: William & Stacy Smith

Date: 10/01/2012

Proposal Name: Smith Family Wealth Accumulation
Plan

Proposal ID: P00003346609

Your Referring Financial Professional is: James Marshall
Marshall Wealth Management, Llc
629 S 4th St
Ste 302
Louisville, KY 40202
502-681-6264
james@marshallcapitalmgmt.com

CURIAN CAPITAL LLC

Proposal and Investment Policy Statement

Prepared for: William & Stacy Smith
Proposal ID: P00003346609
Page: 2 of 23   Date: October 1, 2012

Inside:

INTRODUCTION: Maximizing the opportunity to achieve your investment goals

STEP ONE: Setting personal objectives and identifying your risk profile

STEP TWO: Developing your asset allocation plan

STEP THREE: Creating your personalized Investment Policy Statement

STEP FOUR: Building and implementing your portfolio

STEP FIVE: Monitoring and adjusting your portfolio

STEP SIX: Communicating and rebalancing your portfolio

Other important information

Your suitability questionnaire and response summary

Acceptance and adoption of this proposal

A customized investment solution from Curian Capital, LLC

This proposal is a recommendation to engage Curian Capital, LLC's investment services for your account. Curian is an investment advisor that will be engaged to manage your account assets in accordance with the asset allocation strategy that you have selected in consultation with your Financial Professional.

Your Financial Professional can help guide you through the account opening process, provide information to you and answer questions that you may have about the investment proposal and Investment Policy Statement recommended by Curian, based on your responses to Curian's Suitability Process. However, please bear in mind that your Financial Professional is not authorized to provide investment advice in connection with the Curian Custom Style Portfolios. That is the role of Curian Capital® if you choose to open an account.

Proposal and Investment Policy Statement

Prepared for: William & Stacy Smith
Proposal ID: P00003346609
Page: 3 of 23   Date: October 1, 2012

Maximizing the opportunity to achieve your investment goals

As you look toward the future and outline goals for your life, it becomes clear that you will need a plan to meet those objectives. Without a plan, you leave your future to chance. And along the way, it is likely that you may face a number of challenges that may threaten your ability to meet your goals.

Your investment program should be designed to help you meet these challenges, providing an effective strategy to keep you on track toward pursuing your financial goals. Your plan should also help you set proper expectations for your investment strategy. This includes an understanding of the potential risks and rewards of the investment strategy you plan to pursue.

This proposal represents a carefully constructed and fully personalized financial strategy that is designed to reflect your needs, goals and expectations, while helping you to focus on your progress toward achieving your financial objectives.

Your Investment Policy Statement

This proposal is designed to facilitate a clear and comprehensive discussion of the recommended investment program for you to pursue your investment goals. It describes the investment process and an investment strategy designed to help you pursue your financial goals. It also includes a recommended asset allocation, as well as the specific money managers and implementation strategies that will be used to fulfill your proposed asset allocation.

Together, we can have a frank discussion of these investment recommendations, including risks and limitations, to help you make decisions to meet your personal situation and comfort level. As you review this proposal, please let us know if you have any questions or concerns.

Once you approve this proposal, this document will become your **Investment Policy Statement (IPS)**. This will be a written plan outlining your investment goals and how you plan to pursue them.

Your Custom Style Portfolio

The proposed investment solution is called a **Custom Style Portfolio**. The benefits of a Custom Style Portfolio include:

- A completely **customized portfolio**, based on your financial goals, needs, expectations, and investment beliefs and preferences.

- A **well-diversified portfolio** that may help reduce your exposure (risk) to any single part of the market.

- An **actively managed portfolio** with an institutional investment approach that reflects a disciplined investment process, helping you stay focused on your goals.

Curian Capital, LLC
A Registered Investment Advisor

Proposal and Investment Policy Statement

Prepared for: William & Stacy Smith
Proposal ID: P00003346609
Page: 4 of 23   Date: October 1, 2012

A disciplined investment process

Not only is this recommended strategy tailored to your individual needs and goals, but it also employs a disciplined approach to achieving your goals.

This disciplined approach involves a six-step process:

1. **Setting personal objectives and identifying your risk profile.** This step helps you and your Financial Professional understand your specific financial goals as well as your comfort level with risk.

2. **Selecting your asset allocation plan.** This involves identifying the right asset classes and investment vehicles for you based on your risk profile, objectives and investment time horizon.

3. **Creating your personalized Investment Policy Statement.** This formalizes your investment strategy by creating a written, customized IPS.

4. **Building and implementing your portfolio.** This process is designed to provide the appropriate investment strategies based on the financial information documented in your IPS.

5. **Monitoring and adjusting your portfolio.** This helps ensure that your portfolio remains true to your needs and objectives.

6. **Communicating and rebalancing your portfolio.** This step is designed to keep your portfolio aligned with your investment goals, and provides ongoing communication so you can see how you're progressing toward reaching your goals.

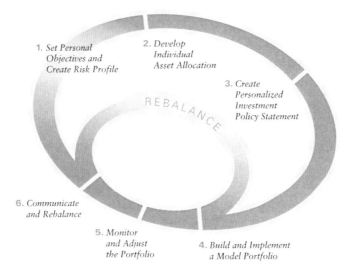

The proposal detailed in the following pages reflects a recommended investment strategy and has been customized to pursue your unique financial needs and objectives.

Proposal and Investment Policy Statement

Prepared for: William & Stacy Smith
Proposal ID: P00003346609
Page: 5 of 23   Date: October 1, 2012

STEP ONE: Setting personal objectives and identifying your risk profile

Understanding your goals, needs and feelings about risk

Personal Objectives

Your financial objectives are determined by your current circumstances, the length of time you have to invest, your personal needs and goals, and your investment beliefs and expectations.

Your stated goal, proposal amount and type of account are:

Goal:	**Retirement**
Proposal Amount:	**$365,000**
Type of Account:	**Traditional IRA**

Time Horizon

The amount of time you have available to work toward attaining your financial goals is an important factor in determining an appropriate investment strategy. Typically, a longer investment time horizon allows for an increased ability to take on investment risk. A shorter time horizon may indicate a decreased capacity for risk, as the portfolio will have less time to rebound from potential losses. Other factors that may influence your time horizon include your liquidity needs, emergency fund availability, and regular contributions to or withdrawals from the account.

The time horizon you have indicated is: Medium-Term Investment Time Horizon

Risk Profile

As part of this investment process, you have been able to identify what type of investor you are. The **Suitability Questionnaire** you have completed includes a series of questions that establishes your risk profile based on your time horizon, objectives, and feelings about risk and return.

This proposed investment strategy is designed to help you balance the return potential you seek with the amount of risk you feel comfortable with as you seek to achieve your objectives within your time horizon.

This proposal is designed to help set reasonable expectations about the potential results of your overall investment strategy based on your risk comfort level, helping you gain a sound understanding of the characteristics of the investments within your portfolio.

A complete review of your risk tolerance can be found in the Suitability Questionnaire results found later in this document.

Your Investment Profile

Based on your identified investment objectives, time horizon and risk tolerance, your investment profile is:
Moderate Conservative

Your Moderate Conservative portfolio will be invested with a slight majority of the assets allocated to fixed-income types of investments and a minority allocated to equity investments. The objective of the portfolio is to provide balance between current income and long-term capital growth. The investor is willing to take on a moderate level of risk. The time horizon on these portfolios is expected to be moderate with minimal liquidity requirements. There is no guarantee this objective will be met *and you could lose money.*

Please note: Investment returns will fluctuate in response to general market and/or economic conditions and this investment entails the risk of possible loss of principal.

Proposal and Investment Policy Statement

Prepared for: William & Stacy Smith
Proposal ID: P00003346609
Page: 6 of 23   Date: October 1, 2012

STEP TWO: Developing your asset allocation plan

Your personalized portfolio

The next step is developing recommended strategies and specific solutions that can lead to achieving your goals. Again, this recommended strategy is personalized based on your risk profile, time horizon, and investment goals and preferences.

Asset allocation is the process of selecting the types and relative amount of investments that are designed to meet your specific financial objectives. Different types of investments involve different degrees of returns and risk, and they tend to react differently to changing economic conditions.

Through proper asset allocation of your assets, you have the potential to maximize your return while decreasing your risk. This process provides you with an asset allocation strategy based on your objectives and risk comfort level.

Your Asset Allocation Strategy

Based on your investment objectives, your proposed asset allocation strategy is:

- Curian Strategic Allocation - Base asset allocation is selected at the time of investment and maintained through systematic rebalancing.

Asset Class Preferences

In addition, you have the ability to further customize your portfolio by either including or excluding international equity, real estate and/or alternative asset classes.

You have identified a preference to include the following additional asset class(es) in your portfolio:

- **International Equities**
- **Real Estate Securities**
- **Alternatives**

Curian Capital, LLC
A Registered Investment Advisor

Proposal and Investment Policy Statement

Prepared for: William & Stacy Smith
Proposal ID: P00003346609
Page: 7 of 23 Date: October 1, 2012

Recommended Allocation of Assets

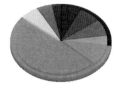

Domestic Equity	27.00%
Large Cap Core	6.82%
Large Cap Value	7.83%
Large Cap Growth	7.83%
Small-Mid Cap Core	4.52%

International Equity	10.00%

May contain Developed Markets and Emerging Markets holdings

Fixed Income	49.00%

May contain U.S., High-Yield, Investment Grade, Mortgage-Backed, Tax-Exempt, Short-Term Treasury, Treasury Inflation-Protected Securities, International Treasury, Emerging Market Fixed Income and Derivative holdings

Real Estate	6.00%

May contain U.S. and International REIT holdings

Alternatives	5.00%

May contain Commodities, Currencies, Long/Short Equity, Managed Futures, Merger Arbitrage, Natural Resources and Private Equity

Reserve Allocation	3.00%

May contain Domestic Equity, U.S. Short Term Treasury or Tax-Exempt Fixed Income holdings

Your Implementation Strategy

Markets experience ups and downs over time, and in the short run, those swings can be dramatic. However, investors who have historically implemented a well-diversified investment strategy and stuck with it have been rewarded.

While your asset allocation decision is critical, you should also consider an **implementation strategy** that makes you most comfortable with your investment decisions. The implementation goal is to select a mix of money managers whose performance tendencies will maximize the likelihood that you will stick to your investment program over the long term.

You may have an implementation strategy for both the equity portion and the fixed-income portion of your investment portfolio.

The goal of the implementation strategy is to help you stay committed to your long-term course of action, one that maximizes the probability that you will meet you investment objectives.

We have identified the following implementation strategies for your equity and fixed-income asset classes:

- **Active-Core Equity Implementation**
- **Core Fixed Income Implementation**

Note: A further explanation of these implementation strategies is included in the back section of this proposal.

Proposal and Investment Policy Statement

Prepared for: William & Stacy Smith
Proposal ID: P00003346609
Page: 8 of 23 Date: October 1, 2012

Securities Exclusion

Your Custom Style Portfolio enables you to exclude a variety of social categories and/or individual securities from your portfolio.

You have identified the following exclusions from your portfolio:

Protestant Values

Social exclusion categories and criteria are supplied by a third party vendor. Selecting a religious values exclusion may select multiple individual social category exclusions associated with the selected preference. Religious values may include parameters that differ from the associated social category and will supersede the parameters for all related categories.

Performance of accounts with exclusions or restrictions may differ from that of accounts without such limitations, including the possibility of lower overall results and deviation from stated investment objectives. The greater the number of categories or securities selected for exclusion, or the selection of a religious values preference, exchange traded-fund (ETF), mutual fund or other forms of investment companies, the greater the likelihood and magnitude of potential performance deviations and the potential for a less diversified portfolio. If a particular security or type of security is excluded, the resulting gap will be filled by proportionately increasing the amount of other securities in the model portfolio. Securities may be added or removed from the social categories on a periodic basis. If a security is added to a social category, that security will be sold from all accounts that have excluded the category. If a security is removed from a social category, that security will be eligible for purchase going forward. Exclusion preferences apply only to separately managed equity portfolios and will not impact the underlying securities within an exchange-traded fund (ETF), mutual fund, or other forms of investment companies. Certain investment companies may be unavailable for exclusion. For additional descriptions and information concerning exclusion preferences, please review Many Ways to Make the World a Better Place (IADV14354).

Dividend Preference

You may select how dividends are reinvested into your account. Cash and other distributions will be temporarily invested in a money market fund on your behalf until they can be reinvested in your portfolio if directed.

The dividend option you have selected is: **Reinvest in Program**

When dividends or interest is paid on the account holdings, this selection will trigger a reinvestment in the securitized reserve or across the entire model (depending on the amount of the dividend payment).

STEP THREE: Creating your personalized Investment Policy Statement

Key to success in a volatile and unpredictable market

Once you have approved this proposal, this document becomes your personalized plan to help you reach your goals. This is called an **Investment Policy Statement** – a written plan outlining your investment goals and how you plan to pursue them.

Your customized Investment Policy Statement:

- Ensures that your objectives and constraints are considered in the portfolio management process.

- Promotes effective communication with regard to your objectives, time horizon, risk tolerance and return expectations.

- Promotes investment discipline, increasing your chances of reaching your financial goals.

- Allows you to set reasonable expectations for your investments.

- Provides a framework for measuring your progress toward your goals.

- Serves as a financial "blueprint" that can be updated and adjusted as your individual situation changes.

This step of the process is fulfilled by signing and approving this document on the signature page at the end of the proposal.

Over time, relying on this Investment Policy Statement to guide decisions with regard to your portfolio helps ensure that you are intelligently pursuing your goals and not letting emotional reactions to short-term market fluctuations derail your progress.

STEP FOUR: Building and implementing your portfolio

Focused on the process – not performance – to meet your investment goals

Your Custom Style Portfolio provides access to institutional money managers and institutional research partners for your account assets. The process also provides ongoing model performance analysis, investment structure review, and money manager oversight to ensure those managers remain on track with their stated philosophy and strategy.

Once a money manager has been selected, a rigorous and ongoing review process ensures that the manager selection criteria are maintained.

Proposal and Investment Policy Statement

Prepared for: William & Stacy Smith
Proposal ID: P00003346609
Page: 10 of 23   Date: October 1, 2012

Investment Managers and Investment Vehicles

Based on the information you have provided, we have selected the following investment vehicles for your portfolio:

Domestic Equity	**27.00%**
Large Cap Core	
UBS Asset Management	6.82%
Large Cap Growth	
Columbus Circle Investors	7.83%
Large Cap Value	
Epoch Investment Partners	7.83%
Small / Mid Cap Core	
Ironwood Investment Management	1.62%
Schroder Investment Management	2.90%
International Equity	**10.00%**
Int'l Dev. Small / Mid Cap Growth	
International Small Cap Growth Portfolio	1.50%
Int'l Equity	
Diversified International Equity	8.50%
Fixed Income	**49.00%**
Core Fixed Income	
Total Return Bond Portfolio	49.00%
Real Estate	**6.00%**
Real Estate	
Real Estate Portfolio	6.00%
Alternatives	**5.00%**
Alternatives	
Alternative Core	5.00%
Securitized Reserve	**3.00%**
Reserve Allocation - Equity	
Reserve Allocation - Equity	3.00%

Asset categorization of mutual fund holdings is based on the most recently disseminated public information, which is expected to occur quarterly, but could be more or less frequent. Please refer to the manager's tear sheet for additional information.

The cash allocations of Curian's model portfolios will be invested in ETFs that track either the S&P 500 Index (Reserve Allocation - Equity) or Barclays Capital 1-3 Year Treasury Index (Reserve Allocation - Fixed-Income) depending on the investment objective of the portfolio. Monthly fees will be deducted from this allocation.

Curian Capital, LLC
A Registered Investment Advisor

Proposal and Investment Policy Statement

Prepared for: William & Stacy Smith
Proposal ID: P00003346609
Page: 11 of 23   Date: October 1, 2012

Your Account Growth Forecast

Based on your current investment amount, the model you chose to invest in and any cash flows into or out of your account, this tool is designed to give you a hypothetical illustration of potential account outcomes over the next 30 years. It illustrates three different outcome scenarios – one optimistic, one pessimistic and one median.

Although the tool cannot predict future investment results, it can help you manage uncertainty and realistically assess the likelihood that your investment goal can be reached.

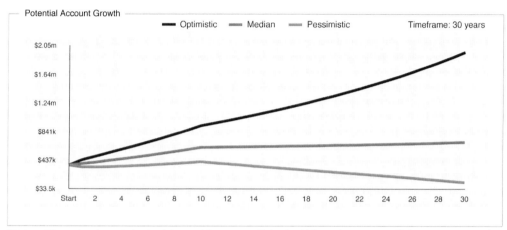

Potential Account Growth — Optimistic — Median — Pessimistic — Timeframe: 30 years

Return expectations are based on passive investments in an asset class as measured by benchmark indexes and represents a possible future investment outcome for a portfolio comprised of those various asset classes. All returns used in the forecast are nominal and include an inflation assumption. Returns from active management and the various implementation strategies (Blend, Defensive, Core, Income, Tactical, Advanced and Research Select) will generate the same results as the passive model forecast. The forecast is estimated at three different success rates or percentiles. These three different percentiles are 5%, 50%, and 95%. The bottom line on the graph shows a Pessimistic outcome. The middle shows the Median outcome (similar to the average outcome). The top line shows an Optimistic outcome. Statistically, one would expect an outcome worse than the Pessimistic outcome only 5% of the time. Similarly, one would expect an outcome better than the Optimistic outcome only 5% of the time. The middle outcome is the Median outcome, for which 50% of the outcomes were worse and 50% were better. It provides a reasonable estimate of the performance you could expect from the asset allocation. All return expectations are reduced by 2.99% to reflect the maximum applicable program fee. The tool does not differentiate between taxable, tax-deferred or tax-exempt investments. The tool does not contain any assumptions related to taxes. **The projections or other information generated by the tool regarding the likelihood of various investment outcomes are hypothetical in nature, do not reflect actual investment results, and are not guarantees of future results. Results may vary with each use and over time. Please read the Account Growth Forecast Tool disclosure document for a more detailed explanation.**

	Will you be making deposits to the account?	What is the amount of the deposits?	When will the deposits start?	How long will you be making deposits for?	Will you be making withdrawals from the account?	What is the amount of withdrawals?	When will the withdrawals start?	How long will you be making withdrawals?
Smith Family Wealth Accumu	Yes	$5,000	1 years	10 years	Yes	$24,000	11 years	20 years

Curian Capital, LLC
A Registered Investment Advisor

Proposal and Investment Policy Statement

Prepared for: William & Stacy Smith
Proposal ID: P00003346609
Page: 12 of 23   Date: October 1, 2012

STEP FIVE: Monitoring and adjusting your portfolio

Managing the details

Pursuing your investment goals is an ongoing process. Periodic reviews are critical to determine that your portfolio remains consistent with your goals, expectations and any lifestyle changes. As necessary, you can adjust or revise your portfolio based on the changes that are important to you.

We recommend periodic meetings with your Financial Professional to review your investment needs and objectives. These review meetings will typically cover:

- Changes in your financial situation that may necessitate adjustments to your investment plan
- Level of risk represented in your portfolio
- Portfolio performance and expectations with respect to your investment objectives

STEP SIX: Communicating and rebalancing your portfolio

Keeping you informed

Your Custom Style Portfolio provides regular, detailed reporting on your portfolio's activity and performance to keep you informed of your progress. You have online access to comprehensive monthly statements and performance reports so that you can keep abreast of your account.

These documents can be accessed through your account online at www.curian.com (located in your Filing Cabinet).

Account Rebalancing

Although your portfolio's asset allocation is important, it may change over time. Because various asset classes perform differently, a portfolio that is not periodically reviewed and rebalanced may become over- or under-weighted in certain asset classes, potentially adversely impacting its risk/reward profile.

Your Custom Style Portfolio enables you to select either an annual or semiannual rebalancing review based on your specific goals and preferences. This ensures that your asset allocation remains in line with your Investment Policy Statement.

The rebalancing review schedule you have selected is: **Semiannual**

Curian Capital, LLC
A Registered Investment Advisor

Proposal and Investment Policy Statement

Prepared for: William & Stacy Smith
Proposal ID: P00003346609
Page: 13 of 23   Date: October 1, 2012

Other important information

FEES

Your Total Program Fee is 2.00% based on the information provided during the creation of this proposal.

This fee amount is subject to change over the life of the account due to several reasons including market value fluctuation, deposits, withdrawals and/or house holding arrangements. For a detailed explanation of your fees, please refer to the Asset Management Services Agreement.

Note: The Total Program Fee does not include expenses imposed or incurred by mutual funds, exchange traded funds or other forms of investment companies within your portfolio.

Helping you pursue long-term financial success

As your Financial Professional, we help make certain that your financial needs and objectives are carefully considered as we help you develop a personalized plan to pursue your goals.

This proposal was created for you based on your unique needs and objectives. It is not a contractual obligation but a guideline and a tool to help you achieve the objectives for your account.

By approving this proposal, you are making an important first step toward pursuing your investment objectives. Your Investment Policy Statement can serve as an invaluable guide and resource for all of your future investment decisions.

Proposal and Investment Policy Statement

Prepared for: William & Stacy Smith
Proposal ID: P00003346609
Page: 14 of 23   Date: October 1, 2012

SUITABILITY QUESTIONNAIRE AND RESPONSE SUMMARY

The model portfolio for this account may have been selected through Curian's online suitability questionnaire or offline though Curian's Paper Account Application. This section restates the suitability questions and highlights the answers that best describe the suitability for the selected model portfolio. Where you have directly selected an investment objective (i.e., Conservative, Growth, etc.), the responses to these questions have been automatically matched to correspond to your predetermined objective and incorporated in your Investment Policy Statement. Please contact your Financial Professional if you have any questions regarding this information.

A) How many years from now do you wish to begin making withdrawals?

      1. 1 Year
      2. 2 Year
      3. 3 Year
✓   4. 4 Year
      5. 5 Year
      6. 6 Year
      7. 7 Year
      8. 8 Year
      9. 9 Year
      10. 10+ Year
      11. Custom Model

B) How long do you expect withdrawals to last once you begin?

      1. Lump Sum Withdrawal
      2. 1 Year
      3. 2 Year
      4. 3 Year
✓   5. 4 Year
      6. 5 Year
      7. 6 Year
      8. 7 Year
      9. 8 Year
      10. 9 Year
      11. 10+ Year
      12. Custom Model

C) How much risk will you be willing to take in an attempt to achieve higher returns?

      1. Low Risk
✓   2. Low Medium Risk
      3. Medium Risk
      4. Medium High Risk
      5. High Risk
      6. Custom Model

Curian Capital, LLC
A Registered Investment Advisor

Proposal and Investment Policy Statement

Prepared for: William & Stacy Smith
Proposal ID: P00003346609
Page: 15 of 23   Date: October 1, 2012

D) **What level of short-term fluctuations are you willing to accept in order to increase the potential of exceeding inflation?**

    1. Low Fluctuations
✓ 2. Medium Fluctuations
    3. High Fluctuations
    4. Custom Model

E) **Hypothetically, considering fairly extreme performance potential, what percent of gain/loss are you comfortable with for this portfolio at the end of the *first* year?**

    1. +14%/-6% Gain/Loss – 1 Year
    2. +18%/-11% Gain/Loss – 1 Year
✓ 3. +23%/-16% Gain/Loss – 1 Year
    4. +28%/-21% Gain/Loss – 1 Year
    5. +34%/-26% Gain/Loss – 1 Year
    6. Custom Model

F) **Hypothetically, considering fairly extreme performance potential, what percent of annualized gain/loss are you comfortable with for this portfolio at the end of the *third* year?**

    1. +10%/-2% Gain/Loss – 3 Years
✓ 2. +13%/-4% Gain/Loss – 3 Years
    3. +15%/-7% Gain/Loss – 3 Years
    4. +18%/-10% Gain/Loss – 3 Years
    5. +22%/-13% Gain/Loss – 3 Years
    6. Custom Model

G) **Which probability of incurring a loss in one year, in order to achieve the corresponding possible return over the longer term, are you most comfortable with?**

    1. 6% Potential Gain / 14% Probability of Loss
    2. 7% Potential Gain /19% Probability of Loss
✓ 3. 8% Potential Gain /24% Probability of Loss
    4. 9% Potential Gain /28% Probability of Loss
    5. 10% Potential Gain /31% Probability of Loss
    6. Custom Model

Proposal and Investment Policy Statement

Prepared for:	William & Stacy Smith
Proposal ID:	P00003346609
Page:	16 of 23 Date: October 1, 2012

The investor has the option of including or excluding International Equities from the recommended asset class mix in order to more closely match their specific objectives.

Investing in the International Equity asset class has unique risk factors not normally associated with domestic asset classes, like currency risk, political risk, and information risk. However, when combined with other asset classes, international equities provide diversification benefits resulting in the potential for enhanced risk and return characteristics for the overall portfolio.

A significant majority of the International allocation includes stocks in developed foreign markets, which have mature economic and market infrastructures similar to the United States. A lesser allocation is in emerging foreign markets, those that have less developed economic and market infrastructure and as a result may involve more risk.

Mutual funds, which may include funds managed by Curian, or Exchange Traded Funds (ETFs) may be used to gain efficient and well diversified exposure to the International Equity asset class.

I wish to…

✓ Include International Equities

Exclude International Equities

The investor has the option of including or excluding Real Estate investments from the recommended asset class mix in order to more closely match their specific objectives.

Investing in the Real Estate asset class has unique risk factors not normally associated with other asset classes, like interest rate risk, vacancy trends, and other risks unique to the real estate industry. However, when combined with other asset classes, real estate investments provide diversification benefits resulting in the potential for enhanced risk and return characteristics for the overall portfolio.

Exposure to the Real Estate asset class is facilitated through investments in real estate investment trusts or REITs. Traded like stock securities, REITs hold income-producing investments like shopping centers, office buildings, hotels, apartments, retirement communities, as well as mortgages secured by real estate. Selection of this option may or may not include investments in domestic and/or international real estate.

Mutual funds are used to gain efficient and well diversified exposure to REIT securities and the Real Estate asset class.

I wish to…

✓ Include Real Estate

Exclude Real Estate

Curian Capital, LLC
A Registered Investment Advisor

Proposal and Investment Policy Statement

Prepared for: William & Stacy Smith
Proposal ID: P00003346609
Page: 17 of 23   Date: October 1, 2012

The investor has the option of adding Alternative assets to the recommended asset class mix to enhance the portfolio's overall potential risk/return characteristics.

Investing in Alternative asset classes or strategies presents unique risks not normally associated with traditional asset classes. In fact, the volatility of a single alternative investment like currency, commodities or publicly traded private equity can involve a higher degree of risk compared to more traditional investments like common stocks or fixed-income investments. However, when combined in a broader portfolio context, the complementary performance tendencies of alternative investments may potentially work to reduce overall portfolio volatility while maintaining or enhancing total return over the long term.

The Alternative allocation includes mutual funds that track certain investment strategies that include, but are not limited to, equity long/short, managed futures, merger arbitrage, natural resources and listed private equity.

Curian Capital will select the mutual funds in the portfolio, make any necessary allocation changes, and at its discretion, add other non-traditional investment vehicles. The underlying securities and strategies employed by the mutual funds are managed by the fund adviser and/or sub-adviser.

Investments in the Alternatives asset class may generate a Schedule K-1 tax form. This may result in delayed tax filings and additional filing requirements. Please consult with your tax advisor before making an investment decision.

I wish to…

✓   Include Alternative investments
    Exclude Alternative investments

Implementation Strategy

Equity Implementation Options:
The Active - Core Equity strategy provides a portfolio of money managers and/or securities executing separate investment strategies, which incorporate the manager's stock picking, sector selection fundamentals and qualitative ideas.

The Active - Defensive Equity strategy provides a portfolio of money managers and/or securities executing separate investment strategies, which incorporate the manager's stock picking, sector selection fundamentals, and qualitative ideas with a focus on reduced price volatility in declining markets.

The Active - Income strategy provides a portfolio of money managers and/or securities executing separate investment strategies incorporating the manager's stock picking, sector selection fundamentals and qualitative ideas with a focus on the stability and growth of dividends. The primary consideration is generating a stream of reliable income that has the potential to increase over time, with a secondary consideration of controlling principal fluctuation.

The Quantitative strategy, in contrast to Active management, is managed by Curian Capital and represents a structured approach to selecting securities aimed at providing risk and return characteristics similar to a stated benchmark.

The Blend strategy represents a combination of both Active and Quantitative managers and/or securities in an attempt to leverage off the qualitative and quantitative strengths of these two management styles.

Curian Capital, LLC
A Registered Investment Advisor

Proposal and Investment Policy Statement

Prepared for: William & Stacy Smith
Proposal ID: P00003346609
Page: 18 of 23   Date: October 1, 2012

Fixed Income Implementation Strategies:
The Core Fixed Income strategy is a portfolio of fixed-income mutual funds that may include funds managed by Curian. The portfolio allocation of the Core Fixed Income strategy is managed by Curian Capital with the objective of seeking to provide income from a diversified exposure across the broad spectrum of the global bond market. The funds may invest in fixed income instruments such as bonds, debt securities and other similar instruments issued by various U.S. and non-U.S. public- or private-sector entities, as well as derivative instruments such as options, futures contracts or swap agreements, or mortgage- or asset-backed securities.

The Tax-exempt strategy is a portfolio of fixed-income mutual funds with the objective of seeking to provide tax-exempt income through investment exposure across the broad spectrum of the municipal bond market. Curian manages the allocation of the Tax-exempt strategy. Curian offers both a national tax-exempt allocation, which includes municipal bonds issued across multiple states, and state-specific tax-exempt allocations, which are limited to municipal bonds issued in New York or California. Underlying bond investments are domestically issued, investment-grade municipal bonds, whose interest payments are generally exempt from income taxes, and in certain cases, state income taxes in California and New York. In addition, the underlying bond investments are expected to be exempt from Alternative Minimum Taxes (AMT). Investors should consult with their Financial Professional and/or tax advisor to review their financial and tax situation when selecting this strategy. *The Tax Exempt - New York and Tax Exempt - California Fixed Income Strategies are intended for use by residents of those states only. The tax benefits offered by these portfolios do not apply to residents outside of these states.*

The Income Bond strategy is a portfolio of fixed-income mutual funds that may include funds managed by Curian, and preferred stock ETFs. The portfolio is managed to provide diversified exposure to global bonds and preferred stocks, with a focus on income generation. The funds may invest primarily in fixed income instruments that include investment grade debt securities and high yield securities, and may also invest in securities issued in foreign currencies, emerging markets and derivative instruments such as options, futures contracts or swap agreements, or mortgage- or asset-backed securities.

You have identified the following Implementation Strategies for your Equity and Fixed Income asset class:

- **Active-Core Equity Implementation**
- **Core Fixed Income Implementation**

Proposal and Investment Policy Statement

Prepared for: William & Stacy Smith
Proposal ID: P00003346609
Page: 19 of 23   Date: October 1, 2012

The investor has the option of choosing from multiple Asset Allocation Strategies to more closely match his or her specific investment objectives.

Strategic Asset Allocation	Tactical Asset Allocation	Advanced Asset Allocation	Research Select Asset Allocation
Strategic asset allocation strategies allocate a percentage of a client's portfolio to various asset classes, such as stocks, bonds, alternatives and cash. They incorporate a set of capital market assumptions with a client's risk, return and time horizon to create a formal target asset allocation policy. Generally, the asset mix is passively maintained over time through periodic rebalances to the target policy weights.	Tactical asset allocation strategies are the result of actively managing a client's strategic asset allocation. The target mix of asset classes, such as stocks, bonds, alternatives and cash, can change in an attempt to enhance risk-adjusted returns over time. Tactical adjustments can be made based on changes in the market (reactive) or perceived short-term opportunities (proactive).	Advanced asset allocation strategies are designed to meet additional client investment objectives and may focus on a select group of asset classes or strategies. The asset mix can be managed strategically or tactically.	The Curian Research Select (RS) Portfolios combine several existing Curian strategies to form a series of portfolios designed to meet specific objectives. The RS Portfolios all employ a level of risk control to acknowledge the potential volatility and cyclical nature of the capital markets. The RS solutions serve two broad investor objectives: the **accumulation** or growth of assets and the generation of **income.** The two objectives are complemented by the risk control features of the Curian Dynamic Risk Advantage® Strategies.
Strategy Options	**Strategy Options**	**Strategy Options**	**Strategy Options**
Equity: *Active - Core:* Similar equity characteristics compared to broad stock market benchmarks measured by risk, quality, sector exposure and market capitalization. Goal is out performance over complete market cycles. *Active - Defensive:* Defensive equity characteristics compared to broad stock market benchmarks measured by lower risk, larger market capitalization and higher quality. Goal is out performance focused on down-market cycles. *Active - Income:* Income equity characteristics compared to broad stock market benchmarks measured by dividend yield, risk and higher quality. Goal is market out performance focused in current income. *Quantitative:* Very similar equity characteristics compared to broad stock market benchmarks measured by risk, quality, sector exposure and market capitalization. Goal is to deliver performance very similar to the benchmark over complete market cycles. *Blend:* A combination of Active-Core and Quantitative strategies. Goal is out performance over complete market cycles. **Fixed Income:** Taxable, Tax-exempt or Yield Focus℠	*Tactical Advantage:* Incorporates a proactive approach to managing asset allocations within defined parameters around the strategic, or base, asset allocation policy. The strategy seeks to identify relative opportunities and/or risks in various asset classes by overweighting and underweighting areas of perceived relative opportunity and areas of perceived higher risk. The goal of Tactical Advantage is to add value relative to the returns associated with a static mix of asset classes. *Dynamic Risk Advantage (DRA):* These strategies incorporate a clearly defined set of trading rules to shift allocations in response to changing market conditions between a diversified market portfolio and a lower risk portfolio. The lower risk portfolio for all strategies contains low volatility, high quality fixed income assets. The strategies manage market exposure (beta) by allowing for substantial shifts among the underlying asset classes. The goal of the DRA strategies is to enhance risk-adjusted performance over time relative to returns associated with a static mix of asset classes. *Dynamic Risk Advantage – Income:* This portfolio is designed to provide total return with an income focus. The diversified market portfolio contains income-oriented asset classes that have growth potential. *Dynamic Risk Advantage – Diversified[1]:* This portfolio is designed to provide balanced capital appreciation and income. The diversified market portfolio contains growth oriented assets. *Dynamic Risk Advantage – Aggressive[1,2]:* This portfolio is designed for long-term capital appreciation. The diversified market portfolio may contain global equities, commodities and managed futures.	*Alternative Select[1,2]:* The portfolios seek long-term capital appreciation by investing in Exchange Traded Funds (ETFs) and mutual funds whose underlying investments are oriented to non-traditional asset classes. The primary objective is to mitigate the risks associated with fixed-income and equity markets by investing in non-correlated asset classes and strategies. *Enhanced Real Return[1]:* Incorporates asset classes that have historically been highly sensitive to inflation. The strategy is appropriate for clients with moderate to high portfolio risk characteristics. The goal is to provide appreciation to the investment portfolio when inflation is present.	*Accumulation RS portfolios* Two versions of Accumulation portfolios draw on the merits of strategic asset allocation and tactically managed portfolios with an added focus on risk control. They are constructed to serve a range of objectives, from a priority for growth with some risk control potential, to more of a risk control priority while seeking growth over time. The Accumulation RS portfolios are a combination of existing Curian strategies: Strategic Active-Core with Dynamic Risk Advantage - Diversified or Dynamic Risk Advantage - Aggressive and Tactical Advantage with Dynamic Risk Advantage - Diversified. *Income RS portfolios* The Income Priority RS portfolios are designed with several distinct income objectives in mind and an added focus on risk and inflation control. Income-oriented investors can choose from portfolios designed to prioritize **maximum** income potential or **rising** income potential, or a **balance** between the two. As with the Accumulation portfolios, each includes a risk control aspect to buffer the downturns in capital markets as well as an option to fend off the erosionary risks of inflation. The Income RS portfolios are a combination of existing Curian strategies: Strategic Active-Income, Dynamic Risk Advantage - Income, and Enhanced Real Return.

I wish to select...

✓ Curian Strategic Allocation
  Curian Tactical Advantage
  Curian Dynamic Risk Advantage® - Income
  Curian Dynamic Risk Advantage® - Diversified
  Curian Dynamic Risk Advantage® - Aggressive
  Curian Alternative Select
  Curian Enhanced Real Return
  Curian Research Select

[1] These portfolios invest in alternative asset classes that may generate a Schedule K-1 tax form. This may result in delayed tax filings and additional filing requirements. Please consult with your tax advisor before making an investment decision.

[2] This portfolio may invest in leveraged or short position ETFs that seek a return that is a multiple or inverse multiple of the return of an index or other benchmark (target) **for a single day**, as measured from one NAV calculation to the next. Due to the compounding of daily returns, the ETF's returns over periods other than one day will likely differ in amount and possibly direction from the target return for the same period. These effects may be more pronounced in funds with larger or inverse multiples and in funds with volatile benchmarks. **These ETFs are not suitable for all investors.**

Curian Capital, LLC
A Registered Investment Advisor

Proposal and Investment Policy Statement

Prepared for: William & Stacy Smith
Proposal ID: P00003346609
Page: 20 of 23   Date: October 1, 2012

Acceptance and adoption of this proposal

I (we) have reviewed, approved and adopted this Proposal and Investment Policy Statement for the investment program prepared with the assistance of James Marshall.

_____   _____
(Investor's Signature)   (Date)

I have discussed this *Proposal and Investment Policy Statement* with this client but have not provided investment advice in connection with this Proposal.

_____   _____
(Financial Professional's Signature)   (Date)
James Marshall

Account Growth Forecast Tool

Introduction

Your Account Growth Forecast is intended to help you see potential investment outcomes based on the model you choose to invest in, your investment amount and any cash flows into/out of your account. And although the tool cannot predict future investment performance, it can help you manage uncertainty and realistically assess the likelihood that your investment goal can be reached.

Your personal and financial situation, the macroeconomic environment, and federal and state tax laws will change over time. Please note that the tool is not a substitute for a comprehensive financial plan and should not be relied on as your sole or primary means of making investment-planning decisions. Strategies that may be appropriate at one stage of life or point in time can become inappropriate. Changing needs and circumstances, including changes in the economy and securities markets in general, call for a review of your strategy to determine whether it should be updated. You should discuss your situation with your financial professional, tax adviser or an estate planning professional to identify specific issues not addressed by the tool.

Assumptions

- The asset classes included in the forecast are domestic equity, developed market equity, emerging market equity, U.S. fixed income, global REITs, inflation-linked bonds, and commodities
- Return expectations are based on passive investments in an asset class as measured by benchmark indexes and represent a possible future outcome for a portfolio comprised of those various asset classes. All returns used in the forecast are nominal and include an inflation assumption. Active investment strategies (core, defensive, income, blend, tactical, and advanced) may result in actual returns which differ from those achieved by the passive benchmark indexes and should be considered when reviewing forecasted growth.
- Fee calculations are not dynamic based on assets under management. All return expectations are reduced by 2.99% to reflect the maximum annual applicable program fee. Curian Capital, LLC ("Capital") makes no revisions, adjustments or modifications to the assumptions (except to reduce returns by 2.99% for fees).
- Only annual periods are used in the forecast (i.e., monthly, quarterly and semiannual values are not available).
- All cash flows, if any, are treated as end-of-period flows. Any cash flow frequency less than one year is not allowable (i.e., the cash flow frequency has to match the return frequency). All cash flows are stated in dollar terms (i.e., no percent of market value, percent of moving average, etc.).
- The forecast displays a 90% degree of confidence (i.e., 95th and 5th percentile) and the median outcome only.
- The forecast is not a Monte Carlo simulation.

Forecast Methodology

The criteria used in the forecast are return, risk and correlation assumptions for the primary asset classes in the Curian Custom Style Portfolios ("CSPs"). The assumptions are developed by an unaffiliated independent Capital Markets Group, based on a 10-year to 15-year forward-looking time horizon. They are reviewed at least annually and updated as deemed necessary by that group.

The assumptions are developed by first examining relationships across assets through historical compound annual returns, volatilities and correlations and then applying an intellectual overlay to reflect forward-looking views for real-return expectations. Capital then simulates real-return expectations and inflation rates to create its nominal expected returns.

All calculations and results from the tool are generated through a forecast methodology. The process first derives an expected compound rate of return and volatility for a portfolio based on the underlying asset class assumptions. Using the expected return and volatility, the forecast then derives return assumptions at varying levels of probability over multiple periods of time. These returns are applied to principal values to graph changes in account value.

The forecast will take into account only domestic equity, international equity, fixed-income, REIT investments, inflation-linked bonds and commodities. Securitized reserve is "equitized," and its weight should be added to the fixed-income weight for conservative and very conservative Model Account Templates ("MATs") and added to domestic equity for moderate conservative through maximum growth MATs.

Except for the Enhanced Real Return (ERR) strategy, if the alternative exposure is selected and the combined allocation to fixed income is greater than or equal to 60%, then the allocation to alternatives is added back to fixed income. If the combined allocation is less than 60% but greater than or equal to 50%, then half the allocation to alternatives is added to domestic equity and half is added to fixed income. If the allocation is less than 50%, the allocation to alternatives is added back to domestic equity.

In addition, the forecast does not provide expected risk and return for preferred stocks. As such, any weight to preferred stocks is always added to fixed income.

Forecasted returns for the Alternative Select offerings are derived using domestic equity, international equity and fixed income allocations. For the Alternative Select – Conservative portfolio, 19.5% is allocated to domestic equity, 10.5% to international equity, and 70.0% to fixed income. For the Alternative Select – Moderate portfolio, 32.5% is allocated to domestic equity, 17.5% to international equity, and 50.0% to fixed income. For the Alternative Select – Growth portfolio, 45.5% is allocated to domestic equity, 24.5% to international equity, and 30.0% to fixed income.

The Global Tactical strategy represents active management of the asset classes within defined parameters of an appropriate benchmark. Forecasted returns are based upon the benchmark returns of the static neutral allocation of the specific tactical strategy selected (please see the appropriate tactical model tear sheet for the selected models neutral allocation) and do not include adjustments for the impact of active management. Actual allocations for the Global Tactical strategy will deviate from these weights over time as a result of the tactical asset allocation approach. The results shown in the tool may not adequately reflect the real returns of your account.

The ERR strategy represents active management of two asset classes within defined parameters of an appropriate benchmark. The strategy incorporates fixed income and commodities based securities. The underlying asset mix changes over time at the discretion of an independent advisor. ERR maintains a base allocation of 50% fixed income and 50% commodity.

Other than "cash," it is not possible to invest generically in any of the above asset classes. All assumed rates of return include reinvestment of dividends and interest income. Other investments not considered might have characteristics similar or superior to the asset classes identified above.

Portfolio returns are based on each economic scenario. For each year in the forecast, the tool takes the portfolio balances after all withdrawals and calculates the income and capital gain/loss ratios based on historical averages. Income and capital gains are added to the portfolio balance. In addition, portfolio returns assume the reinvestment of interest and dividends. Fees or expenses generally will reduce performance returns for actual investments. The tool reflects the impact of these fees and expenses in the hypothetical illustration.

Curian Capital, LLC
A Registered Investment Advisor

Proposal and Investment Policy Statement

Prepared for:	William & Stacy Smith
Proposal ID:	P00003346609
Page:	22 of 23 Date: October 1, 2012

Calculations and Results
Results are based on the investing style you entered in the tool, even if you have implemented a different investing style for your existing accounts. The investing styles (unless modified by you) are applied until you reach the end of the specified time range.

All forecasts are derived at the asset class level. Capital market assumptions are applied to determine the simulated returns and yields for each asset class for every year the forecast is run. Of course, the estimated rates of return figures only represent our assumptions and should not be viewed as predictions or guarantees of future performance.

Interpreting the Results
The forecast begins by accepting information that you provide. Each scenario is based on the forecast of various asset classes as measured by benchmark indexes and represents a possible future investment outcome for a portfolio comprised of those various asset classes. Of course, past performance is not an indication of future results.

The forecast is estimated at three different success rates or percentiles. These three different percentiles are 5%, 50%, and 95%. The bottom line on the graph shows a Pessimistic outcome. The middle shows the Median outcome (similar to the average outcome). The top line shows an Optimistic outcome. Statistically, one would expect an outcome worse than the Pessimistic outcome only 5% of the time. Similarly, one would expect an outcome better than the Optimistic outcome only 5% of the time. The middle outcome is the Median outcome, for which 50% of the outcomes were worse and 50% were better. It provides a reasonable estimate of the performance you could expect from the asset allocation.

Thus, you can be 90% confident that the return for any given year will fall between the 95% and 5% probability returns (this is a 90% confidence interval with 95%-5% = 10% uncertainty). The difference between the highest and lowest probability return should converge to the median over time (50% probability/50% uncertainty).

It is important to note that there is no one ideal simulation success rate or "confidence level" appropriate for everyone. People with significant income from Social Security and a pension may be willing to settle for a lower success rate, while those who will depend almost exclusively on their retirement assets may prefer a higher simulation success rate. It is also important to remember that the future could include any of the projected outcomes as well as outcomes that could be better or worse than the represented forecast.

Tax Considerations
The tool does not differentiate between taxable, tax-deferred or tax-exempt investments. The tool does not contain any assumptions related to taxes. You should discuss your situation with your financial professional, tax adviser or an estate planning professional to determine how your personal tax situation may impact the results of the forecast.

Material Limitations
IMPORTANT: The projections or other information generated by the tool regarding the likelihood of various investment outcomes are hypothetical in nature, do not reflect actual investment results, and are not guarantees of future results. Results may vary with each use and over time.

Material limitations of this tool include, but are not restricted to, universe of investments, investment selection and customization, market performance, and inflation and taxes, as described below.

Universe of Investments
The benchmark proxies used to develop the return assumptions are as follows: domestic equity-Russell 3000; developed markets (unhedged)-MSCI EAFE; emerging markets-IFC Global Index; U.S. fixed income-Barclays Capital Aggregate Bond; Global REITs-FTSE EPRA NAREIT Global; inflation linked bonds - BarCap U.S. Treasury Inflation-Linked Bond Index and Commodities - the Standard & Poor's Goldman Sachs Commodities Index (GSCI).

Investment Selection and Customization
The forecast is based on the strategic asset allocations developed by Curian Capital, which in turn are based on mean-variance optimization. The forecast will pull data based on the model(s) selected by the client. For multiple accounts, the forecast will derive the weighted average allocation based on proposal amounts to each model. Any social sector or security exclusion you may place on your account is not reflected in the tool. Also, any tax-loss harvesting that may be done in your account is not reflected in the tool.

Market Performance
Except for the Enhanced Real Return (ERR) strategy, the tool considers the probabilities that certain asset classes might achieve certain results under different market conditions. The tool assumes a level of diversity within each asset class consistent with a specific market index. There is a distinct possibility that market extremes may occur more frequently than we have assumed and that our asset class forecasts may not reflect actual investment returns of the asset classes. Future results for all asset classes may materially differ from those assumed in our calculations.

The tool does not take into consideration all asset classes. For example, asset classes such as alternatives are excluded from consideration. Asset classes not considered may have characteristics similar or superior to those being analyzed.

Inflation
Long-term inflation within the tool is modeled with an assumption of 3%. This means that over the life of your forecast, the inflation rate assumed is 3%, but the actual rate of inflation may vary from year to year.

CHURCH ENDOWMENT FUND

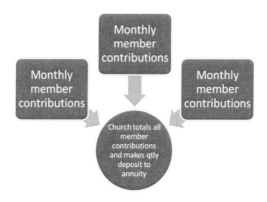

10 STEPS FOR MANAGING THE STORE HOUSE

Step 1   Track and Record all church expenses and complete an outside audit by a CPA.

Step 2   Establish and fund church emergency funds equal to a minimum (6) months operating expenses.

Step 3   Clearly define and record short term, intermediate and long term goals; i.e. debt reduction, community outreach, community cooperative trust, after school program, adult training program and church expansion.

Step 4   Establish a 10 year, 15 year, 20 year and 25 year endowment goal, i.e. $1 million, $2 million, $3 million and $5 million.

Step 5   Structure a clearly defined and realistic accumulation plan i.e. $5000 per month.

Step 6   Encourage 20 percent of the active membership to take ownership and commit financially to their share of the monthly accumulation plan (example: 1000 active members x 20 percent = 200 trustees. This equates to $25 per month for each trustee.

Step 7   Direct monthly accumulation funds to appropriate accounts i.e. 25 percent 10 year fund, 25 percent 15 year fund, 25 percent 20 year fund and 25 percent in the 25 year fund.

Step 8   Establish and maintain an Investment Policy Statement to clearly define your risk tolerance and investment parameters. Create an asset allocation model that corresponds to the IPS. Choose investment vehicles that correspond with the asset allocation model.

Step 9   Structure a distribution and reinvestment plan for each fund.

Step 10 Make this plan perpetual

THE NEED FOR FINANCIAL PLANNING

You could get in your car with no map, GPS, or tour guide and attempt to drive to an undetermined destination. If you are lucky, patient, and have enough resources, you just might succeed. The best course of action however, is to know your destination, map out your course, and consider contingencies for unexpected events. Financial planning is that map with contingency plans.

Many financial problems occur in each of our lives. How we face these problems can determine the quality of our lives and the lives of those we love.

Common Problems

Some of the financial issues which each person can expect to face during his or her lifetime include the following:

Cash management: More than just keeping a balanced check book, cash management includes preparing (and following) a budget, using credit wisely and keeping the income tax burden to the lowest level possible.

Risk management: There is risk of loss of both life and property. Life insurance can be used to protect a family against the risk of premature death. Disability insurance can protect against the loss of a person's ability to earn a living. Property and casualty insurance can protect our worldly goods against accident and such perils as fire, earthquake and theft.

Accumulation goals: We all need to save money for some reason. Educating our children, buying a home, and building an investment portfolio are typical accumulation goals.

Financial independence: It is important to take steps now to ensure that the golden years are, indeed, golden.

Estate planning: This means recognizing that death is inevitable and planning for the ultimate transfer of assets to your heirs.

Solving Common Problems in a Complex World

Solving these problems in today's world is not easy. Two basic steps are involved. The first step is to recognize that in our complex, ever-changing world, expert help is required. There is a need to assemble a financial planning team – trained professionals such as your attorney, CPA, insurance agent, securities broker, and financial planner (who quarterbacks the team).

With the help of your team, the second step can be taken – the development of a systematic, integrated plan for dealing with each of these issues. This will become your financial plan.

Some people choose to ignore these problems until it is too late. A better choice is to begin the process to develop a financial plan. The most important step is the first one – getting started!

WHAT IS FINANCIAL PLANNING?

Financial planning is the process that helps you take better control over your financial assets and manage your money more successfully.

You start with the recognition that you have distinct needs and goals, and that your plan must be specifically designed to achieve your objectives. This brings up several questions: How exactly do you go about sorting out and setting your goals? How do you then select from the tremendous variety of financial "products" and choices available? How do you choose from stocks, bonds, mutual funds, money market funds, CDs and the many other investments? How do you choose between savings and retirement plans (including annuities), and the new type of protection plans and estate planning tools (such as trusts) and many others?

You must be aware of not only the advantages of these alternatives, but also their risks and disadvantages as well. It is important to determine which are best suited for achieving your objectives.

How can a financial advisor help you?

Unlike some investment or insurance sales people, true financial planning professionals concentrate first on identifying your needs rather than only promoting specific products or investments. A financial advisor can help you make the right financial decisions and if necessary, coordinate them with those suggested by the other specialists you may use. This important step is part of a comprehensive financial plan that takes into consideration your overall financial situation.

WHAT SHOULD YOUR FINANCIAL PLAN INCLUDE?

A sound financial plan should cover a broad spectrum of areas related to your present security and future well-being. It should include an analysis of your situation and needs, as well as recommendations on how to achieve your goals. Financial planning typically considers six areas:

ONE: FINANCIAL POSITION

A sound financial plan begins with a thorough understanding of your financial position – a cold hard look at the good, the bad, and the ugly. This involves asking key questions covering three major areas:

Where do you stand today?

What is your net worth after subtracting all of your liabilities from all of your assets? Exactly how much of this is readily available in case of emergency? How much discretionary income do you have after meeting fixed expenses? And how much can you comfortably afford to save and/or invest?

What do you hope to accomplish?

What are your goals for yourself and your family (WDYWFY)? A first (or second) home? College for your children? Setting yourself up in business? Almost surely you want to minimize taxes and assure yourself a comfortable retirement (It's never too early or too late to start).

How can you reach your goals?

How much time do you have to achieve your goals and how much money will you need? It is the job of a financial advisor not only to help see that you have a plan that is right for you, but also to help make sure that your plan is properly implemented.

First, you may have short-term concerns. Everyone should have a "cushion" to fall back on when an emergency arises, an unexpected repair or replacement is needed, or an attractive investment opportunity presents itself. By definition, your reserves should be "liquid", easily convertible to cash when you need it. It also should be money you can definitely count on – not tied up in the kind of investments whose values fluctuate. The amount of your reserves depends on the size of your family, your income, your lifestyle, and your own assessment of the possible problems you may have to face. The general rule is to set aside three to six months of living expenses in cash reserves.

TWO: PROTECTION PLANNING

Protecting yourself against the unexpected is a vital element in financial planning. This means having adequate protection. As situations change over time, your protection needs also change. This is why it's important to regularly review your protection needs at least annually. A financial planner can help you discover ways to meet your protection needs more efficiently and economically. He/she can also show how certain life insurance products can provide savings or accumulation opportunities, while meeting your protection requirements. These benefits can help you achieve such goals as saving for retirement or meeting college education expenses. While protection needs and goals vary, there are certain "bases" that should be covered.

You should always cover your family's health. By this I mean having the resources to be proactive with healthcare, and deal quickly with medical issues, if they should arise. And don't forget about you and your spouse's ability to earn a living. Your greatest asset is your ability to earn a living! In purely economic terms, a serious disability can be disastrous. Disability insurance can protect you against this kind of misfortune. And of course there should be coverage on your personal property...Liability...and/or your business, if you have one. Adequate protection is fundamental to sound financial planning. Proper protection planning assures that your family will realize your goals even through death, disability, or destruction. We can greatly reduce poverty in our community with the proper amount of life insurance in each family.

THREE: INVESTMENT PLANNING

An almost endless array of choices is available to you as you try to select the right investment for current and future needs. This is all the more reason why comprehensive financial planning is vital before making any decision. Before you invest, you must review your goals, the amount of risk you are willing to assume and the time frame within which you hope to achieve your objective.

Investments basically fall into two categories: fixed assets and equity assets.

Fixed Assets funds invested at fixed rates of return, usually for a specific period of time. Examples include long-term bonds (corporate, municipal, state, or federal), some unit trusts, and long-term certificates of deposit. The objective of these investments is usually income and safety of principal.

Equity assets investments whose market values and rates of return can go up or down. Unlike fixed asset investments which are usually bought to produce income, equity assets are purchased for growth, or growth and income. Your home, for instance, is an equity asset as is all real estate. Stocks are also equity assets; they may pay varying dividends, or none at all, and the value of a share of stock will fluctuate depending on the market.

Equity asset investments can be made for either the long or short term. In any case, it is important to weigh the risk involved. This entails looking at an investment's history, the quality of its management, future trends and other factors. Naturally, it also involves looking at your own financial situation.

Keep in mind that a good investment portfolio is driven by financial goals, or your "final number." Knowing your final number, risk tolerance, and the amount you can afford to save or invest, will greatly influence how you invest.

Example: If you have a retirement income goal of $30,000 per year, you will need approximately $600,000 generating 5 percent of income annually during retirement. Here your number is $600,000; from here you back into what you need to do to accomplish this accumulation goal.

FOUR: INCOME TAX PLANNING

Intelligent tax planning can be a powerful element in protecting and building your assets. When seeking to minimize your tax bite, it is important to know how deep that bite is. One way to reduce this bite is through tax-exempt investments.

Virtually all of these investments are free from federal income tax. Many are also free from state and local taxes when purchased by residents of those areas.

The interest and dividends paid on contributions to certain tax-deferred products such as deferred annuities and universal life insurance are not immediately taxable. But unlike tax-exempt returns where the income is never taxable, tax deferred simply postpones the payment of taxes until receipt of this income at a later date – preferably when you are in a lower tax bracket. Of course, a major way for individuals with earned income to defer payment of taxes is through an individual retirement account (IRA) or 401(k). For certain investors, an IRA or 401(k) may also be a tax – deductible investment.

Other ways of lowering your taxable income are through gifts and trusts. If your child is over age 14, you may benefit by shifting investment income to him or her. The taxable income from funds will then be taxed at the lower rate of the individual to whom you make the gift. You should note however, that the income generated by trust and gifts to children under age 14 may be taxed at the parent's tax rate if the income is over $1,000. So in such instances, this may not be an effective means of lowering your taxable income.

FIVE: RETIREMENT PLANNING

"…those who look only to the past or present are certain to miss the future." John F. Kennedy said this, and it is certainly true of preparing for retirement. If we continue to expect that the ways of the past will see us through to our futures, we will be left behind. The methods that helped prepare us for retirement are quickly disappearing, and we must start using others. Today's companies are rewriting the retirement rules for working Americans. Traditional pension plans which gained prominence in the 20th century, are rapidly disappearing because of the high costs involved in funding them. Some corporations are defaulting on their plans, and an increasing number of companies have underfunded or at-risk plans. To help protect employees with corporate pensions, the federal government has enacted laws requiring employers to meet a 100 percent funding target for their defined-benefit plans. Companies that sponsor pension plans are also required to pay higher insurance premiums to the Pension Benefit Guaranty Corporation (PBGC), which was created by Congress in 1974 to help protect American workers from the risk of pension default. Premiums have increased because the PBGC itself is facing a deficit as a result of more companies defaulting on their pension plans.

Because of these costly requirements, it is becoming less and less attractive for companies to provide traditional pensions to retirees. Employers with underfunded plans may simply choose to eliminate them, and even companies with healthy plans may decide that defined-benefit plans are not worth the cost. As a result, it is likely that more companies will offer defined-contribution plans like the 401(k) to attract new employees and to help employees fund their own retirements.

Thus, it is important to be aware that you will have less help from your employer and will have to rely more on your own savings and investments to fund your retirement. The government has tried to help by raising contribution limits to most employer-sponsored retirement plans. You can contribute money to these plans on a pre-tax basis. Your contributions and any earnings accumulate on a tax-deferred basis. Of course, remember that distributions from most employer-sponsored retirement plans are taxed as ordinary income and, if taken prior to reaching age 59 1/2, may be subject to an additional 10 percent federal income tax penalty.

A number of companies are taking steps to help workers fund retirement. Many have instituted automatic enrollment in their defined-contribution plans to encourage more employees to participate. Some are enhancing the benefits of their plans by increasing the amount they contribute to employee accounts and/or enhancing matching contributions. Many companies that still have traditional pension plans should be able to pay their promised benefits. But in light of recent trends, it would be wise to consider all possible sources of retirement income when reviewing your retirement strategy. With the changing retirement landscape, there may be no better time than now to size up your current situation. Your company-sponsored retirement plan will be just one piece of your retirement funding pie.

There are basically 4 slices to the retirement income pie:

1. Pension income
2. Investment income
3. Social Security
4. Employment income

The key is to get the majority (60 percent to 70 percent) of your retirement income from your investments – qualified and tax-deferred, non-qualified plans such as, 401(k), 403(b), IRA, and tax deferred annuities.

Many Americans realize the importance of saving for retirement, but knowing exactly how much they need to save is another issue altogether. With all the information available about retirement, it is sometimes difficult to decipher what is appropriate for your specific situation.

One rule of thumb is that retirees will need approximately 70 to 80 percent of their pre-retirement salaries to maintain their lifestyles in retirement. Depending on your own situation and the type of retirement you hope to have however, that number may be higher or lower.

Fortunately, there are several factors that can help you work toward a retirement savings goal:

Retirement Age: The first factor to consider is the age at which you expect to retire. In reality, many people anticipate that they will retire later than they actually do; unexpected issues, such as health problems or workplace changes (downsizing, etc.), tend to stand in their way. Of course, the earlier you retire the more money you will need to last throughout retirement. It's important to prepare for unanticipated occurrences that could force you into an early retirement.

Life Expectancy: Although you can't know what the duration of your life will be, there are a few factors that may give you a hint.

You should take into account your family history – how long your relatives have lived and diseases that are common in your family – as well as your own past and present health issues. Also consider that life spans are becoming longer with recent medical developments. More people will be living to age 100, or perhaps even longer. When calculating how much you need to save, you need to factor in the number of years you will spend in retirement.

Future Health-Care Needs: Another factor to consider is the cost of health care. Health-care costs have been rising much faster than general inflation, and fewer employers are offering health benefits to retirees. Long-term care is another consideration. These costs could severely dip into your savings and even result in your filing for bankruptcy if the need for care is prolonged. Factoring in higher costs for health care during retirement is vital, and you might want to consider purchasing long-term-care insurance to help protect your assets.

Lifestyle: Another important consideration is your desired retirement lifestyle. Do you want to travel? Are you planning to be involved in philanthropic endeavors? Will you have an expensive country club membership? Are there any hobbies you would like to pursue? The answers to these questions can help you decide what additional costs your ideal retirement will require.

Many baby boomers expect that they will work part-time in retirement. If this is your intention and you find that working longer becomes impossible, you will still need the appropriate funds to support your retirement lifestyle.

Inflation: If you think you have accounted for every possibility when constructing a savings goal but forget this vital component, your savings could be far from sufficient. Inflation has the potential to lower the value of your savings from year to year, significantly reducing your purchasing power over time. It is important for your savings to keep pace with or exceed inflation.

Social Security: Many retirees believe they can rely on their future Social Security benefits. However, this may not be true for you. The Social Security system is under increasing strain as more baby boomers are retiring and fewer workers are available to pay their benefits. And the reality is that Social Security currently provides only 20 percent of the total income of Americans aged 65 and older with at least $44,000 in annual household income.[*] That leaves 80 percent to be covered in other ways.

And the Total Is... After considering all these factors, you should have a much better idea of how much you need to save for retirement.

For example, let's assume you believe that you will retire when you are 65 and spend a total of 20 years in retirement, living to age 85. Your annual income is currently $80,000, and you think that 75 percent of your pre-retirement income ($60,000) will be enough to cover the costs of your ideal retirement, including some travel you intend to do and potential health-care expenses. After factoring in the $12,000 annual Social Security benefit you expect to receive, a $10,000 annual pension from your employer, and 4 percent potential inflation, you end up with a total retirement savings amount of $760,000. (For your own situation, you can use a retirement savings calculator from your retirement plan provider or from a financial site on the Internet.)

The estimated total for this hypothetical example may seem daunting. But after determining your retirement savings goal and factoring in how much you have saved already, you will be able to determine how much you need to save each year to reach your destination. The important thing is to come up with a goal and then develop a strategy to help reach it. You don't want to spend your retirement years wishing you had planned ahead when you had the time. The sooner you start saving and investing to reach your goal, the closer you will be to realizing your retirement dreams.

1) Income of the Population 55 or Older, 2004, Social Security Administration, 2006. Breakdown based on people aged 65 and older with at least $44,000 in annual household income.

SIX: ESTATE PLANNING

Have you ever seen a trailer hitched to a hearse? When we leave this earth – and we will – nothing can be taken with us.

Ben Franklin referred to two certainties of life – death and taxes. Some may take comfort in the belief that death at least brings an end to taxes, but that is not always the case.

So what are you going to do if you can't take it with you?

Congratulations! You've worked hard all of your life; in fact, you've done so well you may not need all of your assets for retirement income. How can you make sure your money is passed on to the people you care about most?

The estate planning process will help you make a smooth transition of your wealth to those you love. The good goodbye.

Planning is a part of nearly everything we do in life. It's even a part of dying. How will you preserve your assets from estate taxes and probate fees? How will you ensure distribution according to your wishes? Who will make financial and medical decisions in the event of your incapacity? By taking steps in advance, you have a greater say in how these questions are answered. And isn't that how it should be? Now let's learn the basics:

Wills and Trusts: Wills and trusts are two of the most popular estate planning tools. Both allow you to spell out how you would like your property to be distributed, but they also go far beyond that.

Just about everyone needs a will. Besides enabling you to determine the distribution of your property, a will gives you the opportunity to nominate your executor and guardians for your minor children. If you fail to make such designations through your will, the decisions will probably be left to the courts. Bear in mind that property distributed through your will is subject to probate, which can be a time-consuming and costly process.

Trusts differ from wills in that they are actual legal entities. Like a will, trusts spell out how you want your property distributed. Trusts let you customize the distribution of your estate with the added advantages of property management and probate avoidance.

Wills and trusts are not mutually exclusive. While not everyone with a will needs a trust, all those with trusts should also have a will.

Durable Power of Attorney for Finances: Incapacity poses almost as much of a threat to your financial well-being as death does. Fortunately, there are tools that can help you cope with this threat. A durable power of attorney is a legal agreement that avoids the need for a conservatorship and enables you to designate who will make your legal and financial decisions if you become incapacitated. Unlike the standard power of attorney, durable powers remain valid if you become incapacitated.

Now that you have the basic outline of the wealth-building process it is time to learn about some of the particulars. But before we go into some frequently-asked questions about wealth creation and protection, let's take a look at a sample financial plan for reference.

Financial Needs Assessment

William and Stacy Smith

Anywhere, Texas

Prepared by: James Marshall, Senior Advisor

Marshall Wealth Management, LLC

October 27, 2008

Table of Contents

Disclaimer.. 3

Overview... 4

Current Financial Position.. 5

Asset Allocation.. 6

Retirement..7

Attainable Retirement.. 8

College savings... 9

College savings... 10

Goal Attainability... 11

Conclusion... 12

Projections are based on assumptions that are believed to be reasonable.
Actual results may vary, perhaps to a material degree.

2

Disclaimer

This financial plan is hypothetical in nature and is intended to help you in making decisions on your financial future based on information that you have provided and reviewed.

IMPORTANT: *The projections or other information generated by this financial plan regarding the likelihood of various investment outcomes are hypothetical in nature, do not reflect actual investment results and are not guarantees of future results.*

Criteria, Assumptions, Methodology, and Limitations of Plan

The assumptions used in this financial plan are based on information provided and reviewed by you. Those assumptions must be reconsidered on a frequent basis to ensure the results are adjusted accordingly. The smallest of changes in assumptions can have a dramatic impact on the outcome of this financial plan. Any inaccurate representation by you of any facts or assumptions used in this financial plan invalidates the results.

We have made no attempt to review your property and liability insurance policies (auto and homeowners, for example). We strongly recommend that in conjunction with this financial plan, you consult with your property and liability agent to review your current coverage to ensure it continues to be appropriate. In doing so, you may wish to review the dollar amount of your coverage, the deductibles, the liability coverage (including an umbrella policy), and the premium amounts.

This plan does not constitute advice in the areas of legal, accounting or tax. It is your responsibility to consult with the appropriate professionals in those areas either independently or in conjunction with this planning process.

Results May Vary With Each Use and Over Time

The results presented in this financial plan are not predictions of actual results. Actual results may vary to a material degree due to external factors beyond the scope and control of this financial plan. Historical data is used to produce future assumptions used in the financial plan, such as rates of return. Past performance is not a guarantee or predictor of future performance.

The results are based on your representation of risk and include information current as of October 26, 2008. You are responsible for confirming that the answers you provided to determine your individual risk tolerance used in this financial plan are accurately represented. The proposed asset allocation presented in this plan is based on your answers to a risk tolerance questionnaire and may represent a more aggressive and therefore more risky investment strategy than your current allocation mix. Actual return rates and performance may vary to a significant degree from that represented in this financial plan.

Investments Considered

This plan does not consider the selection of individual securities; the plan provides model portfolios. The results contained herein do not constitute an actual offer to buy, sell or recommend a particular investment or product. All investments are inherently risky. The asset classes and return rates used in the plan are broad in nature. The illustrations are not indicative of the future performance of actual investments, which will fluctuate over time and may lose value. Refer to the Asset Allocation section of this report for details on return rate assumptions used throughout this plan.

There are risks associated with investing, including the risk of losing a portion or all of your initial investment.

Overview

The following report is an assessment of your current financial position. Throughout this report, you may find the following symbols:

$ = Opportunity   ✓ = Success   ✗ = Problem

In performing this assessment, we have made the following observations:

Net Worth and Cash Flow

$ You have a **net worth of $500,007** and you currently have a cash flow surplus of approximately **$3,075 in** 2008.

Asset Allocation

✗   Based on our analysis of your current asset mix, you may be incurring less risk than your risk tolerance indicates you would be comfortable with in your investment portfolio. We recommend a rebalancing of your portfolio to more closely represent your risk tolerance and time horizon.

Retirement

✓   It appears that no additional savings are required to meet the Retirement goal.

College savings

✗   Additional savings of **$367 per month**, or a **lump sum of $33,835**, may be required to meet the "College savings" goal.

College savings

✗   Additional savings of **$267 per month**, or a **lump sum of $26,334**, may be required to meet the "College savings" goal.

Goal Attainability

✗   You currently may not have sufficient cash flow resources to meet the additional savings requirements for your goals.

Projections are based on assumptions that are believed to be reasonable.
Actual results may vary, perhaps to a material degree.

4

Current Financial Position

Analysis $

To determine your Net Worth we take the current value of all of your assets, and then subtract the current value of all of your liabilities. Based on the information you have provided, you currently have a **Net Worth of $500,007**.

We have also evaluated your current Cash Flow position. We determine your cash flow surplus or deficit by adding together all of your cash inflows, then subtracting all of your cash outflows, which include lifestyle expenses, savings, and taxes. Based on the information you have provided, you currently have **a cash flow surplus of $3,075** in 2008.

Net Worth	**Cash Flow**
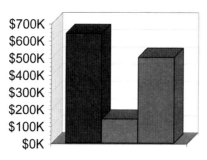	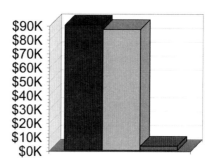

| ■ Assets | ■ Liabilities | ■ Net Worth | | ■ Incomes | ■ Outflows | ■ Surplus |

Net Worth	
Qualified Assets	$365,000
Non Qualified Assets	$0
Lifestyle Assets	$275,000
Liabilities	($139,993)
Net Worth	$500,007

Cash Flow	
Income	$90,000
Lifestyle Expenses	$52,800
Savings	$14,000
Taxes	$20,125
Surplus	$3,075

Consider the Following

- Decide on the sacrifices you are currently willing to make to achieve your financial goals.

Notes

Asset Allocation

Objectives

To realize the projected rate of return that is based on your personal risk tolerance and investment time horizon.

The average weighted return rate assigned to your current portfolio is 8.11%. Your risk profile is Conservative, which represents a proposed average return rate of 12.04%.

Analysis ✖

Based on our analysis, your current weighted average return rate is lower than the proposed average return rate. We recommend that you review and rebalance your portfolio to bring it in line with your risk profile.

Proposed Asset Mix

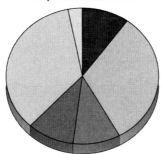

▲ Large Cap Growth (10%)	▲ Growth & Income Equity (10%)	△ US Govt/Treasury/Mortgage Backed (35%)
△ Large Cap Value (32%)	▲ Investment Grade Debt (10%)	△ Money Market (3%)

	Current	Proposed
Rate of Return	8.11%	12.04%
Standard Deviation	0.00%	9.39%
Proposed Risk Profile		Conservative

The above values represent the high level asset class groupings, rather than the individual asset classes displayed in the graphs.

Consider the Following

- A proper asset allocation helps you maximize your return rate for the level of risk that is within your comfort zone.

- A well diversified portfolio also reduces the risk of having "all of your eggs in one basket."

Notes

6

Retirement

Objectives

William plans to retire in the year 2022 at age 65. Stacy plans to retire in the year 2022 at age 62. Your retirement income goal in the year 2022 is $50,000, in today's dollars.

Analysis ✓

Based on our assessment, it appears you have sufficient savings strategies in place, or sufficient capital allocated, to meet your retirement goal.

Monthly Savings for Retirement

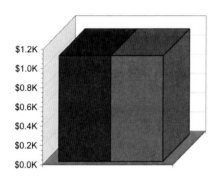

$1.2K	
$1.0K	
$0.8K	
$0.6K	
$0.4K	
$0.2K	
$0.0K	

Capital for Retirement

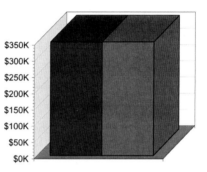

$350K	
$300K	
$250K	
$200K	
$150K	
$100K	
$50K	
$0K	

■ Current Savings/Capital	▨ Additional Required Savings/Capital	■ Total Required Savings/Capital

Current Savings	$1,100 /month*
Assets Currently Allocated	$350,000
Estimated Rate of Return	8.00%
Additional Savings Required	$0 /month
or	
Additional Capital Required	$0

*May include surplus savings.

These projections are based on the average weighted return rate assigned to your current portfolio.

Consider the Following

- The additional required monthly savings amount is based on savings to non-qualified assets.

- Maximize contributions to tax-advantaged qualified retirement plans such as IRAs, Roth IRAs, and 401(k) plans.

- If you have not already done so, begin investing on a regular basis.

Notes

Attainable Retirement

Objectives

William plans to retire in the year 2022 at age 65. Stacy plans to retire in the year 2022 at age 62.

Analysis ✓

In order to achieve your retirement income goal, it appears you may be able to **retire early, in the year 2011,** when William is 54 and Stacy is 51.

If you were to retire in the year 2022, when William is 65 and Stacy is 62, it appears your current savings strategies and retirement capital may provide you with the ability to cover **205% of your planned retirement expenses**.

Attainable Retirement Age
$50,000 /Year

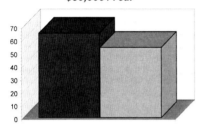

Attainable Retirement Expenses
Retire At 65/62

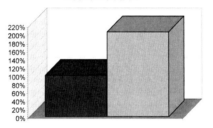

■ Planned Age/Expenses   ▨ Attainable Age/Expenses

Attainable Retirement Age

	Planned Retirement	Attainable Retirement
William	65 (2022)	54 (2011)
Stacy	62 (2022)	51 (2011)

Attainable Retirement Expenses

Retirement Start Date	% of Retirement Expenses
2022	205%

Consider the Following

- If the amount of required savings is unmanageable, we should review your goals to find a solution.
- If your projected savings exceed your need, you may be able to spend more in retirement.

Notes

College savings

Objectives

You want to accumulate sufficient assets to fund William, Jr's education goals for 4 years at a total cost of $15,000 per year, in today's dollars, beginning in the year 2017.

Analysis ✖

Based on our assessment you currently may not have sufficient savings strategies in place or sufficient capital, allocated to meet your goal.

Based on your assumptions, to meet your goal you would need to save an **additional $367 per month** or allocate an **additional $33,835 today**.

Monthly Savings

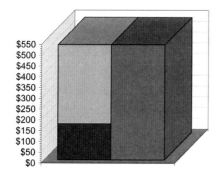

Capital Allocated

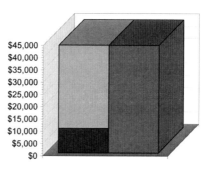

■ Current Savings/Capital	▨ Additional Required Savings/Capital	■ Total Required Savings/Capital

		Consider the Following
Current Savings	$167 /month	• Determine realistic values for tuition and related college expenses. Factor in the effects of inflation. College costs have historically increased at a significantly higher rate than inflation.
Assets Currently Allocated	$10,000	
Estimated Rate of Return	10.00%	
Additional Savings Required	$367 /month	• Invest regularly for your children's education, starting as early as possible.
or		
Additional Capital Required	$33,835	• Where possible, take advantage of educational savings vehicles such as Coverdell ESAs, 529 Plans, UTMA accounts and UGMA accounts.

These projections are based on the average weighted return rate assigned to your current portfolio.

Notes

Goal Attainability

Analysis ✖

Based on our assessment, you currently may not have sufficient cash flow resources to meet the additional savings requirements for your goals.

We recommend you review your current cash flow and prioritize your current and future goals appropriately.

The *Average Monthly Surplus* shown in the graph below is an average of your cash flow surpluses and/or deficits through the next five years. If the final average is a deficit, the graph will show zero.

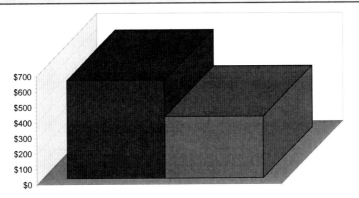

$700
$600
$500
$400
$300
$200
$100
$0

■ Additional Savings Education /mth   ■ Average Monthly Surplus
□ Additional Savings Retirement /mth

Additional Savings for:	
Retirement	$0/month
Education:	
"College savings"	$367/month
"College savings"	$267/month
Average Monthly Surplus/Deficit*	$398

*Represents your average surplus/deficit over the next 5 years.

These projections do not take into consideration potential premium increases for additional Life Insurance, Disability Insurance and Long Term Care Insurance.

These projections are based on current asset mix and rate of return.

Consider the Following

- It is important to balance future goals with current lifestyle needs.

- Assess the priority future goals based on available cash flow.

Notes

Projections are based on assumptions that are believed to be reasonable.
Actual results may vary, perhaps to a material degree.

11

Conclusion

Now that you have an overview of your current financial situation, where do you go from here? Our recommendations are as follows:

- **Review this document** and ensure you understand the information contained in the report. Be sure to ask us questions on areas that need clarification.

- **Assess the original objectives.** Are they realistic? Can you afford to implement all of your objectives? What are your priorities? If you are unable to fund all of your objectives, consider alternative goal dates, revised goal amounts, and alternative investment strategies. We will work together in the process.

- **Review various strategies** that will help you to achieve your goals and determine a time frame for these strategies.

- **Decide on a course of action.** Together, we will evaluate the alternative that is consistent with your objectives and your financial ability.

- **Review your plan** on a regular basis, generally once a year. In addition, review it whenever a major change occurs in your family (e.g., changes in employment, birth of a child, new income or expenses, etc.). You may need to adjust your plan in light of any of these new circumstances.

One final thought!

Remember to maintain a long-term focus with your plan. Do not expect to anticipate every curve in the road but be prepared to adjust your plan when necessary. Your financial plan is not a single event but a journey that can cover ten, twenty, thirty years or more.

Notes

Investing

Investing can be as simple as committing extra cash each month into a savings account, or it can involve complex decisions about choosing stocks, annuities, mutual funds or other investments that best meet your needs. Once you understand the basic principles, however, you can add to your knowledge step by step, either through reading about different investment options or through the guidance of a financial advisor.

How do I start my investment program?

First, have your basic financial situation in order. This means that you should have no high interest credit card accounts or other excessive unsecured debt. You will also need six months of 'rainy day' savings and fully participate in your employer-sponsored retirement plan, such as a 401(k) account or in an Individual Retirement Account if you are not eligible for an employer's plan.

With these basics covered, next you need to determine your investment goals, timeline and risk tolerance. Is your goal to invest for retirement, purchase a second home, start a business or take a year off to travel the world? Whatever your financial aim, the first step is to

The hypothetical case study results are for illustrative purposes only and should not be deemed a representation of past or future results. This example does not represent any specific product, nor does it reflect sales charges or other expenses that may be required for some investments. No representation is made as to the accurateness of the analysis.

determine how much money you will need. Next, estimate when you will need it. Your investing approach differs greatly if retirement is five years away instead of twenty-five years down the road. Timing will influence the amount of money you need to invest as well as the best ways to invest it.

Next consider the risk you are willing to take to reach your goal. Larger yield investments also carry the highest risk, either temporarily or permanently. Likewise, the safest investments return relatively lower gains. You need to decide whether you will be comfortable if a sizeable portion of your nest egg rides on highly volatile investments. On the other hand, you may have to postpone retirement, take on a second job, scale back your lifestyle or downsize your financial goals if low-risk investments cannot produce the returns you need to reach your goals.

A final consideration is how much money you have to invest. If you are starting with a small sum and want to make regular additions to a plan, then you will choose different investments than if you have a six-figure inheritance to invest.

Once you understand these factors, start your research, on your own or with a financial planner, to structure the investment plan that best suits your individual situation.

There seems to be many ways to invest. People talk about stocks, funds, gas and oil futures, precious metals, venture capital, real estate and even pork bellies. How do I find my right investment?

The cardinal rule of investing is never to invest in something you do not understand. This rule is especially true for do-it-yourself investors, who might be swayed by a story in the newspaper or postings on an Internet chat board. Even when you work with an investment professional, you need a clear understanding of the investment, how its market generally works to raise or lower its value and the amount of risk and volatility it carries. You need not be an expert in every technical detail, but you must grasp the basics to determine how a particular investment fits into your overall investment plan. You gain this background through your own research, through research services or from an advisor. The bottom line is never to buy investments you do not understand.

Provided it makes money in the end, why should the volatility of a stock or other investment affect my decision?

Volatility – or the rise or decline in value – is an important consideration in two ways: Your risk tolerance and your *time horizon* – when you need the money.

More volatile stocks frequently make big swings between their highs and lows. The stock worth fifty cents a share in the morning may be down to fifteen cents by evening. If you will stress about money 'lost' on paper that day, then highly volatile investments are not your best choice. Through panic you may sell out at the wrong time and at a loss just to end your anxiety.

Volatile investments can give you greater returns, but what if its value is down when you need to sell? While you may be an investor who can watch a stock swoop and dive over the long term, confident that over time it is likely to finish on the upswing, what if it is in a prolonged down period when you need the money to buy your retirement home or when junior's tuition is due at State U? You then end up missing substantial future gains, and perhaps selling at a loss.

The standard investing approach is to diversify investments from more volatile vehicles, such as stocks, into more stable instruments, such as bonds, as you get closer to needing the money. For example, one widely accepted rule of thumb for retirement portfolios suggests that your percentage of assets in stocks should be 110 percent minus your age in years, with the balance invested in cash or bonds. Therefore, if you are fifty years old, you should not have more than sixty percent of your portfolio in stocks or other risky investments. There is, of course, a wide range of different approaches and strategies regarding asset allocation, and you should tailor these assumptions to your individual needs.

What are the different types of investments and how do I evaluate each?

There are a wide variety of investments, but most fall into one of four dominant *asset classes*: different vehicles that share risk factors and market influences. The four major categories are: Cash and cash equivalents, fixed-income securities, equity investments, and tangibles and property.

> Using diversification/asset allocation as part of your investment strategy neither assures nor guarantees better performance and cannot protect against loss in declining markets.

Is cash really an investment?

Cash and cash equivalents are the safest category of investments. Generally speaking, they give you guaranteed returns on your money, although the rate may change periodically. Bank savings accounts are one example and possibly the safest, since deposits are currently insured up to $250,000 per single account. Other cash accounts include certificates of deposit, money market accounts, short-term Treasury bills and short-term bonds.

What about fixed-income investments?

Fixed-income instruments cover a larger group of bonds, including government, municipal corporate, high-yield and foreign bonds. While there are certain classes of risky, high rate bonds on the market, often called *junk bonds*, for the most part bonds are used by conservative investors who want a steady stream of income and protection for their invested principal. *Fixed* refers to a set rate of interest that the bond pays over its term. While the performance is not always guaranteed, bonds are considered safe investments, especially government bonds. Bonds are ranked or rated according to risk and the credit rating of the issuer.

What is an equity investment?

Equity is stock ownership in a business enterprise. Equity investments include blue chip and large-capitalization stocks to mid- and small-capitalization stocks sold in the US markets, as well as international stocks. Stocks can be possibly more speculative then bonds and might carry higher rates of risk, although the risk from owning shares can vary greatly between an established, blue-chip manufacturing company that pays a steady dividend and a tiny biotechnology start-up that may never earn a profit. Unlike bonds and cash accounts, stockholders assume more risk concerning the performance of the company since there is no guarantee the value of stock will increase or that the firm will pay a dividend. Poor management or changes in the marketplace may even drive the company into bankruptcy. Because of this greater degree of risk, stocks reciprocally reward investors with higher returns than bonds and bank accounts.

What about investing in tangibles and property?

Tangibles and property include real estate, but also precious metals (gold and silver, etc.), Commodities (grain futures and pork bellies, etc.) and even collectibles (automobiles, art, coins, wine and antiques). These investments are more specialized and subject to bigger valuation swings than stocks, partly because the market is much smaller for a rare painting, a house or a ton of grain. These investments are *illiquid* and difficult to sell at certain times.

For example, an investor might have to hold onto property for years until it can be sold profitably. At other times – especially with commodities – investors cannot wait out a bad market, such as when oranges that underlie orange juice futures are ready to be picked. To invest in tangibles requires expert knowledge of the investment and its unique market.

How do I factor inflation?

The first step is understanding your investment goal. How much must your investment return in the end, what is your timeline? How much must you invest and what rate of return do you need to successfully reach your goal and keep pace with inflation?

Assume your goal is to purchase vacation property in the next ten years. The property you want may sell for $100,000 today. The historical average rate of inflation is about three percent. Compounded; then you need about $134,000 to have the same purchasing power in ten years, assuming the price of your desired property matches the rate of inflation. If the property you want has increased in value at a rate faster than inflation, then you must save more. To compute that amount use one of the many online loan calculators and average the rate of increased value during the past few years. If your desired property has increased in value at ten percent per year, then it will take about $259,000 to buy the same property in ten years.

That seems like a huge increase over the years. Is it hopeless to try and beat inflation and other cost increases?

The influence inflation has on savers and investors can really hurt as it compounds year after year, but that same compounding is what gives investors the edge. Compound interest, of course, is the effect of gaining interest on top of interest or gains on top of gains as you reinvest the money your investments are earning. When combined with regular contributions, compounding results in what Albert Einstein once called, 'the eighth wonder of the world.'

For example, a $100 investment that pays five percent annual interest yields $105 at the end of the year. Leave that $5 gain in place and you collect five percent interest on the entire sum next year, for a total of $110.25. If you think that extra quarter-dollar will not amount to much, leave it all in for a total of ten years, and it builds to $162.89. Add $5 per month to your investment and after ten years the total is $952.15 – almost ten times your original investment.

Once I have figured out my goal and timeline, how do I reach it?

Balance the amount of money you have to invest now against how much you can continue to regularly contribute each week, monthly or annually, along with the rate of return you can expect from your investments for the risk you are willing to bear. Also figure how much of your investment gains will be lost to taxes. You can calculate those factors with inflation and investing calculators found online, or with help from your financial advisor.

For example, to reach the $259,000 goal in our vacation property, you could put $25,000 into an investment with a five percent rate of return. Add $1,550 per month for ten years, and assume a twenty-eight percent federal tax rate, not counting any state or local taxes. Increase that initial investment to $50,000 and you need to add a bit less, $1,300 per month. If you pick an investment that is riskier but pays a ten percent rate of return, you only need to add $900 per month to your $50,000 initial investment.

In practice, investing can be just this simple or far more complicated, combining various tax considerations and many combinations of investment vehicles, risk factors and other details. The basics are the same, however, and once you grasp them you are well on your way to making the important strategic decisions to meet your financial goals.

CASH AND CASH EQUIVALENTS

What are the different types of cash accounts and how do they work?

Savings accounts: The most basic cash account is simply a savings account. You can withdraw or deposit money and the bank pays you interest at set intervals on the balance in your account. The rate of return is typically low, but these accounts offer two big advantages: Virtually no risk, thanks to deposit insurance, and complete liquidity, which allows you to add or withdraw money at almost any time.

Federally insured savings accounts are currently guaranteed up to a balance of $250,000; any amount over that in a single account could be lost in a bank failure. A couple who keeps larger amounts of cash on deposit can triple that amount by titling $250,000 into two single accounts, one in each spouse's name, and another $250,000 in a joint account. To avoid risk on additional cash, they would open accounts at a different bank.

Money market accounts: Also available through banks, offer many of the same benefits of a savings account, with a bit less liquidity. They also pay higher interest. Most money market accounts are structured like checking accounts, with a set limit on the number of withdrawals that can be made during any one month. Additional withdrawals are subject to service charges that erode your interest. Money market accounts are typically used to hold money for transactions such as monthly bills or other fixed expenses, at which point the saver simply transfers one lump sum to pay the month's bills into a checking account.

Certificates of deposit: These also are insured bank accounts that can pay higher rates of interest than savings accounts or money markets, but also have more restrictions. Certificates of deposit, also referred to as CDs, pay set rates of interest for fixed terms ranging from fourteen days to five years or more.

CDs are used to hold cash for a fixed period of time and you are charged penalties if you withdraw from the account early. To obtain the higher rates of interest on CDs, savers often divide a lump sum among several shorter term CDs, or a combination of long- and short-term CDs. This strategy is called laddering.

For instance, instead of $30,000 invested into a three-year CD where you could not access the money without penalty for three years, you could put $10,000 into a combination of a one-year CD, a two-year CD and a three-year CD. Although you would collect less interest, you would have penalty-free access to $10,000 each year while collecting the maximum amount of interest available for those accounts. If you did not need the money, you could then re-invest each year's CD at the higher three-year rate. This strategy is especially effective when interest rates rise and savers don't want to be locked in to a low, long-term CD rate.

What are the best ways to use these accounts?

Since these accounts typically do not pay high interest, CDs, money markets and savings accounts are generally called "*s*" by professional money managers. They secure your cash until it is ready to be spent or invested elsewhere, as they gain little interest while the money is on hold. Of course, retirees with accumulated nest eggs in stocks, bonds and other investments methodically move their gains out of riskier, more volatile investments because of the safety of these accounts, the liquidity in case of a medical or other emergency and their total lack of volatility.

For younger folks, savings vehicles offer a good way to hold emergency cash, such as a rainy day fund or to accumulate money to invest. If, for example, you want to invest in a mutual fund or other vehicle with a minimum investment, which is often $1,000, a money market or even a savings account is a good way to put a little money aside from each paycheck until you have enough to invest. Savings accounts are also good ways for parents and other grown-ups to teach youngsters about banks, money and interest, as well as to get them into the savings habit.

Do all bank accounts pay the same rate of interest, or should I shop around?

You should definitely shop around if you are parking money for any length of time in one of these accounts. On accounts such as CDs and money markets you can improve your rate by more than a point with just a few minutes of research. Most newspapers and several online sites survey the highest-yield bank accounts across the country on a weekly basis. In most cases, savers simply call a toll-free number to get the specifics for opening an account, mail in an account form and then wire transfer the money to the bank.

How important is the rate of compounding?

It can be very important. Some accounts compute and pay interest quarterly, while others compute interest monthly or even daily. The more frequently that interest is paid, the more it increases the effect of compounding, resulting in a higher yield on your savings.

What do I look for in choosing one of these type of investments?

When you compare CD and money market accounts, look beyond the rate to the *annual percentage yield* (APY). This number takes the interest rate and compounding method for the account and computes the total annual yield of the investment. For instance, if two accounts offer the same interest rate but one compounds interest monthly and the other compounds quarterly, then the monthly compounding account produces more interest for the saver in a year's time. Assuming both banks offer the same service and are equally safe, you would want the higher APY.

> An investment in a money market fund is not insured or guaranteed by the Federal Deposit Insurance Corporation or any other government agency. Although the fund seeks to preserve the value of your investment at $1 per share, it is possible to lose money by investing in the fund.

How do I evaluate a bank for safety?

A financial institution's financial soundness is rated by several different national services all based on the reports the banks and thrifts file with government regulators and insurers. The FDIC publishes a list of these services, and others are offered online from sites such as *www.bankrate.com*.

In most cases, for accounts less than $250,000, a bank in poor financial condition only presents a question of convenience, not risk of losing money. Typically, a bank that fails is closed for a period of a few days or weeks and then reopens under government supervision, which protects your money but prevents you from gaining access to your accounts during this temporary period. If, however, you have more than $250,000 in any account, the over-limit amount is not insured and you could lose some or all of it if the bank fails.

What about Treasury bills and short-term bonds?

Short-term US Treasury bills and highly rated short-term bonds are considered as safe as money in the bank based on the credit rating of the issuer and the maturity of the bond, which in this case is one year or less. With Treasury bills, the terms are one year, twenty-six weeks or thirteen weeks; the interest rate is guaranteed and the bond is backed by the federal government. In the case of other bonds, perhaps state or municipal bonds or high quality corporate bonds, the basic principal is the same: A credit-worthy institution issuing a quality short-term bond for a period of weeks or months is considered a safe investment.

BONDS AND FIXED-INCOME INSTRUMENTS

What exactly is a bond?

A bond is essentially a loan, either to a government or a corporate entity. The investor loans a certain amount of money at a fixed rate for a fixed period of time and receives regular interest payments on the loan until the end of the bond's term, when the invested principal is returned as well.

How do bonds work?

A government or corporate entity issues the bond, which is sold through investment banks, brokers or, in the case of some US Treasury bonds, directly through the government. The bond has a fixed interest rate or *coupon rate*. The investor pays the *par value*, also called *face value* or *maturity value*, of the bond as principal and receives regular fixed interest payments during the term of the bond. At maturity, the investor's principal is returned. Some bonds, such as zero coupon bonds and some savings bonds, are issued at less than par value.

These regular interest payments and protection of principal are what make bonds appealing to investors who need regular income with lower risk, such as retirees, parents saving for college or investors who want to balance their portfolios by locking in guaranteed returns over a period of time.

For example, if a $1,000 par value bond pays six percent annual interest during a term of ten years, therefore the bond yields six percent annual interest. The investor loans to the bond issuer $1,000 and then receives $60 in interest every year for the next decade, for a total return of $600. At the end of ten years, the investor also receives his original $1,000. In most cases, the interest is taxed as the investor receives it, but certain government and municipal bonds are tax-free at various levels, either federal, state, local or some combination of the three.

Are there other ways to profit from bonds?

Once they are issued, bonds can lose or gain value based on the difference between the bond's fixed interest rate during its term and the rise or fall of interest. If interest rates fall below the bond's fixed rate, the bond's value appreciates. If rates rise in comparison to the bond, the bond's value depreciates.

What are the risks of investing in bonds?

One risk is that as interest rates fall below the bond's rate, you can earn less return on the bond than you could by investing elsewhere. Rising interest rates also are a sign of inflation, and you could end up losing money on a bond that pays a rate that is lower than the rate of inflation. Bonds also can lose value if the issuer's credit or bond rating is downgraded, which lowers the bond's value in the secondary market. We saw this often occur in the financial markets of 2008. You, as the investor, then hold a shakier investment than you expected, while receiving a lower rate of interest than you should for that risk. Finally, the issuer of the bond could default or go bankrupt and fail to make regular interest payments or return your principal.

What kind of interest rate can I expect on bonds?

Bonds reflect the prevailing interest rates for similar investments of the same risk and term. A quality ten year corporate bond pays an interest rate that reflects the current rate for a ten year US Treasury note, plus an additional premium, since bonds from corporate entities are less safe than Treasury issues, which are backed by the full faith and credit of the US government.

Bonds pay higher rates of interest as their term increases to offset the long-term risk of inflation and other factors. Bonds also pay higher or lower rates of interest depending on the credit level of the corporation issuing the bond. The lower the credit rating, the more risk to the investor in buying the bond, but it offers a greater potential return. Most risky are corporate junk bonds, which pay high yields but also carry a good chance of issuer default.

What does it mean when a bond trades at a discount or a premium?

Bonds trade at a discount or premium in the *secondary market*, where the original bondholder sells the bond before maturity. This can happen because the bondholder needs the money and wants to liquidate the bond or, more typically, because interest rates have moved significantly up or down in relation to the fixed interest rate of the specific bond.

For instance, most bonds pay a yield approximating the prevailing interest rate when issued. If interest rates rise after the bond is issued, it is now a less attractive investment than new bonds, or it might become a losing investment if inflation rises above the bond's interest rate. The bondholder may then sell the bond before maturity at less than its face value. This results in a loss, but allows the bondholder to reclaim his principal early with a penalty to spend or to reinvest the money at the current higher rate of interest, rather than waiting until the bond matures and loses more money. The discount allows the secondary buyer to more closely match the current prevailing interest rate at a shorter term to maturity and avoid losing money on the re-sold bond.

When a bond trades at a premium, that means prevailing interest rates have dropped since the bond was issued, making the existing bond a more attractive investment. The bondholder can now sell the bond at more than its face value, scoring an early profit without having to keep the bond until maturity. Although the profit is not as much as would have been received for the entire term of the bond, the money can now be spent or reinvested. The buyer pays more than the principal amount, but offsets that price hike by receiving more interest than at prevailing rates.

In each case, the person buying the bond is essentially raising or lowering the bond's overall yield by paying less or more than the principal that will be received when the bond matures.

Can you give an example of buying a bond at discount?

Let us say an investor buys a ten-year, $1,000 face-value bond paying five percent interest, which is the prevailing rate. The investor receives ten payments of $50, and then gets the original $1,000 back with a profit of $500 and a yield of five percent.

After two years, the prevailing interest rate has risen to seven percent. The bondholder decides to sell the bond, either to free up cash or to invest the money elsewhere. The bond is sold for $800 to another investor after receiving $100 in interest from two years of $50 payments. This results in a $100 loss for the original bond buyer. In turn, the secondary buyer receives eight payments of $50, plus the entire $1,000 principal, for a profit of $600 and a resulting yield of 6.25 percent. The buyer has raised the yield by essentially purchasing the right to receive $1,000 in cash eight years from now for $800.

How does it work when buying a bond at a premium?

Take the same ten-year, $1,000 face-value bond paying the prevailing rate of five percent interest, yielding five percent for a $500 return. Two years later, though, instead of interest rates rising, rates drop to three percent. Since it is now more difficult to find an investment yielding five percent, the bondholder can sell the bond for above its face value.

In this case, the $1,000 face-value bond is sold for $1,300 after receiving two $50 interest payments, for a total return of $400. The buyer still receives the eight remaining interest payments of $50, plus the entire $1,000 principal, with a return of $100 and a resulting yield of 3.85 percent. Although $1,300 was paid for the right to the $1,000 principal in eight years, the $400 of interest payments offset that premium and still allow for a profit.

How do I buy or sell bonds?

You can buy and sell bonds through a regular full-service or discount brokerage, many financial institutions or through a bond broker. You can bypass brokers and avoid commission charges by purchasing US Treasury bills and notes directly from a Federal Reserve bank or the government. These transactions are handled at *www.treasurydirect.gov*, or over the phone at 800-722-2678. In the auctions you can bid competitively or noncompetitively, meaning you agree to accept whatever rate or yield is determined at the auction. This is a good way for beginners to start. You need to open an account and register. The minimum amount to invest is $1,000. A step-by-step set of instructions is on the website or you can call and request an investor information kit. A good way to start is with the weekly Monday auctions, when the government sells thirteen and twenty-six week $1,000 face-value bills to individuals and institutional investors.

What is a government bond?

The US Treasury issues, or *floats* bonds to pay for governmental operations and to finance the national debt. Federal government bonds are considered very safe because the Treasury's source of money to pay interest and repay principal is its ability to collect taxes, compared to a corporation that may be unable to sell its products or services.

Treasury issued bills are available in thirteen, twenty-six and fifty-two week maturities and notes are floated in two, five and ten yearterms. The Treasury also issues bonds called *Separate Trading of Registered Interest and Principal of Securities*, or *STRIPS*. These are deeply discounted zero-coupon government bonds, and *Treasury Inflation-Protected Securities* or *TIPS*, which are inflation-protected bonds.

Five and ten year Treasury notes are issued in February, May, August and November. The two year notes are issued monthly. The fifty-two week T-bills are issued every four weeks, and the thirteen and twenty-six week issues are floated weekly.

What are savings bonds?

Savings bonds also are issued by the government and are familiar to savers who have participated in savings programs at work or received or purchased them as gifts. Savings bonds differ from other government bonds in that they cannot be traded in the secondary market, although they can be cashed in early. Savings bonds can be purchased directly from the Treasury, through *www.treasurydirect.gov*, through most banks and other financial institutions and through many employer savings programs.

Savings bonds can be purchased in your name or in another name to be given as a gift. Bonds can be registered in the owner's name, under the name of two co-owners or with a designated beneficiary. Two types of savings bonds are currently issued: Series EE and Series I, while several older series of bonds are still in circulation. Series HH Bonds were discontinued.

Series EE Bonds: These bonds are purchased for one-half of the face amount, in denominations of $50, $75, $100, $200, $500, $1,000, $5,000 and $10,000 (although

$50 and $75 denominations are unavailable through the Payroll Savings Plans and other employer savings plans). Much like a zero-coupon bond, these bonds do not offer regular interest payments. Instead, interest accrues until the bond is cashed. Series EE Bonds can continue gaining interest even after they reach face value (for up to thirty years). Individuals are limited to buying $30,000 of face-value Series EE Bonds in any one calendar year. EE Bonds are guaranteed to reach face value in twenty years.

Series EE Bonds increase in value every month, with interest compounded semiannually. The Treasury announces EE Bond rates each May and November, and that rate applies to the bonds for the next six months. The rate is based on ninety percent of the average yields on five-year Treasury securities for the preceding six months. If you cash such a bond before it is five years old, you are penalized for the amount of the last three months of interest, and EE Bonds must be held for at least twelve months before they can be redeemed.

Gains on EE Bonds are exempt from state and local income taxes, and federal tax is deferred until the bonds are redeemed or stop earning interest after thirty years. There are also special tax benefits when savings bonds are used to save for college or other education purposes.

Series I Bonds: Similar to EE Bonds, Series I Bonds are sold at face value and earn interest based on two different rates: a fixed rate of return and a variable semiannual inflation rate. The fixed rate is set every May and November and remains the same throughout the life of the I Bond, while the semiannual inflation rate can be adjusted every six months. The semiannual inflation rate is based on part of the Consumer Price Index reported by the Bureau of Labor Statistics. Interest is paid when the bond is redeemed.

I Bonds are sold at face value in denominations of $50, $75, $100, $200, $500, $1,000, $5,000 and $10,000. Like EE Bonds, they earn interest for up to thirty years; individuals are limited to purchasing no more than $30,000 in face-value bonds in one year. Tax treatment of gains on Series I Bonds is the same as for Series EE Bonds. Likewise, I Bonds must be held for twelve months before they can be cashed, and they carry the same three months interest penalty if cashed before being held for five years.

Series HH/H Bonds: These bonds were purchased for face value and pay interest directly to the bondholder every six months. The government stopped issuing Series HH Bonds in September 1, 2004. Prior to that date, HH Bonds could only be purchased by exchanging Series EE/E Bonds or reinvesting older Series H Bonds. Series HH Bonds issued after January 1980 mature in twenty years, while H Bonds issued between February 1957 and December 1979 mature in thirty years. When those bonds mature, the Treasury notifies the owners and provides reinvestment information.

Interest on HH/H Bonds is paid at a fixed rate set on the day of the bond's purchase and locked in for the first ten years of the bond's term. Interest rates are reset on the tenth anniversary of the HH Bond's issue date and on the tenth and twentieth anniversaries for H Bonds.

What is a Patriot Bond?

Patriot Bonds are Series EE Savings Bonds specially inscribed with the words Patriot Bond. You can purchase them through banks and other financial institutions, but not through payroll savings plans. After the terrorist attacks of September 2001, many Americans wanted a 'war bond' to express their support for the anti-terrorism efforts. Patriot Bond revenue, however, goes to the general Treasury fund and is not earmarked to pay for specific anti-terrorism efforts.

What about Treasury TIPS?

TIPS are a marketable Treasury security. TIPS pay interest every six months and return your principal when the security matures. The interest and redemption payments for TIPS are tied to inflation. TIPS are sold at face value and pay a fixed rate of interest, but both the redemption value at maturity and the interest payments are based on adjusting the principal for inflation against the Consumer Price Index. To guard against deflation, TIPS are guaranteed to pay at least the face value or the inflation-adjusted face value, whichever is greater.

TIPS are sold in five, ten and twenty year maturities, cannot be reinvested in new TIPS, and offer the same tax advantages as other Treasury vehicles.

What are Treasury STRIPS?

STRIPS are Treasury bonds where the principal and each interest payment have been separated into single components, creating independent individual invest-ments. With STRIPS, investors (especially pension funds, retirement investors and others) can guarantee themselves a known payment at a specific future date.

STRIPS are sold at discount like zero-coupon bonds and only make one scheduled payment. They are traded in the secondary market, where their prices tend to fluctuate more than the prices of the whole bonds from which they are derived. The minimum investment in STRIPS is $1,000 face value, and all Treasury notes and bonds are *strippable*.

You mention T-bills, T-Notes and Savings Bonds, but you have not discussed US Treasury Bonds.

Treasury Bonds were known as 'the long bond' because of their extended thirty-year term. They were considered the benchmark risk-free investment in the US and were widely monitored throughout all global financial markets. However, the Treasury Department suspended issuing new thirty year bonds in October 2001, began issuing them again in April of 2006. At the time, federal budget surpluses made the thirty year bond unnecessary and expensive to US taxpayers because of the higher interest rates paid on the long-term issue. The long bond is still traded in the secondary market, although some of the older thirty year bonds have been redeemed.

What is a Municipal Bond?

States, counties, cities and towns issue municipal bonds to supplement local government operating budgets and to finance schools, road projects, sewer construction and other building projects. *Muni* bonds, as they are called for short, are not subject to most federal taxes, although they can sometimes be subject to the Alternative Minimum Tax. Municipal bonds are exempt from state and city taxes, if you live in the particular state or city that floats the bonds. Out-of-town investors, however, pay the applicable tax on interest gains in their home state (if state has income tax).

There are two main types of municipal bonds: *general obligation* and *revenue bonds*. General obligation means the bonds are backed by the full faith and credit of the issuing government and are repaid with tax collections and other general income. Revenue bonds are issued to finance specific projects and are repaid with proceeds from those operations, such as toll road collections or water plant charges. Revenue bonds are considered riskier because of their dependence on a single operation to generate money to pay interest and repay principal.

Other forms of municipal bonds include private activity bonds, which are issued in connection with some private businesses, such as a public-private partnership to develop a sports arena or other facility. Depending on the issue, it may or may not be subject to federal or state taxes. Another type of municipal bond is the insured municipal bond. As the name implies, these bonds carry private insurance against default. The cost of insurance is seen in the lower interest rate of the bond, which reflects the lowered risk factor.

Because states and other municipalities may default on bonds or, in extreme situations, even declare bankruptcy, not all municipal bonds are considered as safe as government bonds (with the exception of insured municipal bonds). Municipal bonds are reviewed and rated by the large bond-rating services.

What is a corporate bond?

Corporate bonds are issued by individual businesses to finance operations, expand operations, plants and other facilities, or to finance takeovers or other adjustments to the corporate financial structure.

Unlike federal, state and local governments, corporations can issue stock to raise money, which does not require regular interest payments or even guarantee the return of the original investment. However, many corporations do not want to issue new stock because it can dilute the ownership interest of the current stockholders. Many investors and analysts also prefer to see businesses issue bonds because the guaranteed payment schedules and fixed terms of bonds are more dependable and require the business to be more disciplined in meeting revenue and profit goals. Bonds also can provide tax advantages to the corporate issuer.

Are there different types of corporate bonds?

There are several basic types of corporate bonds:

Commercial paper: These are short-term, unsecured bonds that usually mature in thirty to ninety days.

Convertible bonds: These can be very attractive bonds that allow investors to profit from a company in two ways. In addition to your investment return, they can be converted into company stock, either when the stock hits a set price, at the bond's maturity, at the investor's option or under other specified circumstances.

Debentures: These are bonds that are secured only by the general operations and credit of the corporation.

Revenue bonds: Like municipal bonds, corporate revenue bonds can be tied to the proceeds of specific operations, subsidiaries or product lines.

Mortgage bonds: These are often used to purchase specific pieces of equipment or to build or expand plants and facilities. They are secured by the purchased asset.

What is the difference between a registered bond and a bearer bond?

A registered bond is a bond issued in the investor's name, historically through certificates held by the buyer, his or her broker or some other representative. A bearer bond is not issued in any one investor's name, and can be redeemed by whoever presents it. Most bonds issued today, however, are tracked in book entry form, where investors' names are registered on electronic lists. Investors receive a simple paper receipt instead of fancy printed certificates.

What is a zero-coupon bond?

A zero-coupon bond is one that does not make regular interest payments, but instead accrues the interest until maturity, when it is paid along with the return of the principal. *Zeroes*, as they're called, are sold at deep discount from their face value, and then paid at face value when they mature. Because they do not pay regular income, zero-coupon bonds are not attractive to investors looking for fixed income, and prices for zeroes in the secondary market are subject to broader swings as interest rates fluctuate.

'Phantom taxes' are another drawback for some investors who buy taxable zeroes because taxes are due each year on the accrued interest of the bonds even though no actual income has been received by the bondholder. However, if you hold them in a traditional IRA, Roth IRA, or other retirement plan, the Phantom tax would not be a problem since the earnings are tax-deferred or tax-free. This is offset by the fact that no tax is then due when the bond matures.

The notion of a 'coupon' originated with registered bonds that came with attached coupons that were redeemed for each interest payment. That is why a bond's interest rate still is often referred to as its *coupon rate*.

What's a baby bond?

Baby bonds are those with a face value of less than $1,000. Baby bonds are issued when issuers want to make bonds more affordable to a greater number of investors, often by municipalities that want to encourage greater public participation in financing operations or a specific project.

How are bonds rated?

Bonds are rated by several research services, with the two most widely known being Standard & Poor's and Moody's Investors Service. These services investigate the financial stability and resources of the bond issuer, its debt and income, the dependability and likelihood of projected revenues, market conditions, financial stability and prospects of the issuer compared to similar firms in its industry (or similar municipalities) and many other factors. The subsequent ratings are ranked on an alphabetical scale, ranging from *triple* A (AAA for Standard & Poor's, Aaa for Moody's) all the way down to being in default (unrated for Moody's and D for Standard and Poor's).

What are investment-grade bonds?

Investment-grade bonds are the four highest-graded types of bonds. They are considered the safest and most reliable by the rating services, issued by stable and dependable corporations, states or municipalities. Because of this lower risk, they tend to pay lower rates of interest than riskier, lower-rated issues.

Rating refers to the symbol assigned by the rating agency, i.e., A+, A, BBB, etc. Descriptor refers to rating agency's description for the symbol, Superior, Excellent, Very Strong, etc.

Moody's Investor Services:
[Rating], [Descriptor] Moody's rating reflects a company's financial security. Rating is [x] out of 21 possible.

Standard & Poor's:
[Rating], [Descriptor] S&P's rating reflects [strong] financial security. Rating is [X] out of 20 possible.

What are junk bonds?

Junk bonds are the three classes of lowest-graded bonds (plus those in default) by investor research services. These bonds are regarded as highly speculative investments, with a great deal of risk, often issued by financially unstable entities with a high probability of default. Some lower classes of junk bonds may already be in default.

Why aren't Treasury issues rated?

US government bonds are not rated because they are considered absolutely safe and collectible, since the government has the authority to raise taxes to pay its debts and simply could never afford to consider default.

What happens when bonds are downgraded?

If one or more of the research or rating services discovers or anticipates that the financial stability of a bond issuer is decreasing, the issuer's bond rating is lowered. This instantly sends the price of its existing bonds down in the secondary market as buyers demand a higher yield, creating what is called a *fallen angel*. Naturally, any new bond that might be issued by the downgraded firm or government would have to be floated at a higher interest rate, creating even more doubts about the financial security of the issuer.

What does yield to maturity mean?

Yield to maturity is a somewhat complicated bond-pricing model that takes into account not only the total return a bond provides when purchased at a given price and held for its full term, but also assumes that all interest payments are reinvested at the same rate and compounded. For example, a six percent, $1,000 ten year bond purchased at face value would have a yield to maturity of about 6.11 percent if all the coupon payments were reinvested at six percent.

What is a bond call?

A bond call occurs when the issuer exercises the right to redeem the bond early. Calls are often attached to longer-term bonds as a kind of refinance measure that allows the issuer to pay the bonds early and re-issue new bonds at lower interest rates. Call terms are disclosed in advance, and often stipulate that a specific bond won't be called before a certain number of years or a certain date. Because callable bonds are less attractive to investors overall (especially those seeking regular bond payments as income); these are usually priced lower than regular bonds. In some cases only part of a bond issue is called, with the selection of bonds to call made by lottery.

What is paper?

Paper is only another word for bonds, referring to the paper certificates and receipts used when bonds are issued.

EQUITY INVESTMENTS

How do stocks work?

When you buy stock, you buy an ownership stake or equity in the company by becoming a shareholder. You then literally own a share in the company. This gives you, along with all the other shareholders, a claim on the company's earnings and assets, as well as a voice in how the company is operated. It also gives you the same degree of risk that the company might be unprofitable or even fail, resulting in the entire loss of your investment.

Why do companies issue stock?

Corporations issue stock to finance start-ups and expansion, support operations, research and development, acquisitions and other business activities. Stock is attractive because once the company sells its offering, it can use the proceeds of the sale without being obligated to regular interest payments or by having to directly pay back the shareholders' investment, as with a loan, bond or other type of financing. Besides raising money, stock also spreads the risk of owning the company throughout the marketplace.

What is an IPO?

An initial public offering (IPO) takes place the first time a company issues shares to the public, first by registering the issue with the Securities and Exchange Commission. The stock is then purchased by underwriters, such as investment banks, who sell the shares to the public. An IPO is accompanied by a prospectus, which describes the operation of the company, its products and financial history and sets out the risks of investing in the offering.

What is a secondary offering?

A secondary offering is any subsequent public offering of additional stock, often in different classes or forms, such as preferred stock or convertible bonds. A secondary offering is usually undertaken when a company's stock is priced high; otherwise the new issue dilutes the holdings of other investors by reducing the size and value of their shares.

What are stock options?

Stock options allow individuals the right to purchase shares of stock at set prices at a time in the future. Options are exercised when the stock price of the company is higher than the *exercise price*, or *strike price*, of the option, resulting in an immediate profit for the option holder. Options are usually granted to key managers of the company as a tool to motivate them to ensure a high stock price so that their options will be profitable.

What do we generally mean by the stock market?

The market refers to overall business and investment conditions; when the market is up, stock prices rise and the general business climate is considered good, with most firms growing and operating profitably and with ample demand for products and services. When the market declines, share prices fall or stagnate, and business conditions are considered unfavorable because of rising costs, shrinking profits or both, and consumer demand for products and services also weakens.

Besides the market, investors and business analysts also refer to Wall Street when discussing overall investment conditions. It is located in New York, which is home to scores of investment banks and financial institutions, and is considered one of the global financial capitals. Still, the term *Wall Street* tends to refer generally to all of the major investing and financial institutions in the US and their combined outlook on the economy and business conditions.

This overall market is made up of several different trading venues for investments, including stocks. The major stock exchanges are the New York Stock Exchange, which is also called the 'big board' because of its dominant position in the market, and the smaller American Stock Exchange, or Amex, also located in New York. These are markets for stocks, options and other investments where traders actually meet on the floor of the exchange. The NASDAQ stock market has no physical exchange; it is a computerized, electronic marketplace operated by the National Association of Securities Dealers.

The NASDAQ is the nation's busiest stock exchange, especially for new, small and emerging companies, although firms as large as Microsoft also trade on the NASDAQ. The NASDAQ and Amex exchanges merged in 1998, but both still operate separately.

How can I make money with stocks?

There are two basic ways to make money with stocks. One is through price appreciation and trading in the secondary market. Once a company has issued stock, it makes no more money from the issue, but uses the proceeds to invest in the business. If successful, the company becomes increasingly profitable and the overall business increases in value, which usually raises the underlying value of your shares in the company. You can now sell those shares to other investors at a profit in the secondary market.

You can also make money on a stock through receiving dividends. As a company becomes established and stable, it may possibly turn from reinvesting its profits in the business and instead distributes some of that money to its shareholders in the form of dividends. Dividends are announced ahead of time, and usually paid quarterly, semi-annually or annually.

The rate and regularity of dividends influences the stock price of the firm. Companies tend to be careful about paying dividends, since once established, investors expect dividends to continue or even increase. Reducing or suspending dividend payments is sometimes seen as a sign that the business is having financial difficulty.

Are there different types of stocks?

Common stock, as the name implies, is the most common form of stock. With common stock there is no guarantee you will receive a dividend or see profits on the investment, or that the stock won't lose value or become worthless. In exchange for this risk, you receive a stake in the company that can possibly appreciate in value, deliver consistent cash dividends or do both if the company is successful.

Preferred stock is sold and traded like common stock, but offers investors less risk. Dividends are set with preferred stock, and paid before dividends on common stock are issued. Preferred shareholders also are paid before common stockholders if the company fails. As always, less risk means less reward, and preferred stock is no exception. While the dividend has priority over preferred stock, it also won't increase if the company is successful, and could pay a smaller dividend than common shares. Preferred stock tends also to appreciate more slowly than common stock, which limits profit.

In addition to these two forms of stock, shares can also be issued in different classes, which are listed separately, as with preferred and common shares. Any class of stock can:

- be limited to ownership of a specific subsidiary or portion of the business,

- have limited or special voting rights,

- come with specific dividend rights or restrictions,

- sell at different market prices from the common shares.

What is market capitalization?

Market capitalization, or market cap, for short, is simply the financial size of a publicly traded company. Market cap is calculated by multiplying the current share price of a company's stock by the total number of outstanding shares. For example, a company with 100 million outstanding shares currently trading at $20 per share would have a capitalization of $2 billion. Market cap allows investors to compare companies to similar-sized firms in the following categories.

Large-caps: These firms have a market capitalization of more than $5 billion. They have large volumes of daily trades in their stocks, often pay regular dividends and have little risk of failure, but sometimes carry high stock prices. Because they are so large and established, they usally do not offer the highest potential growth. This includes blue chip stocks and many of those found in the Dow Jones Industrial Average, the S&P 500 index and other top indexes.

Mid-caps: These firms have capitalizations of more than $1.5 billion and also are widely traded fairly large companies. They usually offer more potential share price appreciation than most of the large-cap stocks, and often show up on many of the same indexes.

Small-caps: These companies with less than $1.5 billion in capitalization offer potentially bigger gains and higher risk, and do not usually pay any dividends. Some of these firms can be difficult to trade because of their small trading volume. They do not appear on the major stock indexes and often are not covered by analysts or other financial analysts.

Why are some stocks called blue chips?

Blue chip designates stocks considered to be the most valuable, stable and regularly profitable. They tend to represent shares of the largest, most established corporations, and form a type of unofficial benchmark for the market.

There is no standard, official list of blue chip stocks, and some old-line companies have fallen out of the category while others have joined. Some analysts and brokers might be more selective, holding their own basket of blue chips to a few dozen companies, while others might extend the category to several hundred.

What are income stocks?

Income stocks regularly pay dividends to provide a reliable income for investors. These include mature, stable companies that lead their industries and have stable, unthreatened markets. Until deregulation, utility stocks – especially electrical utilities – were considered good investments for retirees and others who depended on these investments to provide a regular income. Income stocks also have stable prices and do not typically present opportunities for significant capital gains unless the structure or strategy of the firm significantly changes direction. At the same time, that stability tends to guard against share price depreciation which preserves the investor's capital investment.

What are growth stocks?

Growth stocks are almost the opposite of income stocks. Rather than distributing their profits to shareholders, growth stocks are usually typified by younger, aggressively expanding companies that reinvest their profits to expand. Because these firms are expansionary, the opportunities for share price appreciation are significant, as is the level of risk. Growth stocks have more volatile price swings.

What are cyclical stocks?

Cyclical stocks are shares of businesses that react predictably to the condition of the economy, either following the business cycle up when times are good and falling when times are bad. Sometimes they move in a contrary direction. Cyclical stocks can include shares of mortgage lenders and others that are sensitive to movements in interest rates or companies that operate in discretionary spending categories, such as airlines, hotels and travel agencies, where spending falls during recessionary cycles and soars during business booms.

What are DRIPs?

This acronym stands for Dividend Re-Investment Program. These are stocks that can usually be purchased directly from a number of large companies for a small fee, rather than through a broker or securities dealer for full commission. Investors have the option to have their stock dividends automatically reinvested in new shares, or fractions of new shares. Investors can usually purchase additional shares for cash, sometimes on a regular monthly basis, in what are called *Optional Cash Purchase Plans* (OCPs).

DRIP plans are attractive to small, individual investors with a long timeline who are looking for stable shares and low investment fees, for investors who want small, regular investments, or for inexperienced investors who want inexpensive investments they can directly control. Some DRIPs discount the sale of their shares to the public, while others allow for small initial investments (as little as ten dollars).

What is a stock split?

When the price of a stock increases drastically, it can become too expensive for small, individual investors to buy in the usual minimum lots of one hundred shares. The high share price dissuades investors who feel the issue has reached the top of its potential value. In a stock split, the number of shares increase and the stock's price is cut proportionately. This leaves the stock with the same overall capitalization and investors retain the same dollar value in their holdings.

Besides the benefits of liquidity and affordability, shares of split stocks tend to rise back toward the pre-split price, either for psychological reasons (as many investors still feel it is a $200 stock, for instance) or because investors sense the company split its stock in order to leave the share price room to grow because they expect more growth and profit. The most common stock split is two-for-one, but stocks can split three-for-two or in any combination.

For example, a stock that reaches $200 per share could split, offering investors two $100 shares for each share they hold and leaving them with the same total value.

Do stock splits ever work the opposite way?

There is a reverse stock split, although it is not always as positive an event as a normal stock split. Reverse splits work to raise the price of a stock by taking shares out of circulation and proportionally raising the value of the remaining shares. This often is done so that the stock price meets the required minimum set by some exchanges, or to make the stock more attractive to institutional investors that often do not want to hold low priced issues.

As an example, a fifty-cent stock that split one-for-three would give stockholders one $1.50 share for every three, fifty-cent shares they hold, since the price is now set above the $1 minimum it can be carried on the NASDAQ exchange.

How do I know the value a stock is at?

A stock is only worth what someone else will pay you for it. But in truth, valuing a stock can be a very complicated process. There are some rules of thumb such as price/earning ratios and dividend yields – but these must be considered within the overall market, the business sector in which the company operates, the financial structure and management talent of the firm, its competitive environment and investor psychology. There is also that risk factor, called the future. Businesses can decline – or soar in value – because of advances in technology, government deregulation, nationwide demographic shifts or just unpredictable, drastic changes in global politics or local consumer attitudes.

One common (but not simple) approach used by financial analysts is to measure a company's predicted growth and projected revenue and profits, then discount those future earnings to their current worth together with the value of the firms tangible assets (plants, machinery, patents, cash and cash equivalents). After arriving at a total value for the company and adjusting for risk and other factors, this value is divided by the number of shares of stock issued to arrive at a current pershare price. This discounted cash flow method allows investors to recognize when a company is trading above or below its real value and to buy or sell shares accordingly.

What is the P/E ratio?

The price/earnings ratio, illustrates, to some extent, the balance between a stock's price and the company's profits for the prior four quarters (not calendar year). P/E ratios are used to compare the market value of different stocks. A stock is said to be 'cheap' if its P/E is lower than the overall market or similar competitors. Likewise, a high P/E in comparison makes a stock expensive. P/E ratios are a useful but limited tool, mostly because they rely on past performance instead of future earnings and because they rely on current market price, which may already be over- or understated by the investing public – especially in the case of a popular 'hot' stock or an effectively managed company operating in an unpopular market segment. In addition, a company's P/E may appear expensive if it is going through a rapid growth phase where heavy expenses are incurred before earnings climb.

Commonly, the P/E ratio is referred to when a stock is said to be trading for 'X' times its earnings. A stock with a P/E of twelve would trade for twelve times its earnings.

How do analysts compute the forward P/E ratio?

The forward P/E ratio attempts to get around some of the limits of the standard P/E by combining the last two quarters of results with the financial performance projected by analysts for the next two quarters.

What is the percent yield?

Percent yield, also called dividend yield, applies to stocks that pay dividends. It illustrates the relationship between current share price and expected rate of dividends as a percentage. This allows investors to make side-by-side comparisons of stocks, as well as comparing the yield to other investments, such as bonds. Obviously, a percent yield cannot be computed on stocks that will not pay dividends.

What is meant by total return?

Total return is another, more useful barometer of stock performance that allows you to compare individual stocks or entire portfolios against other investment vehicles. Total return adds your dividends plus the change in stock price since your purchase to calculate gains or losses. Taxes and broker commissions must also be factored.

What does volume refer to?

Volume is simply the number of shares trading in any one day or period. The higher the volume of a stock, the more often it is traded, meaning that the stock price stays current in the market and that your investment is fairly liquid or easy to sell. Marked increases or dips in volume indicate that traders are acting on new information affecting the stock's future. Low-volume stocks, which are said to be *thinly traded*, can pose a risk in that the price can be easily influenced by a relatively few trades, and may not be followed closely by analysts and forecasters, leaving the price to reflect out-of-date information about the company's prospects.

What does book value mean?

Book value is the pershare value of the equity (or net worth) of a firm, which is computed by subtracting assets from liabilities, minus intangible items such as goodwill. This is, literally, the company's stated financial worth 'on the books'. If a firm has substantial assets, including significant cash, relative to the stock price, it will have a high book value and can represent a good investment. On the other hand, a high book value might result from over-valued assets or understated liabilities, making the stock a poor investment. Likewise, a low book value might result from a company's assets being undervalued, which can make it a good buy for investors, or it might result from heavy debt, which can make it an unattractive stock.

Is EPS important?

EPS stands for earnings per share, and is useful to see whether profits are increasing in relation to the price per share. EPS is calculated by dividing the company's net earnings, or profits, by the number of outstanding shares of stock. A high EPS means the company is increasing in value by making a greater percentage of profits for each shareholder than if its EPS were lower. EPS can be compared annually to see if the company is increasing its profits, or in relation to other similarly structured competitors or other companies.

What is ROE?

This is return on equity, a percentage derived by dividing earnings per share by the stock's book value or equity. This illustrates how efficiently and effectively the company uses its assets to produce earnings or profits. The higher the ROE number, the better. Some investors prefer to look at ROA, *return on assets,* to measure how productively a company's assets are being deployed, rather than just considering the equity balance of the assets.

What is the payout ratio?

Payout ratio is the amount of net income or earnings, the company uses to pay its dividends. This is normally somewhere between fifty and twenty-five percent. If a company uses a higher percentage of income to pay its dividends, it may have profitability problems, lower revenue, excessive debt or high operating expenses.

What is a stock's range?

A stock's range is the span between its high and low prices over a day, week, year or some other period. Wide fluctuations in price mean that a stock is volatile, or subject to wide movements in its price, either up or down. Volatility, though, is not always bad, if you know what to expect and if the stock moves decisively upwards.

Typically, stock prices are accompanied by a list of the fifty-two week high and low – which represents the highest and lowest price the stock has traded at in the preceding fifty-two weeks (not calendar year). Stocks also have historical highs and lows, which measures their all-time extreme prices at both ends of the scale.

How do I buy and sell stocks?

That depends on how much help you want and how much you are willing to pay. You must buy or sell through a stock broker, except in the case of DRIPs and some other direct-sale stock issues. Brokers work for brokerage houses, which are investment firms that have purchased seats and become members of a stock exchange. Brokers handle your orders in exchange for a commission, although the actual sale or purchase at the exchange is handled by a dealer or trader. There are several different types of brokers:

Full-service brokers: These are brokers who also act as investment and financial advisors and have access to research services that help them recommend specific stocks or other investments. Full-service brokers usually work with clients to develop strategies to reach long-term investment goals and provide personal attention and assistance.

Discount brokers: These brokers charge lower commissions than full-service brokers, offering more limited services to customers in terms of personal investment planning, but still supplying some research and other assistance in executing trades.

Deep-discount brokers: For investors who make many big trades and do not need assistance in choosing stocks and designing investment portfolios. These brokers handle trades at lower commission rates.

Online brokerages: These Internet-based services, often operated by large, well-established brokerages, offer the lowest commissions on trades, as well as provide online research, support and other services (sometimes for additional fees).

What kind of order do I place?

There are several ways to set price when you buy or sell stock through a broker. Most orders are *market orders*, when you buy or sell stock at or near its current trading price or market price. There are however, other order strategies:

Limit order: This is used to place a ceiling or floor on your trade by instructing the broker to make the trade only when the stock is at a designated price or better. Limit orders are used with volatile stocks or when you expect changes in the price.

Stop order: This instructs your broker to buy or sell the stock when it hits a specific price target, called the *stop price*. In most cases, the trade will not execute at exactly the stop price, since share prices continue to rise or fall after they reach any one level. Stops more typically are used to sell stocks before their prices drop too far to cause a loss or erode profits.

Good 'til canceled order: This means you want the order to stand until the trade is executed or you cancel the order. This differs from a *day order*, which automatically expires at the end of the market's trading day without any further action from you.

What is day trading?

Day trading is a form of arbitrage, where investors aim to take advantage of temporary shifts in a stock's price by rapidly buying and selling shares, buying and selling several different stocks throughout the day. Day trading is highly speculative and often requires a substantial initial investment. It can be quite profitable and therefore quite risky.

What do investment advisors mean by buy-and-hold?

The buy-and-hold philosophy is the direct opposite of day trading. This approach to investing involves educating yourself about a particular company's stock or a segment of the market or particular industry, buying that stock and holding onto it during market ups and downs to realize a long-term gain. Practitioners of buy-and-hold say they invest in companies, not stocks, and tend to look for stable or growing well managed firms with experienced management. This approach is seen with buying market indexes.

What is market timing?

Market timing is a stock investing approach where investors anticipate the ups and downs of particular stocks or market segments, buying when those shares are depressed but ready to rise and selling as prices peak. Timing the market or any particular stock, involves being intimately familiar with the management and financial condition of the firm, its growth prospects and opportunities, the competitive landscape in its major markets, its ability to profitably expand, the strength of its management and general economic factors that influence the company's operations and profitability.

While some professional money managers are effective market timers, most individual investors lack the time, resources and expertise to effectively time the market, which can result in larger losses and smaller gains than the traditional buy-and-hold approach to investing.

What is short selling?

Short selling is a strategy in which you believe that the stock price will decrease instead of increase. In short selling, you borrow stocks from a broker, order them to be sold and then wait to buy them back at a lower price. You then replace the more expensive borrowed stocks you already sold with cheaper shares you just bought, keeping the difference between the two trades as your profit (minus commissions and fees, including interest you pay your broker on the borrowed shares).

For example, you borrow 100 shares of stock trading at $12 per share from the broker and immediately sell them for $1,200. You now owe your broker 100 shares of the same stock. If the stock price drops to $10, you can buy 100 shares for $1,000, which is called covering your position. You then hand those shares over to the broker and pocket the $200 profit, minus interest fees and commissions.

The advantage of short selling is that you do not make any initial investment of your own. Of course, that return comes with risk. Short selling is called *betting against a stock* because you are gambling that the price will go down. If the price of the stock does not drop in the time period you expect, you are faced with holding your borrowed shares and will continue to pay interest on them. Over time the interest can reduce or eliminate any gain you can make when the stock price eventually drops. The stock price may also increase and cause you to pay interest while waiting for the price to decrease which forces you to cover your short position at a loss.

For example, you borrow the same 100 shares of stock trading at $12 per share from the broker, immediately sell them for $1,200 and now owe your broker 100 shares. Instead of dropping, however, the stock price climbs to $14. Your interest on the borrowed stock continues to climb, meaning the stock has to drop even lower to result in any profit – and that assumes that the share price won't continue to increase. To limit your losses you cover your position at $14, resulting in a $200 loss, plus interest fees and commissions.

In some cases, short sellers end up working against their own interests if too many traders short a particular stock. If that stock begins to rise, many short sellers buy to cover their positions and limit their losses. This results in an increased demand for the stock, which drives the price even higher and prompts larger losses for the short sellers who have not yet covered their positions. This cycle is a *squeeze play*.

What's the opposite of shorting a stock?

That is buying a warrant, a type of option that has less risk than short selling. For a small fee, a warrant guarantees an investor the right to purchase a stock at a set price during a specified period of time. Warrants are used when investors believe a stock's price will rise past the warrant price. If the stock price does not rise, or fails to reach a level where the warrant holder wants to exercise the option, then the warrant expires at the end of the fixed period, which results in a loss.

For example, you buy warrants in a stock for $1 per share that allows you to get the stock for $20 a share within the next year. If the stock price hits $25 you can exercise the warrant and save $5 per share on the trade. You can then sell the stock for its price of $25, for a net profit of $4 per share, after the cost of your warrants and minus commissions.

Warrants are relatively inexpensive, and are traded on the markets after issue, usually marked with a 'wt' after the stock's name. Companies may sell warrants to the public if the firm plans to issue new stock or market stock held in reserve.

Should I buy stocks on margin?

Buying on margin leverages your existing shares of stock. It can   significantly raise the potential for profit in your trades but, as with short selling, carries great risks. Buying on margin means you borrow money for part of your trades from your broker. To trade on margin, you set up a margin account with a brokerage, funded with cash, securities or a combination of the two. You can then borrow up to half of the cost of any stocks you buy. Most margin accounts require a minimum deposit of $2,000 in cash or securities.

In a profitable scenario, you buy 1,000 shares of stock at $12, using $6,000 of your own money and $6,000 borrowed on margin. If the stock rises to $20 you sell for $20,000, repay the $6,000 margin loan and net an $8,000 gain on your original investment of $6,000, plus interest and commissions. In this case, you have earned about twice what you could have, had you used only your own cash.

As with short selling, if the stock price drops you can be forced to either sell the stock at a loss or put more money into your margin account in order to protect your broker from losses on the loan. At minimum, the NYSE and the NASD require margin accounts to maintain a balance minimum twenty-five percent of the price of the securities purchased and held in the margin account. If your holdings drop to the minimum balance, the broker issues a margin call. If you do not meet the call by adding more money or securities to the margin account, you can sell the stock, repay the loan and incur the loss. Brokerages can also liquidate the stock without your approval if you do not meet your margin call.

What is the purpose of stock indexes?

Stock indexes, or market indexes track specific overall segments of the stock market, or even an entire industry, reflecting the historical trend of the measured stocks to return gains over time.

What are the main stock market averages and indexes?

While most investors monitor the performance of their individual stock holdings, market averages and indexes can present a larger picture of how the market as a whole is performing, it mirrors the US economy and current business conditions and investor sentiment. Some indexes and averages track total performance on certain exchanges, while others monitor the performance of specific groups or types of stocks, such as utilities or transportation industries.

The Dow Jones Industrial Average: Also called simply 'the Dow', tracks thirty major industrial companies, but is weighted and adjusted for stock splits and the addition or removal of companies since the Dow expanded to thirty companies in 1928. The original Dow Industrials debuted in 1896, and General Electric is the only original stock still listed. The Dow is designed to measure the performance of firms that are equal to about twenty-five percent of the total of all stocks traded on the New York Stock Exchange.

Other Dow Averages: The Transportation Average tracks a list of twenty railroads, trucking firms and airlines; the Dow Utility Average follows fifteen electric, power and gas companies; the Dow 65 Composite Average covers all sixty-five stocks included in the other Dow averages.

NYSE Composite Index: This includes all stocks traded on the Big Board. The New York Stock Exchange also reports indexes for industrial, utility, financial and transportation shares traded on the exchange.

Standard & Poor's 500: This widely followed index covers a broad range of five hundred companies and is considered a benchmark for investors in major firms. The S&P 500 is weighted to reflect the influence of high market value stocks. It covers four hundred industrial stocks, as well as transportation, utilities and financial firms.

NASDAQ Composite Index: This covers stocks traded on the electronic market system, and usually reflects more volatility because of the number of smaller and emerging companies who have stocked traded on the exchange. NASDAQ also breaks out indexes to cover activity in industrial, insurance banks, computer, and telecommunications firms, as well as an index of one hundred leading NASDAQ stocks.

Amex Composite: This covers the activity of stocks traded on the American Stock Exchange.

Russell 2000: Tracks the activity of the smallest two-thirds of the three thousand largest US publicly traded companies, the Russell 2000 is widely followed as a barometer of small company stock performance.

Wilshire 5000: This index tracks nearly all stocks traded in the US markets, making it the most wide-ranging and broadest popular index.

Value-Line: This covers 1,700 stocks selected by this independent investor research service.

What is the moving average?

A moving average is designed to smooth out the ups and downs of stock prices during a period of time by calculating the average price of a particular stock. A fifty-two week moving average, for example, follows the weekly average of stock prices for the past fifty-two weeks and can give a clearer picture of overall price movement. The movement in a moving average comes from the practice of dropping the oldest average and adding the most recent for each period.

What is the difference between a bear market and a bull market?

Bear and bull markets refer to the current cycle of stock trading. The market may be said to be charging like a bull, with stock prices gaining in an upward trend that can last months or even years. When the market drops by a significant amount, usually about twenty percent, it is likened to a hibernating bear taking to its cave for the winter. Historically, bull markets tend to last longer than bear markets, but bear markets tend to come on quickly with rapid drops in prices.

What are ETFs?

ETF stands for exchange-traded fund. These funds represent a portfolio of stocks that track a specific market index and can be traded on the exchanges just like other stocks, including buying, selling, short selling and purchasing warrants. ETFs are, in essence, a stock of many stocks, similar to a mutual index fund. They cannot exactly replicate the performance of a total index because of commissions and broker fees.

Can you explain American Depository Receipts?

ADRs are a way to trade certain foreign stocks in the US market. They are exchange-traded certificates representing a number of shares of an overseas firm issued by a US bank. ADRs simplify foreign investing by trading in dollars and offer lower trading costs than investing on overseas exchanges. For instance, since the merger of Chrysler Corporation with Germany's Daimler-Benz, the new Daimler Chrysler stock now trades as an ADR in the US.

What rights do I have as a shareholder?

Besides the ability to buy and sell your shares, you also have a voice in the major decisions of the company, including decisions to merge or sell to another firm and choosing a board of directors. In general, the more stock you own, the more votes you can exercise. Preferred stockholders may have fewer voting rights than common shareholders. After a year or so, shareholders can present proposals that meet the requirements of the Securities and Exchange Commission (SEC) to be voted on at the annual corporate meeting.

What is a proxy?

Shareholders who want to vote but do not attend the annual corporate meeting can cast their votes on various proposals by mailing in a proxy statement or paper ballot, or by making a proxy vote over the phone or Internet. Before each annual meeting shareholders receive a proxy statement outlining planned changes and proposals that require the approval of the firm's stockholders.

What is cumulative voting?

While most stockholders have one vote per share of stock, cumulative voting allows you to weight your votes when electing the company's board of directors. This practice is offered in some companies in order to give more weight to small shareholders in voting for the firm's overseers. In traditional or statutory voting, a shareholder with five hundred shares of stock voting on eight directors' seats would cast five hundred votes per desired candidate for a total of four thousand votes. In cumulative voting, those four thousand votes can be distributed differently among the candidates, or can even be cast for one candidate.

Will I get stock certificates when I buy shares?

While some firms still issue elaborately designed stock certificates, most companies and brokerages today simply track stock ownership electronically rather than issuing paper shares. In many cases, investors do not want to hold the certificates, but instead have the stock registered in a street name or the name of the brokerage firm. This allows you to sell the stocks by phone or electronic order, rather than having to deliver the certificates directly to the broker. It also prevents certificates from being lost or stolen.

MUTUAL FUNDS

What are mutual funds?

A mutual fund allows many different investors to invest their money in a large number of stocks, rather than constructing an investment portfolio of individual stocks, bonds and other securities. Investors pool their money under the supervision of an investment company and fund managers who research and direct the funds in many different investments.

In theory, an advantage is that the buying power of many investors allows them to obtain professional portfolio management at lower cost. Another advantage is that a mutual fund can balance the ups and downs of the market between different individual stocks or types of stocks, different markets or even types of securities. Losses in one investment are then offset by gains in another. Plus, the ability to diversify vehicles means that fund managers can lock in investment gains by moving out of one stock or market sector in different investments or even cash.

What are the different types of funds?

Most mutual funds fall into one of three different categories: stocks, bonds or money markets.

Stock funds: As the name implies, are funds that focus their investments in stocks – varying widely in the types of companies in which they invest. Some stocks may focus on young, growing companies in an attempt to deliver significant share-price growth. Others may invest in solid, dividend-paying blue chip stocks, with the primary goal of providing steady income. Still other funds may combine approaches, or even focus on just one segment of business, such as manufacturing or biotechnology.

Bond funds: Like stock funds, bond funds invest in a basket of bonds, including Treasuries, municipal and corporate bonds. Bond funds can diversify, balance or focus, as do stock funds, ranging from risky high-yield corporate junk bonds to stable, income-producing portfolios of government bonds. Bond funds can either distribute interest payments or reinvest them.

Another feature of bond funds is that they allow investors to handle many types of bonds without being locked into rates, terms and yields, and to invest in bonds without having to make large initial bond purchases at specific times of the year. Bond funds can also be divided into taxable and tax-free bonds as well. In some cases, a bond fund can allow investors to shelter their gains from local, state and federal taxes.

Money market funds: Money market funds often are described as 'cash-equivalent investments'. Money markets focus their investments to maintain a $1 per share value, paying dividends that can be reinvested or withdrawn, often with checking account-type privileges. Money markets focus on short-term municipal bonds and corporate debt, as well as T-bills, usually for six months or less. These funds have the advantages of being very safe (few ever have 'busted' the $1 per share level) and very liquid. The down side is that the interest is not much higher than bank deposit accounts such as CDs and the funds are not federally insured. Money market funds are offered in both taxable and tax-free forms, with taxables paying a slightly higher rate of interest.

How are funds targeted?

Within each type of fund there is plenty of opportunity to achieve widely differing investment goals. Each fund is established with a specific philosophy, approach and investment goal, so that you can tailor your choice of funds to your investment needs. Most funds aim to provide either growth, current income or a balance of growth and income.

Growth funds: These funds can vary greatly in their focus, covering everything from aggressive and volatile long-term share price appreciation to value funds that concentrate on buying under-appreciated stocks at a bargain. These funds bypass steady dividends to invest in stocks that are expected to provide capital gains over a period of years.

Income funds: These funds concentrate on adding value primarily through dividends, not price appreciation, investing in US and municipal bonds, corporate bonds and even international currencies. They can be taxed or untaxed, and the risk can range from very safe government issues to high-yielding corporate bonds with a definite risk of default. In general, bond funds are considered less volatile and more dependable than growth funds, while sacrificing some of the high potential gains found in stocks.

Growth and income funds: These funds seek to provide growth over time but with income to balance the fund's risk and volatility. Even within growth and income funds, fund focuses can be very different. Some funds seek to generate their income through equities, investing in blue chips, utilities and other stable stocks, while other funds focus on bonds with fewer stocks.

How important is the fund manager?

Each fund manager has his or her own buying style in managing the fund. Their philosophy and skill guides their choices in the wide range of potential investment options available to even the most narrowly defined fund. Some managers look for bargain-priced stocks that are temporarily overlooked or under-traded, others concentrate on identifying potential high-flyers that are ready to break out, and still others move away from current market trends in what is called a *contrarian* strategy.

What's a focused fund?

Within each fund's target, the manager can select a number of different investments and approaches that define the fund's focus. This might be a specific type of company within a growth stock fund or tax-free bonds that will appeal to investors in certain states.

Sector funds: Sector funds focus on one segment of the market or economy, such as technology, transportation, health care, manufacturing and others. They can be riskier than more broadly focused funds because they are at the mercy of one financial sector. For example, banking stocks can all suffer during a period of rising interest rates, regardless of the quality of the individual stock selections that are made by the fund manager. That risk is offset by the fact that when an industry is growing and attractive to investors, the sector as a whole gets a great deal of interest. Fund managers who understand and concentrate on the sector aim to select the best companies with the greatest potential in a growing market so they can deliver above-average returns.

Metal funds: These are a subset of sector funds that concentrate on mining stocks and their products, such as gold, silver, copper and others. Metal funds are considered more stable than other types of sector funds, and tend to do well during periods of inflation, world political turmoil and other times of insecurity.

Index funds: An index fund is designed to track a particular stock index, such as the S&P 500, the Dow Industrials, the American Exchange and any one of more than a hundred other formal stock averages. The point of an index fund is to match the performance of the market, although most give their managers some discretion in an effort to beat their indexes. More commonly, index funds slightly under-perform their underlying index because of fees and commissions.

Quant funds: These are like index funds but are designed to outperform the specific index by aiming to choose the index's best-performing individual stocks or bonds using quantitative statistical analysis.

Market-neutral funds: These funds focus on a long and short portfolio that aims for a constant annual return that is a few points above US Treasury bills. The goal is to provide an element of stability and predictability within a larger investment portfolio.

Conscience funds: These are mutual funds in which the investment selections are filtered to meet specific investor social goals beyond making money. Some conscience funds are 'green' funds that restrict themselves to companies that have specific environmental practices or screen highly polluting or toxic market segments. Other socially conscious funds may avoid stocks that involve the production of alcohol, tobacco or other products they find objectionable. Still others may invest in companies with certain social practices, such as promoting diversity or adopting corporate policies that are friendly toward certain population segments. While conscience funds have posted some high returns and above-average growth in certain years, they tend to sacrifice performance because of their restrictions.

What is a fund family?

A fund family is a group of funds operated by the same investment company. This allows investors to keep a range of fund investments with a firm they like and trust, and can make it easier to move money between funds as your investment goals and needs change. Each fund, though, is usually separately managed, therefore the performance of one fund in a family is not indicative of how others in the family will perform.

What's a closed-end fund?

Traditional closed-end funds operate more like a stock than a mutual fund. Usually, an open mutual fund continually buys and sells shares to the investing public as new investors come into the fund and existing investors cash out or move their capital. With a closed-end fund, however, a set number of shares are sold only once, although they can be bought and sold in the secondary market, either over the usual exchanges (another example of an exchange-traded fund) or over the counter.

At other times, a conventional open-end mutual fund may close itself to new investors. This often happens when a very popular fund gets too large to be managed and invested without skewing the market or running into other difficulties. In most cases, current investors can continue to invest in the fund.

Are mutual funds taxable?

Unless it is a tax-free vehicle, a mutual fund is taxed. Distributions from the fund are taxed, whether paid out or reinvested, although when losses in a fund offset gains those distributions are not taxed. You do not, however, pay taxes on the gains in share price of your funds until you sell those shares.

Mutual funds that are held in retirement plans such as Individual Retirement Accounts and 401(k) plans are not taxed until distribution, in most cases, although distributions from Roth IRAs are not taxed. Investments in 401(k)s and IRAs that are part of qualified retirement plans are also not taxed until withdrawals are made.

What is hedging?

Hedging is any investment strategy that seeks to offset risk with other positions, such as investing in stocks while also shorting them. Hedge funds are not mutual funds, but privately run investment pools where the money managers have extreme flexibility in choosing what investments to make, including some very complicated strategies. In most cases, hedge funds are open only to high-worth individuals who are sophisticated and experienced investors, often with a $1 million minimal net worth.

How do I evaluate a fund?

You can weigh the performance of any fund by examining three factors: change in net asset value, yield and total return.

Net asset value: *Net asset value* (NAV) is the current price of one share of a mutual fund, or the share price. NAV is calculated by taking the total value of the fund and dividing by the number of shares. The change in NAV over time is the amount of appreciation in the fund's overall value, just like the price of an individual stock.

Yield: *Yield* is the income the fund provides measured against its net asset value, making it possible for you to compare a fund to other investments, such as bonds or bond indexes. Yield is computed by dividing the income distribution by share price.

Total return: Another way to measure the performance of any fund is to add the change in NAV during the time you have owned it with any received dividends, and then divide that total by the cost of your initial investment. This is sometimes called *percentage return*. You can compare the total return of a fund to others and view it over a period of weeks, months or years.

Are mutual funds rated?

Mutual funds are rated by investment and business magazines, brokerages, online investing sites and investor research services. The most widely known are Morningstar Inc., Value Line and Lipper Analytical Services, which can often be found at your local library or you can subscribe. Each service uses its own method and rankings.

How do I buy mutual funds?

You can buy most mutual funds directly from the company, through a broker or other financial service. The advantage of buying directly is that you can save on fees and commissions, although buying through a broker or other advisor may be more than worth the cost as it improves your chances of buying the right funds.

What about fund fees?

Professional management to make a mutual fund work comes at a cost, mostly through mutual fund fees or expenses, of which there are several. Bond and index funds usually have the lowest expenses, since their investment choices are more limited. Expenses are one of the biggest factors to successfully investing in mutual funds, since higher-cost funds with several fees can quickly erode investment gains. The most common are:

Sales charges or loads: *Front-end loads*, which charge a percentage of the total amount you are investing at the time you buy the fund. A *back-end* or *deferred load* takes the sales charge out when you sell shares. A level load collects annual charges while you own the fund, with no charge up front or when you sell. Some funds offer a choice of fee plans, usually rated Class A for front-end loads, Class B for back-end load, and Class C for level loads.

Marketing fees: Also referred to as *12b-1 fees*, allow the fund company to recover marking and advertising costs in running the fund and, in some cases, to pay certain employee bonuses.

Exchange fees: A service charge for moving money from one fund to another.

Redemption fees: Another variety of a back-end load that some companies add to certain funds, usually designed to discourage investors from jumping in and out of the fund.

Annual fees are subtracted from most mutual fund returns, explaining why very similar funds can often produce widely different performances. Sales charges or loads, are not figured into annual returns. In addition, funds may charge more than one expense, such as a 12b-1 marketing fee and a back-end load.

Are no-load funds better?

No-load funds don't charge sales fees, but they can still charge annual expenses, including 12b-1 fees. In theory, a no-load fund returns more money since all your capital is working in your investment, but if the no-load's annual expenses are more than those of a similar load fund, then the no-load might not be a bargain at all. As with any other investment, consider your total return over time to get the best sense of which fund will work best for you.

What are international funds?

International funds invest in specific countries, regions, international indexes or combinations that can include US markets. As well as the normal advantages of allowing liquidity, consistent contributions, diversification and professional management, international funds offer the advantages of allowing you to avoid complex overseas tax implications and fluctuations in foreign currency exchange rates. Of course, the risks involve the volatility of exchange rates, along with all the events that can disrupt markets both at home and abroad. The common classes of international funds are:

International funds: These invest in stocks, bonds or other securities in markets located outside of the United States, often balancing investments in stable, mature countries with others in more volatile emerging markets.

Regional funds: These funds invest in several countries in one part of the globe, such as Latin America, the Pacific Rim, or Eastern Europe. While several countries in one region may enjoy the same trends and have similar economic forces at work, this diversification helps balance the situation in one country with what is going on in its neighboring economies.

Global funds: These are international funds that also include US stocks, bonds and securities among their investments. The investments are shifted in and out of several countries as the economies rise and fall.

Country funds: These funds concentrate their efforts on one country, sometimes including nations where private investors may not be able to participate in the market. Some country funds are offered as closed-end funds and traded through brokers.

International index funds: Similar to domestic index funds, international funds can follow a single foreign exchange, such as the London Stock Exchange, or any one of several averages maintained by investment firms, analysts and brokerages.

What happens when a fund closes or is purchased?

A mutual fund may be closed if it has been consistently under-performing the market, in which case the assets are distributed to the investors and the fund closes. At other times in the age of financial mega-mergers, a fund company may merge with another financial institution with a similar fund, such as a blue chip or index fund. In this case one fund is subsumed into the other, with its shares exchanged for shares in the surviving fund.

What's a prospectus?

The prospectus is the document legally required by the Securities and Exchange Commission that sets out the objectives, management, performance history, fee structure and other details of how the fund works and operates.

Now that you understand the basic principles of investing and its terminology, you will feel more confident in exploring the world of investments to choose the best financial strategy for your personal circumstances.

How do I get started with a retirement plan?

When it comes to retirement planning, perhaps the best advice to keep in mind comes from author and satirist John Sladek, who once wrote: "The future, according to some scientists, will be exactly like the past, only far more expensive."

Retirement planning must focus on the present and the future at the same time. Like all other types of financial planning, you will be much better off the sooner you start. Also like all other types of financial planning, it is never too late to start. Even if you only have a few years left until retirement, it is better to retire with some kind of realistic plan than with no plan at all.

Naturally, financial planning is a big part of retirement. This involves calculating your expected expenses in retirement, your expected lifespan and factoring in the effects of inflation not only between now and when you retire, but also during the twenty years, thirty years or even longer that you live as a retiree. Another financial planning consideration is health care as you age, including consideration of different types of care and medical insurance.

Once you establish financial goals, you can begin to look at the investing and saving tools available to help you get there. This includes several types of tax-advantaged retirement accounts you can set up on your own, employer-sponsored retirement savings plans and other types of savings and investments that help you build your retirement nest egg.

At the same time, you also should factor in any employer pension benefits you might receive, along with any Social Security payments. For those who are near retirement age now, planners say you can depend on collecting all or most of these benefits, while much younger workers with several decades before retirement should make their plans without depending on employer pensions or Social Security income.

Are there non-financial considerations I should consider for retirement?

As important as the financial aspects of retirement planning are, also important is planning what kind of retirement you want to have, including where you want to live and how you want to spend your time. Are you the kind of person who can quit working entirely, or will you want to pursue a new part-time career or business?

Do you want to stay near family members or become a world traveler? How does your spouse envision your retirement together? You may need to coordinate your plans and expectations about life after work. If you've been a two-career couple, then you need to get ready for a two-career retirement.

As the country's 78 million Baby Boomers head into retirement, it is important to remember that nearly 40 million of them are women who aren't likely to be ready to leave work at the exact same time as their husbands. Many of their careers paused for children, while others postponed joining the workforce or launched their careers later in life; many others are simply younger – or older – than their husbands.

In some cases, women are just entering their peak earning years and want to set aside as much money as possible for the longer retirements that come with their generation's greater life expectancy. Women who took time off from working find they need to make up lost ground to save for retirement or to qualify for pension and Social Security benefits.

Sometimes it is the husband who retires early after decades of work, either in a corporate buyout, layoff or for health reasons. In other cases, some women in the workforce are not yet ready to give up jobs they find enjoyable and fulfilling, and others simply can't afford to join their husbands in retirement until they are old enough to qualify for retirement benefits or to start withdrawing money from retirement accounts.

Whatever the reasons, retirement and financial planners say there's a good chance that one half of a working couple – frequently the husband – retires years before the spouse. If you're one of those couples, you need to decide sooner rather than later how you are going to balance the situation when one spouse is home and the other is working. This requires more than just careful planning for finances and health benefits. Several aspects of the marriage must be reviewed as well, including not just who will do the cooking and where to live, but also exploring the expectations you and your spouse harbor for your golden years.

Whether it is a retired husband adjusting his expectations to his working wife's career or the other way around, planners say these lifestyle considerations need to be factored into the financial aspects of your retirement planning.

SAVING AND INVESTING FOR COLLEGE

College planning touches on all aspects for your life, financial as well as personal. Saving and investing for college, however, is much like any other type of financial planning. You need to set your goals, establish a timeline and then review the financial vehicles that can get you there on time.

How can I put together a plan to pay for my children's or grandchildren's college education?

Saving and investing for college and beyond is much like any other type of financial planning: you need to set your goals, establish a timeline and then review the financial vehicles that can get you there on time. Financial planning for college also involves tax planning to reduce the government's bite out of your college fund.

You need to balance retirement savings and other long-term financial goals against saving for college. For example, you face personal decisions, such as assessing the talents and capabilities of the children, deciding how much personal responsibility you want them to take in financing their own education, balancing the needs of one child whose career requires only a bachelor's degree against another who may need postgraduate study, such as law or medical school, and much more.

Finally, financing college involves all kinds of real-world complications that force you to coordinate your investing and savings results with school, state and federal aid and loan programs, each child's academic performance and skills, and each college or university's individual acceptance, enrollment and financial aid policies.

When do I need to start?

As with any long-range financial goal, any adviser will tell you that the sooner you start saving, the better. Maintaining a long-range college financing plan over a period of many years is easier and less expensive and gives you more options than waiting until your children are in high school. In some families, college savings start the day a child is born, while others establish estate plans, inheritances and trusts to send their grandchildren or even great-grandchildren to college.

Long-range planning is more important with college savings than other investing plans because for many years the cost of a college education has been steadily and significantly outpacing the rate of inflation. This means you have to concentrate on investing more money at the best possible rate to beat inflation, while also balancing risk factors so that the money is on hand when your children head off to school.

How much will I need?

You may not need as much as you think you do. The average yearly cost of a four-year public school in 2008-2009 is just $6,585, according to the College Board, the association of colleges, universities and educators that administers the SAT. Even though private four-year schools post annual tuitions that average $25,143 per year, many of those schools award significant amounts of grants, loans and other types of financial aid.

How long will it take?

If college is a long way off for your family, you definitely need more money than you would spend today to cover tuition increases and inflation, but with planning and saving it is definitely an achievable goal. Assuming that college costs rise at an annual rate of five percent, in fifteen years that $6,585 year of tuition at a public, four-year school would cost today's toddler $13,689.75, a little more than double the current annual tab. That looks daunting, but if you invested $100 today and add $49.70 monthly, you would need only a five percent annual return on your investments to hit that goal by the time your child starts college.

The longer you have until college starts, obviously the more options you have for investing and saving. If school is only a few years off, saving and investing probably will not be enough, and you need to consider loans, scholarships, grants and other aid, as well as having the student work, attend part-time or postpone school to work for a few years.

What are the different ways to pay for college?

There are a number of different approaches to paying for college depending on your income, savings and overall financial status.

Income: Assuming you make enough and expect to keep doing so, you can just pay the tuition bills out of your pocket every year. This does not require a lot of planning and investing, but does require that, in an ever-changing world, your income manage to remain stable until your last youngster finishes graduate school.

Savings and investments: With regular savings and investments in stocks, bonds, mutual funds and savings accounts, you gradually build up an educational nest egg for your children. This requires discipline to make continual investments and manage the portfolio effectively over a dozen years or more.

Loans: These can range from student loans in your children's names to your own borrowing, including financing school by borrowing against your home equity or other assets. This shifts some of the burden from saving before the children go to college to paying for their educations after they finish. It also assumes you will have enough investment equity and credit standing to borrow enough money when it is needed.

Gifts: These can include contributions from other family members, inheritances and trusts. If the money is received well ahead of when it is needed, it must be appropriately invested, with investments and trusts structured to guard against taxes and inflation so that enough money is on hand when college starts.

Financial aid: This covers grants, tuition waivers, fellowships, scholarships, work-study and other arrangements, either from state or federal governments, the school itself or private foundations. These types of aid often are predicated on academic or other achievement, and have a number of other students competing for the same assistance. In addition, it is difficult to plan many years ahead since you cannot know whether your student will qualify or what level of aid will be offered.

Are educational savings and investments tax-free?

Properly structured, many types of saving and investment plans are tax-exempt or tax-deferred, which can add greatly to the compounding effect of your money before the college years. This can include simple vehicles from US Savings Bonds to special tax-free accounts, putting money into each child's name, or constructing appropriate annual gifts from relatives or structuring long-term trusts. You also have the option of withdrawing money from some of your own tax-deferred retirement accounts to pay for your children's college education.

Will a prepaid plan take care of everything?

Prepaid tuition plans vary widely from state to state. A traditional prepaid tuition plan allows you to make either a lump-sum payment or pay by installments for several years. This locks in the current tuition rates for your child, so that no matter how much tuition has increased in the meantime, the bill is already fully paid. Some of these plans cover a group of colleges, a single school, or all the schools in one state, including what are known as *529 plans*, a name referring to the IRS tax code under which such plans fall.

The benefit of a prepaid plan is that you are protected from increases in tuition, which have outpaced inflation for the last several years. The plans also allow you to pay for college in a regular disciplined payment program and can cover a wide range of schools. The drawbacks are that there is no guarantee your son or daughter will be admitted to the participating schools. Under typical state plans, the prepayment covers in-state tuition charges, which means that if your family moves out of state by the time your child matriculates, you could be faced with covering the additional charges for out-of-state students.

Another major drawback is that prepaid plans typically pay a very low rate of return on your investment. That means that if your child does not attend school under the plan, the amount of money returned can be much less than if it had been deposited in other standard investment vehicles. In some plans where payments are spread over several years, the only way to discontinue the plan is to cancel participation, withdraw the principal and pay a penalty. Most plans also give you a very low return on your principal if you transfer the plan to an out-of-state or private school. Prepaid plans also affect the financial aid amount your student receives, reducing his or her eligibility dollar for dollar.

In addition to state-sponsored prepaid tuition plans, the Independent 529 plan has been established with more than three hundred participating private colleges and universities. Participants purchase a percentage of tuition at institutions participating in the plan.

Finally, while prepaid tuition plans do cover tuition, as the name implies, in most cases you still need to cover the costs of room, board, books and other living and educational expenses. Each state's prepaid plan can be quite different, so it pays to make sure you research it thoroughly before signing up.

My child is already in high school; are we too late?

If you have only a few years until you face college bills, then you will have to forgo the long-term benefits of compounding small, regular investments in stocks and bonds. Instead, focus on financial aid, grants, scholarships, loans and other strategies. By combining those opportunities with other options such as going to school part time or spending a year or two at a community college, most families and even individuals can find a way to finance a four-year education.

We don't even have children yet so why worry about college costs?

The longer your investment and saving horizon, the more flexibility you have in making your decisions and the more you benefit from compounding and appreciation of investments in stocks, bonds and other vehicles. It also makes good sense to coordinate college savings plans with other long- and medium-term financial goals, such as saving for a home and investing for retirement.

Is a college education really worth that much money?

While college costs are rising, higher education may still be one of the best investments. Students who earn a bachelor's degree are likely to earn $22,000 more annually than students who do not complete high school, according to the College

Board, or more than $1 million during their lifetimes when compared to what they can make without at least a bachelor's degree.

WAYS TO SAVE

How do I figure out how much to start saving for my children's college education?

Like any other investment, look at your financial goal and timeline. In most cases, if you have more than five years to go before your first child heads off to the university, you can take at least some advantage of investing in higher-yielding stocks, bonds and mutual funds.

When it comes to figuring out how much you need, do not succumb to college 'sticker shock'. While many reports contain dire descriptions that you need to come up with nearly a quarter of a million dollars for college twenty years from now, the truth is that many students pay significantly less at most state and even private schools. Even at the most elite, expensive four-year institutions, few but the wealthiest families foot the entire bill.

Start by consulting any one of the dozens of good, informative college planning books and websites to get a reasonable idea of current expenses at different schools. They will guide you in determining what college financial aid offices would classify as your 'expected family contribution' for college costs based on your current family finances. Take those figures, factor in inflation and cost increases, and you get a reasonable estimation of how much money you need to have saved when the first tuition bill comes due so you can adjust your investing, savings and expectations accordingly.

Should I create a special account for college savings?

No matter how you end up saving for education, it is best to create different accounts for each investing purpose for tax reasons, to assist with planning and to help motivate and focus your financial goals.

With college savings, your aim is to balance investment returns and risk against your ultimate tax cost. There are several types of accounts that receive favored tax treatment, but they also come with restrictions and rules that can limit the amount of money invested, how it has to be spent, when it can be withdrawn and even who controls the money. The options include:

Regular savings and investment accounts: This is where you set aside money on your own in stocks, bonds, mutual funds and savings accounts. The benefits are that you can contribute as much or as little money as you want on any schedule, exercise complete control over the investment decisions and withdraw any amount of money at any time, whether for educational purposes, emergencies or any reason at all. Another benefit is that these assets are held in your name, which means that they count less against any college financial aid considerations than money held in the student's name.

The biggest drawback is obvious: Taxes. Both the contributions and the gains invested and saved this way are immediately subject to your normal tax rate. These accounts also are part of your overall assets, which means they could be claimed by any creditors.

Tax-free bonds: Most US Savings Bonds are tax-free or partly tax free if used for educational purposes, including Treasury TIPS and STRIPS. The benefit of these is that you do not need to set up special accounts or even declare that the bonds will be used for education, giving you flexibility during the years you hold them. You can time the bond maturity and redemption dates with your children's college years. Drawbacks are that the deductibility is phased out above certain income levels, and a lower rate of interest is paid on government bonds. There are also certain restrictions on registering the bonds and making sure that the proceeds are used for qualified educational expenses.

Traditional Individual Retirement Accounts: Parents and grandparents can use their own traditional IRAs or SEP IRAs to save for college expenses, too. Early withdrawals (before age 59 ½) from these accounts are penalty-free when used to pay higher education expenses for the IRA owner or the owner's spouse, as well as the children or grandchildren of the owner or spouse. The benefits are a wide range of investment choices, the ability for many people to deduct the annual investment in the IRA, and the tax-free compounding of interest and gains in the accounts. Withdrawals can also pay for most any education-related expense, including room and board if the student goes to school at least half-time. Another benefit is that the IRA does not have to be set up only for educational purposes or one particular student. The drawbacks are that while the withdrawals are exempt from the early distribution penalties on IRAs, the distributions still are taxed at the owner's regular rate.

Roth IRAs: Roth IRAs differ from regular IRAs in that you make after-tax contributions to the account, which allows any earnings to be withdrawn tax-free after age 59 ½. Like traditional IRAs, early withdrawals of earnings are penalty-free when used for higher education expenses. Withdrawals of contributions, however, are always penalty- and tax-free after five years.

Coverdell Education Savings Account or Education IRA: Known as the ESA for short (and formerly as the Education IRA), the Coverdell account can be established for any named beneficiary younger than eighteen. Contributions are not tax-deductible, but earnings are tax-free as long as they are used for qualified educational expenses. The accounts can be invested in stocks, bonds, mutual funds and other vehicles, just like an IRA. ESAs can also be used for pre-college educational expenses, including elementary and high school tuition, books and even computers.

Anyone can set up an ESA for a qualified beneficiary, which means several accounts can be established for one student. That option, however, runs into the biggest downside of the ESA: The annual total contribution limit for any one beneficiary is $2,000. Any amount above that is subject to a 6 percent 'excess contribution tax,' which means you need to coordinate contributions with grandparents or any others putting money into an ESA for the same student.

Other negatives are that all contributions must stop when the beneficiary turns eighteen, and that the money must be used by the time the beneficiary turns thirty, or must be transferred to someone else younger than thirty. (Special needs students may not be required to use all ESA money by age thirty, and may be eligible for contributions after age eighteen.) Finally, you can contribute to an ESA only if your income is less than $95,000 for those filing as single taxpayers, $190,000 if married filing jointly. Limited contributions are allowed for single taxpayers earning up to $110,000 and married couples making up to $220,000. Finally, ESAs are counted as student assets when figuring financial aid, which assumes that most of the account is available for educational expenses.

529 Plans: The 529 refers to a section of the federal tax code that covers this newest type of college financing vehicle. There are two varieties of 529 plans: Prepaid tuition plans, as discussed earlier, and state-sponsored college savings plans. Each plan is independently structured by its sponsoring state, but all share certain attributes.

With 529 plans you can invest a large sum, usually more than $100,000 and in some states more than $300,000 of after-tax money. Even though the plan is sponsored by a specific state, you are free to use savings plan money to pay for expenses at any accredited college or university in the US.

Contribution limits vary by state. Contributions to a Section 529 plan are subject to applicable limits under federal gift tax and generation skipping transfer tax provisions and may be subject, upon distribution, to

Each plan has several investment options, or tracks, that you choose for your investment. In most cases, at least one track is an age-base option that shifts the investment from stocks and other aggressive investments in the early years to bonds and other stable vehicles as the first day of college approaches.

Once you have selected an investment track, you cannot change it. The only way to change your investment option is to roll your 529 plan over to another 529 plan in another state. More than two dozen states operate plans open to any US citizen; however, joining an out-of-state plan eliminates any in-state tax deduction you get with your home state's plan. You can, however, join any number of 529 plans in separate states. Another point to watch for in 529 plans is the fee and fee structure; some plans have higher fees that will eat into investment returns.

Under 529 plans the investment remains under your control, not the student's, which helps with financial aid formulas. Your investment grows tax-deferred, and distributions to pay for the beneficiary's college costs come out federally tax-free. You also can withdraw money from the plans, for non-educational expense although any earnings will be subject to normal taxes plus a ten percent penalty. Money in a 529 plan also can be transferred without tax or penalty to another family member's 529 plan, as well.

What's a super gift in a 529 plan?

Ordinarily, a parent or grandparent is restricted to giving no more than $13,000 a year to an individual without triggering gift

federal income tax if the amounts are not used for higher educational expenses. Penalties, in accordance with IRS guidelines, may apply to distributions that are not attributable to higher educational expenses of the designated beneficiary, made on account of the death or disability of the beneficiary, or due to rollover.

State tax advantages vary from state to state and may depend on whether you are a resident of the state sponsoring the plan. Investment options vary greatly - from high-risk stock funds, to funds that contain a mix of stocks and bonds, to conservative investments that contain money market or short-term bond funds. Most plans offer age- or enrollment based investments that grow more conservatively over time, as the beneficiary gets closer to using the proceeds to pay for college expenses. Many plans also offer static investments where assets are typically invested in a set allocation of one or more mutual funds.

As with other investments, there are generally fees and expenses associated with participation in Section 529 College Savings Plans. Fees and expenses vary greatly, even among plans offered within the same state. There is also the risk that plan investments may lose money or not perform well enough to cover college costs as anticipated.

Withdrawals may or may not be state income tax-free, depending on the participant's state of residence. Withdrawals of earnings for purposes of paying for qualified higher educational expenses are federal income tax-free. This tax provision is available until December 31, 2010. After 2010, distributions may be taxed at the beneficiary's tax rate unless there is further legislation to extend or change the tax law. Withdrawals for non-qualified educational expenses are subject to a 10 percent federal tax penalty and are taxed as ordinary income taxes with the IRS, which applies at the same rate as the estate tax. With 529 plans, however, you can contribute five years of 'gifts' at once, meaning a single person could give $65,000, or $130,000 for a couple, to jump-start the student's college savings plan.

Can I transfer stocks or other investments into a 529 plan?

Unfortunately, 529 plans are cash only, with one exception. If you have a custodial account or other investments in stocks, bonds or other instruments, you have to liquidate those accounts and pay any taxes due before you can move that cash into a 529. However, under the Education Bond Program, you can cash in US bonds and put those proceeds into a 529 plan without taking the tax hit. (Some IRA qualifications apply. Therefore, review this strategy with your CPA or accountant first.)

What are Individual Development Accounts?

Known as IDAs, for short, these accounts aim to help low-income workers save for college by matching their own savings, usually on a ratio of $2 for each $1 saved, but in some cases by as much as $7 to $1. IDAs are managed by a network of non-profit organizations. A qualified person under the plan sets a savings goal for school and once that goal is met, the matching grant is sent directly to pay for tuition. Money for matching grants comes from nonprofits, financial institutions, foundations, churches and religious organizations, and state or local governments.

What about gifting?

The term usually refers to parents and grandparents who transfer money to youngsters under the Uniform Transfers to Minors Act (UTMA) or the Uniform Gift to Minors Act (UGMA). Under these plans, money is placed in custodial accounts and children eighteen and younger can keep the first $850 in earnings tax free. The second $850 is taxed at their rate. Investment income exceeding $1,700 is taxed at parents' tax rates – fifteen percent for dividends and long-term gains up to thirty-five percent on interest and short-term gains. After the child is eighteen, all earnings are taxed at the child's rate.

In general, financial planners discourage custodial accounts in favor of the Coverdell Educational Savings Accounts and 529 plans, which do not tax earnings at all in most cases, and do not run up against the IRS gift tax rules. Another consideration is that custodial accounts become the property of the child at age eighteen or twenty-one, depending on the state where you live, which can allow the youngster to withdraw the money for any purpose at all.

What are other ways that relatives or friends can help pay for a student's education?

Rather than contributing to special educational savings accounts where the money is factored into financial aid considerations by colleges, friends and relatives can consider making a direct payment of tuition, which won't count against the $13,000 annual gift-tax limit. They might also choose to help the student out with loan payments after graduation.

Other than saving, investing and paying school bills out-of-pocket, what other financial sources can I tap for my child's education?

In addition to various loan programs, these college-financing options include tax credits, financial aid and scholarships.

TAX CREDITS

How much can I save with a tax credit?

There are three federal tax credits available to families with students in college:

Hope tax credit: This gives you a dollar-for-dollar credit right off your income tax, up to $1,500 for a student's freshman and sophomore years of college. Hope credits cover only tuition, not room and board, up to 100 percent of the first $1,000 spent, and fifty percent of the next $1,000.

To be eligible for the credit, a single taxpayer must have a modified gross adjusted income of less than $53,000, or $107,000 for those filing jointly. Taxpayers can receive partial credit if their incomes fall between $43,000 and $53,000 for those filing singly, or $87,000 and $107,000 for those filing jointly. In addition to the income limits, rules for the Hope credit also require the student to be enrolled at least half-time in a program leading to a degree, certificate or other educational credential, and cannot have been convicted of any felony relating to possession or distribution of a controlled substance. The Hope credit can be claimed only in the first two years of the student's college career.

Lifetime Learning credit: The Lifetime Learning credit is similar to the Hope credit, in that it boosts your tax refund dollar for dollar, up to $2,000. The Lifetime Learning credit, however, is much more flexible. It can be applied to any student at any time during college, graduate school or even continuing education classes.

Rules for the Lifetime Learning credit mean that you cannot apply for Lifetime Learning and Hope tax credits in the same year, and the same income limits apply as with Hope credits, although the felony drug rule does not apply. The amount of the credit is based on twenty percent of paid tuition, up to $10,000, for a maximum credit of $2,000 per tax return for you, a spouse or dependent.

Higher Education tax deduction: In 2001 Congress created another tax credit for parents with children in college. Unfortunately, the credit expires after 2005 unless it is extended. Income limits to claim the full credit are modified adjusted gross incomes of $65,000 for single filers, $130,000 for those filing jointly. Taxpayers with incomes between $65,000 and $85,000 for single filers and $130,000 and $160,000 for joint returns can still qualify for a limited $2,000 credit. The other limit on the deduction is that it cannot be claimed in the same year that the taxpayer claims either a Hope or Lifetime Learning tax credit.

Is it important to coordinate these benefits?

Remember, you can claim only one of these tax benefits on any one year's return. In most cases, the tax credits are worth more than the tax deduction, so calculate the savings there. You also need to be sure to claim the Hope credit in the student's first two years of college, or lose out on that benefit altogether. If you qualify, plan to take the Hope credit first, and then apply the Lifetime Learning credit after the student's sophomore year. Of course, if you do not qualify to take the credits, then apply the deduction if it is still available.

Can these tax credits be used with money from educational accounts?

Any expenses you pay from a 529 plan, Coverdell Account or other tax-free educational savings program cannot be counted toward qualifying for any of these tax benefits. Otherwise, you would be engaging in 'double dipping' in the eyes of the IRS when you claim a tax credit or deduction on already untaxed money. These tax benefits also exclude any money from scholarships, grants or other tax-free awards.

One way around some of these limits is to use untaxed education money to pay for room and board, since the tax programs apply only to tuition costs. Scholarships that reduce your student's tuition, however, lower the amount of your tax benefit.

Do we have to pay taxes on scholarships and other awards?

This material was created to provide accurate and reliable information on the subjects covered. It is not intended to provide specific legal, tax or other professional advice. The services of an appropriate professional should be sought regarding your individual situation.

In most cases, scholarship money and similar educational awards are untaxed, as long as they go to pay for tuition, related school fees, required books and supplies and you are pursuing a degree. You have to pay tax on any scholarship money that pays for room and board, or money received as a payment for services, such as working as a teaching or research assistant.

What about my employer's educational benefits?

In most cases up to $5,250 of employer-provided educational assistance benefits can be received tax-free, as long as the money pays for tuition, fees, book and similar costs, at both the undergraduate and graduate-school level, whether the education is work-related or not. These benefits are excluded from figuring your Hope and Lifetime Learning credits, or any other tax deduction or credit.

Are there any other education-related tax deductions?

Yes – student loan interest is deductible (modified adjusted gross income limits apply), up to $2,500 per year and generally including loan origination fees, as long as the money pays for tuition, room and board, supplies and other qualified expenses. While many student loans are repaid by the student some time after graduation, some loans either require or give you the option of paying interest immediately.

FINANCIAL AID

What kind of financial aid can I expect to receive from the colleges?

As opposed to scholarships, financial aid is quite common. Up to ninety-eight percent of all college students receive some kind of federal or state aid, according to experts. Some comes in the form of outright grants, some from tuition wavers and some from work-study programs.

The process requires a great deal of paperwork, attention to timing, your personal variables, such as having more than one child in college at the same time, tax status, and even how your personal finances are structured. Each school can use its own particular formula for calculating financial aid, with each school individually calculating how it will consider your home equity, retirement accounts, income levels, family assets and other financial factors. In some cases, families may want to shift or restructure some assets or expenses to improve their chances for financial aid.

Overall, the financial aid process can be complicated, so it is best to do your homework, starting with your student's college counselor, reference books and guides, online sites, college financial aid offices and financial and tax planners.

What is the key to receiving the best possible financial aid package?

The basic formula for financial aid is the total cost of college minus the *expected family contribution*. Whatever balance is left has to come from either financial aid, scholarships, tuition waivers, work-study programs or loans.

Expected family contribution is the key to financial aid. It is a calculation of how much of your family income and assets the school expects you to put toward tuition, books, room and board and other expenses. In general, schools use their own formulas based on a few set guidelines. One is the Free Application for Federal Student Aid (FAFSA), which almost every college will ask you to submit. This determines the student's eligibility for federal aid at all schools and at most public schools. Schools may also calculate their own aid formula based on additional information from the PROFILE form from the College Scholarship Service. In addition, you may also have to deal with state aid forms in your home state and any additional institutional forms, especially with private colleges.

For your own planning services, you can complete the FAFSA and PROFILE applications early to get an idea of what you would be expected to pay for college today, and calculate an estimate of what you will need from savings, scholarships and other financial aid at specific schools.

SCHOLARSHIPS

I hear there are millions of dollars in scholarships available. How do we qualify?

There are many scholarships available from all kinds of sources. Some experts have stories of individuals who have single-handedly put themselves through Ivy League schools on nothing but scholarships. Other authorities note that applying for scholarships is a lengthy, time-consuming process and that many of them award no more than a few hundred dollars, while the most generous ones attract a huge crowd of applicants.

Nonetheless, when it comes to financing college, nothing beats free money. If you want or need to pursue scholarships, the first step is to leave enough time, perhaps even starting in the student's sophomore year of high school, since many scholarships require work in specific fields or lengthy essays. The next step is to winnow out the many scholarships available, matching the student's skills and capabilities to the requirements and competition, and to balance the size of any award against the time and effort it will take to win it. Some students might be better off just spending several weekends working rather than investing that time polishing an essay for a chance at a $500 scholarship.

One extra benefit of scholarships is that, beyond the money, winning one or more of these awards can also boost the appeal of a student's application.

How do I find appropriate scholarships?

The best sources are your school's college counselors, who have first-hand knowledge of what scholarship monies past students have garnered and how they won. The next best place is in your local community, through service clubs, civic organizations, state or local governments. Another close resource is the workplace, where awards and grants may be available to the children or relatives of employees.

There are many scholarships from professional organizations and businesses, either for children of members or for students focusing on entering a certain profession or industry. Local businesses, politicians and even sports teams also are a good source, as well as organizations related to extracurricular activities, such as Scout troops, drama societies, Junior Achievement and others. Other local sources are unions, religious organizations and even military associations related to parents' or even grandparents' service in the armed forces.

After finding as many local scholarships as possible, there are many annually updated directories, both in print and online. Another good source is the financial aid offices of the schools to which your student applies, which may have special scholarships for certain types of students or fields of study.

What about paying for a scholarship search?

In general, paid scholarship databases and search services probably won't do a better job of finding college money than you can do on your own. Some services 'guarantee' results or refunds, but it can be hard to collect on those promises, experts say. Check your local schools to see what scholarship databases they subscribe to or recommend. The College Board *www.collegeboard.org* offers free and paid databases of grants and scholarships. Other good sites are *www.fastWeb.com* and *www.collegenet.com*.

Will scholarships affect other areas of financial aid?

In most instances financial aid packages from colleges and universities take into account the entire amount of any scholarships the student wins, reducing any overall financial aid package.

What about the National Merit Scholarships?

These are guaranteed scholarships offered to students who score among the highest 15,000 or so students who take the PSAT, the Preliminary Standard Aptitude Test administered by the College Board, usually in the sophomore or junior year of high school. Those students automatically become National Merit Semifinalists, who are then invited to compete for the National Merit Scholarship. About half of the semifinalists receive either a $2,500 National Merit Scholarship or a corporate- or college-sponsored National Merit Scholarship.

Are there any guaranteed scholarships?

Many colleges and states offer grants and scholarships based on SAT scores, grade point averages, ACT scores, class ranking, or some combination of those factors, regardless of need. Other schools also offer scholarships to transfer students and students from community colleges. These offers vary widely from state to state and school to school, but it pays to take them into consideration when applying.

What about work-study programs?

Federal work-study jobs usually award about $1,500 a year at an on-campus job that pays about minimum wage. Work-study is awarded as part of the school's overall financial aid package.

LOANS

What about loans for college?

In many cases, loans of some sort are going to make up part of your financial strategy for college. Many families just won't be able to cover the costs through saving and investing, and college aid packages probably will include some kind of loans. The good news is that college loans have low interest rates for both students and parents, and can often be restructured to offer tax-deductible interest payments.

What are the basic types of loans?

There are several types of federal and private school loans:

Stafford Student Loans: Formerly known as Guaranteed Student Loans, these are made directly to students, either as Federal Direct Student Loans, where your child borrows directly from the government, or as Federal Family Education Loans, where your student borrows from a financial institution with the government guaranteeing the loan.

The terms on these loans are identical. Limits for dependent students are $2,625 for freshman, $3,500 for sophomores and $5,500 for juniors and seniors. Students cannot borrow more than the cost of school after any other financial aid, and cannot borrow more than a total of $23,000, including a fifth year of study, during their course of undergraduate study. Independent students have higher limits: $6,625 as freshman, $7,500 as sophomores and $10,500 as juniors and seniors, including fifth years. The total limit for independent students is $46,000 for undergraduate study. For graduate students, the loan limits are $18,500 per year with a maximum of $138,500, including all undergraduate borrowing in the Stafford loan program. These are variable interest rate loans, with rates adjusted the first of July every year, equal to the rate on ninety-one day Treasure bills plus 2.3 percent, with an interest rate cap of 8.25 percent.

Stafford loans are offered in both subsidized and unsubsidized forms. Unsubsidized loans start charging interest immediately when the loan is made, although interest can be deferred, while subsidized loans have the government paying the loan interest until six months after graduation and during any deferment period. In some cases, students might be offered a combination of subsidized and unsubsidized loans.

Under the Family Education loans you should shop around for a lender, preferably one who resells its loans to the Student Loan Marketing Association, which helps to cut costs. For Federal Direct Student Loans, apply through the school's financial aid office.

Perkins Loans: Colleges and universities make these loans from their own pool of federal money for students with a high level of financial need. Perkins loans offer low interest rates of five percent and do not require repayment until nine months after graduation. The repayment term is ten years and the maximum loan amount is $4,000 per year for undergraduates at most schools. Perkins loan repayments may be cancelled for students in certain situations who work after graduation as a full-time teacher, Peace Corps volunteer, nurse or medical technician, corrections or law enforcement officer or who work with a child- or family-services agency.

PLUS Loans: These loans are available to parents and do not count as part of any school's financial aid package. This is a federal loan program that allows parents to borrow up to the full cost of college, minus other financial aid. The loan is not based on need, but does take creditworthiness into account. Like Stafford loans, the money is either borrowed directly from the government or guaranteed to a financial institution. The interest rate equals the ninety-one day Treasury bill rate plus 3.1 points, and is capped at an even nine percent, adjusted every July 1. PLUS loan terms require repayment to begin sixty days after the school receives its money, either full loan payments or interest-only payments, with average repayment periods of ten years.

EXCEL Loans: These are offered to parents by the private, nonprofit Nellie Mae of Braintree, Massachusetts, the largest source for student loans in the US. These loans are variable rate, with an annual rate of prime plus two percentage points, set each August. Parents can borrow up to the full cost of college each year, minus financial aid. Debt payments, including mortgages and the EXCEL loan, cannot be more than forty percent of your gross monthly income.

SIGNATURE Loans: These loans are offered to students by Sallie Mae, the Student Loan Marketing Association, and are available for the full amount of your college bill, minus any financial aid. These are variable rate loans, based on the prime rate plus anywhere from zero to two points, depending on creditworthiness and any co-borrowers on the loan. These loans can be obtained along with Stafford Loans at the same lenders.

TERI Alternative Loans: These loans from The Education Resources Institute are structured like Signature and EXCEL loans. They are offered to parents and students, although students usually need a parent as a co-signer. TERI loans are offered through several financial institutions, including Bank of America, Chase and PNC Bank, with a rate of prime minus 0.5 points, based on creditworthiness.

Is it true that you can extend repayment terms on student loans for quite a while?

While most students have to start repaying their loans six months after graduation, recent grads who meet certain terms can extend or consolidate loan repayment up to thirty years in some cases under the federal direct loan program. Many private lenders offer similar options. To ensure the most flexibility, take payment extension programs into account when applying for loans. Students and parents also should recognize that stretching loan payments over additional decades substantially increases the amount of interest paid. However, for graduates who have trouble landing jobs or who start in low-paying fields, loan extensions and consolidation programs offer an alternative.

What about borrowing from other sources?

While loans specifically targeted toward college education are generally the least expensive, you may want to consider other sources that may give you better terms or more flexibility, such as home equity loans and lines of credit, loans from life insurance, retirement plans or even margin loans on investment accounts.

The benefits are that you may be able to borrow more money with more flexible repayment terms or lower loan costs, and be able to borrow more than the limits set on student loan programs. Interest on home equity loans, for example, is usually deductible if you itemize your tax return. In all cases, it is best to examine the interest charges, origination fees and repayment schedules and terms to determine what gives you the best cash flow and lowest after-tax cost.

It seems like new 529 plans pop up every day. How can I get more information about them?

Each state has one more plan, and many also offer prepaid tuition plans, each with varying options, benefits and requirements, with some of the basics listed here. You can check out detailed descriptions of the plans at *www.savingforcollege.com* and *www.finaid.org*. Plans are added and changed on a regular basis, so it pays to keep up with the latest developments.

Taxes and Tax Planning

For some citizens, tax planning is fairly simple if their only income is from wages and they have no dependents, real property or any assets beyond their basic investments. However, once you own a home, get married, have children, start saving for retirement and saving money for college, taxes become more of an issue in making your financial decisions and planning your future. Should you own your own business or strike it rich, you not only must consider the effect of taxes on your income and financial status today, but also weigh the effects of taxes on your estate for future generations.

> These materials are not intended to be used to avoid tax penalties, and were prepared to support the promotion or marketing of the matter addressed in this document. The taxpayer should seek advice from an independent tax advisor.

How do I incorporate taxes into my financial plans?

Your savings, investment and estate planning decisions all need to take taxes into account for a number of reasons, but primarily to make sure that you do not pay more than your fair share to the government, to increase and shelter your investment and savings gains, and to pass along a large portion of your estate's assets to your heirs or other beneficiaries.

I dislike paying taxes. Can I structure my finances to avoid them entirely?

Good, honest tax planning with trained professionals can significantly reduce your tax burden in many instances, but it is doubtful you can make any respectable amount of money and not be required to pay some taxes on your income. While reducing the government's tax bite is an important consideration in financial planning, it is also important not to let tax issues warp your priorities or cloud your thinking. In most cases, financial planners and tax experts advise that you keep your financial goals in mind and adjust your decisions to minimize taxes, but avoid making tax considerations your primary goal. In general, any financial decision based solely on the notion of avoiding taxes is too narrow to be successful in the long run.

Do I pay tax on all my income?

There are certain types of income on which you do not have to pay tax, either at any time or in certain situations. The government wants to encourage specific types of behavior, such as saving for retirement and supporting charities. Otherwise, any type of new income to you will be taxed by at least one government body. In addition to salary and wages, the list includes:

- Interest and dividends,

- Business receipts,

- Fees, commissions and bonuses,

- Tips,

- Royalties,

- Rental income,

- Capital gains on investments,

- Pensions, annuities and retirement plan withdrawals or distributions,

- Alimony and maintenance if the payer deducts them,

- Disability payments,

- Unemployment compensation,

- Some fringe benefits or parts of fringe benefits,

- Prizes and awards,

- Social Security benefits in some cases,

- Gambling proceeds, and

- Miscellaneous income, such as money you make selling a used car or holding a garage sale.

What income is tax-free?

In most cases, untaxed sources of income are either not truly income (for example, reimbursed business expenses), have previously been taxed (inheritances are already taxed, when required, as part of the estate tax), to promote a societal goal (profits on home sales under certain amounts are not taxed, for instance, because home ownership is assumed to strengthen communities) or to cut you a break in bad circumstances (including disability payments and worker's compensation). The list includes:

- Interest on municipal bonds, including dividends on municipal bonds held by mutual funds,

- Gifts and inheritances upon receipt,

- Child support payments,

- Life insurance death benefits,

- Gains on the sale of a home up to $500,000 for a couple, $250,000 for single taxpayers, if you have lived in the house for at least two of the last five years,

- Reimbursed business expenses,

- Worker's compensation benefits,

- Disability income from your own policies (but not employer-paid policies),

- Health insurance, educational assistance and many other employer-paid benefits, and

- Some or all Social Security benefits in some cases.

Are there different types of income?

While any money received can be considered income, the federal, state and local tax rules have different definitions of what constitutes income for their various tax purposes. These categories include:

Gross Income: All taxable income.

Adjusted Gross Income (AGI): This is your gross income after it has been reduced by certain 'above the line' deductions, including contributions to qualified retirement plans, moving expenses, student loan interest and so on.

Modified Adjusted Gross Income: This is adjusted gross income with some tax breaks eliminated, such as municipal bond interest, in order to calculate other tax questions, such as whether your Social Security benefits are subject to tax.

Taxable Income: This is the amount on which you actually pay tax. You arrive at this amount by taking your adjusted gross income and further reducing it with your 'below the line' itemized or standard deductions, including mortgage interest, health expenses, property taxes, charitable contributions and more. Generally, you balance your itemized deductions against your standard deduction and claim whichever amount is larger against your AGI.

How can I reduce the huge taxes taken out of my paycheck each week?

The first step is to make certain that too much tax is not withheld by your employer. Withholding is the government's way to regularly collect taxes, instead of waiting until April 15 and hoping that you and your fellow taxpayers have set aside enough cash to pay the tax bill.

Withholding is calculated on your tax filing status, and you have a number of exemptions based on your marital status, number of dependents and whether you file joint or separate returns. This is submitted to the Internal Revenue Service on the W-4 form you fill out when you begin employment. Your employer calculates a percentage of your salary each pay period based on your exemptions. When you file your taxes, you subtract this withheld income from your tax bill and either pay the difference or, if there is a balance, receive a refund.

The problem is that if too much money is withheld from your check, then you give the IRS an interest-free loan all year while forfeiting the use of your own money. You would then want to raise your number of exemptions until you bring the withholding amount in line with your anticipated tax bill.

One way to calculate this is to determine what financial planners call your 'effective tax rate'. While you already fall within certain tax brackets where, for example, your tax is twenty-eight percent of your taxable income, your effective tax rate helps you estimate how much of your net income should be withheld for taxes. To calculate your effective tax rate, review last year's return and divide the actual income tax you paid by your net taxable income before taxes. The resulting percentage is the amount of your pre-tax salary (after pre-tax deductions) that should be withheld. This won't exactly match your tax liability, but it will be close, assuming you have no major changes in your tax situation during the year. You can change your W-4 status at any time during the tax year; just watch the year-to-date taxable gross salary versus federal withholding listed on your pay stub.

Can I reduce my withholding tax to zero?

You cannot if you will owe taxes. In general, taxpayers can claim up to ten exemptions, but can be penalized $500 for each excess exemption over that amount. In addition, if you have under-withheld, you have to pay interest on the amount you shorted the IRS, calculated from the due date for those withheld payments. The IRS can also penalize you for under-withholding up to twenty-five percent of the tax that went unpaid. You can avoid this penalty if you paid at least ninety percent of your current tax bill or a percentage of the taxes you paid in the previous year. This 'safe harbor' percentage is set each year. Lastly, you could face criminal charges for intentionally falsifying a W-4, carrying penalties of up to $1,000 in fines, a year in jail, or both.

I want a big tax refund every spring. Is planning that a mistake?

Some taxpayers over-withhold their taxes as a kind of government-enforced personal savings plan, but you should use this strategy only as a last resort if you lack the discipline to save in some other manner. It is preferable to adjust your withholding and have the amount you were overpaying automatically deducted from your checking account and deposited into a savings account, money market fund or investment account.

Ideally, when you do your taxes, you will owe the government nothing and the government will owe you nothing. It is unlikely that you will precisely hit that target, but if you do end up paying only a small amount every April 15, you are then getting the most out of your paycheck.

What if I get a big raise this year?

In the event of that happy occurrence, your payroll processor should recalculate the withholding, especially if your company awards increases on employment anniversary dates rather than on an annual schedule. If your employer computes withholding allowances only once a year, then your new, higher salary might not be adjusted for an additional tax liability and you will be surprised with a higher tax bill next April 15th.

What if I am self-employed?

If you are your own boss, you have to pay your own estimated quarterly taxes to the IRS. The guidelines are about the same for withholding; either ninety percent of your total taxes due or the safe harbor percentage of the previous year's taxes. Your tax preparer, accountant or other financial advisor can explain how to file and what forms to use, or you can check the IRS website at *www.irs.gov*.

You also need to consider filing quarterly estimated taxes if you receive a significant portion of your income from investments or other non-salary sources of income where withholding does not apply.

What other taxes will be listed on my pay stub?

The only other taxes you will see (besides any state or local tax withheld) are your FICA taxes – Federal Insurance Contributions Act. These are your tax payments for Social Security (it is a tax, not a retirement fund) and Medicare. On your pay stub, you may find these taxes notated as OASDI, which stands for 'old-age, survivor and disability insurance', and HI, for Medicare 'hospital insurance'.

Under the law, 12.4 percent of your salary, up to an annual limit, goes toward financing the Social Security system, while Medicare collects an additional 2.9 percent on everything you earn. If you are a salaried employee you pay only half, and your employer pays the other half. If you are self-employed you pay the full amount, although you can deduct half of the amount, called self-employment tax, as a business expense.

What about state taxes?

There are as many different state tax structures as there are states, unless you live in one of the country's so-called 'tax havens' who have no state income tax. Those states presently include Alaska, Florida, Nevada, South Dakota, Texas, Washington and Wyoming. Otherwise, state rules, regulations and even definitions of income can vary. In addition, some cities charge their own local income tax on residents, or even commuter taxes on suburban dwellers who work in the city. These state and local taxes can be deducted from your federal tax, and usually have filing deadlines similar to federal taxes to simplify some of your paperwork.

What about taxation for my household help?

If you have a nanny, housekeeper or other household employee who works on a regular basis and is paid more than $1,500 in the calendar year, you are officially an employer. You then have to provide each member of the household staff with a W-2 statement of wages by the end of January and file the appropriate reports, such as the W-3 form, with the Social Security Administration by the end of February. You report and pay the actual tax on your federal income tax return.

The taxes you will pay include the employer's portion of FICA and, in some cases, federal unemployment tax. You may also have to withhold income tax if you pay any household helper more than $1,000 per quarter.

What is Tax Freedom Day?

Tax Freedom Day is defined by the Tax Foundation, a nonprofit group that monitors government fiscal policies. According to the foundation, Tax Freedom Day is the first day of the year when US citizens have earned enough to fully pay their entire tax liability for the year. It gives taxpayers an easy way to identify their total tax load. The earlier in the year the Tax Freedom Day arrives, the smaller the average tax bill.

Are income taxes enforceable?

The federal income tax is legal – and enforceable, despite occasional challenges to the constitutionality of the federal income tax. The sixteenth amendment to the US Constitution which authorizes Congress to collect income tax, became official in 1913. History buffs may note that Wyoming cast the deciding vote to ratify the amendment, which assessed taxes at one percent, with only about one out of every 271 citizens paying taxes at that time.

Confusion about the constitutionality of the income tax dates to the Civil War, when a three percent income tax was passed as an emergency measure to raise war revenue in 1862, and lapsed ten years later. A two percent federal tax was passed in

1894, but was ruled unconstitutional by the Supreme Court three years later. The drive for the constitutional amendment was launched when Congress approved the amendment in 1909 and sent it to the states for ratification. The income tax is quite established as part of the law, despite what some protestors and scam artists may try to say. Some promoters charge hundreds or even thousands of dollars for packages of sample letters and other information to challenge the tax law as illegal. Taxpayers who follow this route usually end up paying more in fines, penalties and interest to the IRS.

Is it illegal to falsify my taxpayer identification?

This outright tax scam originated several years ago, and it is illegal. The strategy involves obtaining a separate taxpayer identification number to give your employer and using it to file your taxes so that wages and other money paid under either your Social Security or Taxpayer ID number won't be detected by the IRS. Taxpayer ID numbers are legitimately used by incorporated businesses and by foreign workers in this country who cannot obtain Social Security numbers.

What if I move my money into offshore accounts?

Offshoring, as it is called, is a more recently popular (and illegal) tax-avoidance scheme that involves a series of trusts that move your money to an offshore account, but allow you access to your account through a debit or credit card.

Are there any other tax scams I need to avoid?

There are all kinds of abusive trusts that are marketed purely to avoid paying income tax, as well as schemes for claiming personal costs as business deductions: Bogus African-American reparations credit marketed by some shady dealers, claim to get you a refund of your Social Security taxes, and unscrupulous preparers who promise larger refunds by inflating or claiming non-existent deductions.

What these ploys all have in common is the fact that they sound too good to be true, which they are. They can end up costing you a lot more in fines, interest and penalties than you would pay with an uncontested return. When in doubt, check with the IRS by calling 800-829-1040.

Can I postpone paying my taxes by applying for an extension?

If you find that getting the paperwork together is too complicated to complete your tax return by the April 15 IRS deadline, you can submit an extension to file your taxes, but not an extension to pay. Instead, you pay what you estimate your tax will be at the same time you request the extension, and file a complete return later.

What are the legal ways to reduce my taxes?

There are four different approaches you can take to make sure you are maximizing tax exemptions and deductions, staying within the law, and still paying your legal, fair share of taxes. These include:

- Reducing or minimizing your gross income by moving or reclassifying some income that would normally be counted in your gross. For example, contributions to healthcare savings accounts or qualified retirement plans such as 401(k)s and Individual Retirement Accounts (IRAs), when applicable,

- Reconfiguring your finances and activities so that some of your normal personal expenses can be counted as tax deductions, which reduce both your gross and taxable income. An example would be taking a home office deduction if you are self-employed or otherwise qualify,

- Making sure you take advantage of special tax credits that will reduce your final tax liability, usually dollar for dollar; for instance, the Lifetime Learning or the Hope tax credits, which boost your tax refund dollar-for-dollar up to $2,000 for the education of you or your children,

- Reallocating family income to different members of your family who are in lower tax brackets. An example would be giving income-producing property as a gift to a family member in a lower bracket, such as a child or establishing a trust.

What is a tax bracket?

Your tax bracket determines how much tax you pay on income earned in that category, and how much of your itemized deductions are credited toward your final tax bill. Because of the progressive nature of our tax code, though, you do not pay your top bracket tax rate on all your income. Instead, you pay the bracket rate on the amount of income earned under each separate limit. So, for example, a single filer with a taxable income of $30,000 pays ten percent on the first $7,550 of income; and fifteen percent on everything above $7,550. His top bracket of fifteen percent only applies to the last $22,450 of taxable income.

If the taxpayer paid fifteen percent on the total $30,000, his tax bill would come out to $4,500. Instead, he pays, $755 plus $3,367.50, for a total of $4,122.50, resulting in a difference of $3,262.65 between the two methods.

EXCLUDABLE INCOME

What are the types of income that are excluded?

Excluded income is money you have received that the government does not even include in figuring your taxes, often because it is considered a business expense or other source of money that is a reimbursement, as well as for other reasons, such as Constitutional factors in the case of municipal bond interest, or to promote certain social goals, such as education or home ownership, or in some cases just for efficiency's sake.

The best part about an income exclusion is that it gives you a simple, immediate break on your taxes that does not shift (in most cases) with your income level and tax bracket, as opposed to deductions, which may not apply to you in many cases or may not be worth claiming when compared with your tax write-off under a standard deduction.

Tax planners advise that, whenever possible, you aim to shift taxable income to excludable sources for the best possible tax breaks. At the very least, make sure you are not paying tax on excludable income, such as workplace benefits. They might be part of your total compensation package at the office, but that does not make them taxable.

Does this include some of my regular employee benefits?

Quite a few of your employee benefits are excludable, so check and make sure that you are not paying tax on these items, including:

- Hospitalization premiums, including those for Medicare and other supplementary medical insurance, paid by your employer (or your ex-employer, if you are retired)

- Group term life insurance covered up to $50,000 provided by your employer,

- Group legal service plans provided by your employer,

- Employee death benefits paid directly or indirectly by your employer to your family or your estate,

- Merchandise given to employees on holidays, such as a Christmas ham or other item that is not of substantial value. Cash, however, is not excluded, even if it is just a small holiday bonus,

- Meals and lodging provided at your employer's place of business, for the convenience of your employer, or lodging and related expenses (heat, electricity, water, etc.) required for your employment (such as living on your employer's property as a caretaker),

- Employee and courtesy discounts from your employer, such as a store discount; substantial discounts on buying property from your employer, such as a computer or company car, are considered income,

- Worker's compensation payments if you are injured or incapacitated on the job. If you turn over your compensation payments to your employer in return for continuing to receive your full salary, you are taxed only on the balance above the compensation payments,

- Premiums on flexible benefits plans or cafeteria plans by your employer,

- Dependent care assistance programs provided by employers, with certain restrictions, although payments made for dependents or child care for those younger than nineteen are not excludable,

- Employer educational assistance payments, whether or not job-related, going up to $5,250, but with no limit if it would have been a deductible business- or trade-related training or educational expense by the employee,

- Employee awards up to $400 a year or under certain qualified award plans that also are deductible by the employer, meaning that your $100 employee-of-the-month award will not be taxed, or

- Other fringe benefits, such as employer-negotiated discounts on mass transportation, parking and other services, are not considered income.

Do I have to pay tax on gifts and inheritances?

Money or property that comes to you as a bequest or inheritance is not considered taxable income as long as it constitutes a bona fide gift. However, any investment income or interest that comes to you after you receive the property or cash is considered part of your taxable income.

What about scholarships and other academic awards?

In most cases, scholarships, fellowships and other academic awards are excluded from your gross income as long as you are a degree candidate at a qualified educational institution and the payments go toward tuition, enrollment, books, supplies and required equipment for instruction, such as computers. This exclusion also applies to any qualified tuition reduction an educational institution may give to employees and their families. The exclusion does not apply if you receive the award in return for teaching or other services.

What about other prizes and awards?

Unless you assign your winnings to a charity or arm of the government, anything of value that you win, ranging from your church raffle savings bond to the Nobel Peace Prize check, is taxable as income. The only advantage here is that you pay tax only on the fair market value of the item to you. So, for example, if you win a $2,000 computer but already have a PC of your own, the value to you may be less than the normal market price. If you turned around and sold your newly won PC for $1,200, for example, then you claim only that $1,200 as taxable income.

However, if you discount the sale too much, perhaps for a relative, it could be considered a gift and end up taxed as income to you and counting toward the annual gift limit to your relative. For example, if you won the PC and sold it for $50 to your sister, you could be ruled to have received $2,000 in income and have given a gift of $1,950 to your sister.

Can I exclude interest I receive on municipal bonds?

Yes, interest on state and municipal bonds is excluded from tax. This is one of the factors that make these investments so attractive to investors, particularly those in the higher tax brackets. For example, if you end up in the thirty-three percent tax bracket, a municipal bond with a six percent yield gives you the same yield as a taxable bond paying 8.96 percent interest. The only exception to this rule is the purchase of arbitrage bonds, which are bonds that will be used to buy other, higher-interest paying bonds.

What about welfare payments or other public assistance?

Cash payments or other benefits, including crime victim compensation, are excluded from taxable income.

Does that include Social Security payments?

Yes, for the most part Social Security payments are excluded from your gross income, too, along with basic Medicare benefits and supplementary benefits covering costs not included under basic Medicare. Part of your Social Security payments do count toward your income if your income is above a specific level computed by a three-part formula.

If your income was $34,000 or less (or $44,000 or less for joint filers) the formula involves your adjusted gross income on your federal tax return, plus any tax-exempt interest and any foreign income received during the year; the amount of half of your Social Security benefits received during the year (including any benefits paid to your spouse, if you file jointly); and your base amount, which is $25,000 for single filers, $32,000 for joint filers and $0 for married couples filing separately if they have not lived apart for the entire tax year. The formula adds your income and half-benefit, subtracts your base amount and counts half of the balance as your taxable Social Security benefit. For example, if you were a joint filer with $25,000 in income and $5,000 in tax-exempt interest, and received $10,000 in Social Security payments, your calculation would be $30,000 in income plus $5,000 (one half of your social security benefit), minus your $32,000 base amount, for a balance of $3,000, and a taxable Social Security benefit of $1,500 on your federal income tax. Reference: Turbo Tax 2005.

If your income is above $34,000 (or $44,000 for joint filers) a different formula applies, and up to eighty-five percent of your benefits could be taxed if your income plus half of your Social Security payments are more than $34,000 for a single filer or $44,000 for joint filers. If you fall into this category, you can have some of your benefit payments withheld for taxes by filing Form W-4V, Voluntary Withholding Request, with the Social Security Administration. This allows you to have seven percent, ten percent, fifteen percent or twenty-five percent of your total benefit payment withheld. To reduce or eliminate the withholding later, file another W-4V to adjust or end withholding.

At the state level, several states exempt the federally taxable benefit from state income taxes, while others exclude a portion. Some states simply exempt all Social Security benefits from being taxed.

Are payments from annuities and other retirement benefits excluded?

With annuity payments, you are not taxed on the principal you originally invested, but only on the gain your investments have made. Computing the taxable amount requires figuring your life expectancy and number of annuity payments, for which you can consult the IRS tables or a tax preparer.

In the case of other retirement plans, withdrawals from Roth Individual Retirement Accounts are not taxed at all, while distributions from regular IRAs and 401(k) plans are considered part of your income.

Can I exclude profits on the sale of my home?

Home ownership is one of those areas that the government actively supports and encourages through the tax code, and excluding profits from the sale of your primary residence is one of the biggest breaks the IRS hands out. Since the middle of 1997, joint filers can exclude up to $500,000 ($250,000 for single taxpayers), in profits on the sale of their home as often as every two years. The only requirement is that you live in the house for at least two of the last five years. If you live in the house for less than two years, you can get a partial exclusion. You can also get a partial exclusion on profits if the sale is required because of a change in employment, health reasons or other unforeseen circumstances, based on the time you have occupied and owned the home.

Previous rules and exceptions based on age and rolling over gains from one house into another property all have been eliminated.

Are there other types of income I can exclude?

Several other types of miscellaneous income are excludable for tax purposes, including:

- Carpool receipts,

- Damages awarded by a court or received in settling a lawsuit (except back pay and damages under the Age Discrimination in Employment Act),

- Life insurance payments (unless you paid for the policy),

- Child support payments received by you, or

- Interest and earnings on qualified state 529 tuition savings programs.

TAX CREDITS

How can I use tax credits to my advantage?

Tax credits are the next best thing to excludable income when it comes to lowering your tax liability. While exclusions simply take some of your money out of the tax equation altogether, tax credits give you a substantial break that comes right off your total tax bill.

Unlike deductions, which give you a percentage of the write-off based on your level of taxable income, tax credits are 'dollar-for-dollar' tax cuts; that is, if you qualify for a $1,000 tax credit, your tax bill is reduced by exactly $1,000. If, however, you qualify for a $1,000 deduction and are in the twenty-eight percent tax bracket, your tax savings comes out to only $280.

The few downsides to tax credits are that several of them phase out according to your level of income, either awarding only a partial credit as your income rises or eliminating your eligibility altogether. The other drawback is that to get the most tax credits, you first have to owe enough in taxes so that you can apply the credits to your annual tax bill. There are some refundable tax credits that are paid to you, even if you owe no taxes; otherwise, tax credits are non-refundable – they can cut your taxes down to $0, but not beyond. The child tax credit, though, is partly refundable for some lower-income taxpayers with only one or two children.

One more caveat: To claim most of these credits, you have to file additional paperwork, itemize and provide supporting information (Social Security number for dependent children, for example), which means you cannot file the simple 1040EZ tax return.

What are the refundable tax credits?

Excess Social Security tax credit: If you work for more than one employer during the year and make enough money, you could end up having too much Social Security tax withheld. The amount of income taxed is capped at $97,500 for 2007, but if you worked for more than one employer, both of them would apply Social Security taxes up to the cap during the year. This is one tax credit you can claim even if you owe no tax for the year.

Other credits for withheld taxes: This includes any federal tax you have had withheld during the year, estimated taxes you have paid, and tax withheld on interest, investment gains or other sources of income, such as gambling winnings (tax is withheld if you win more than $5,000) or early distributions from retirement plans.

This is where it pays to keep an eye on your taxes all year and to have your paperwork at least minimally organized. You will find interest and dividends that were subject to withholding listed on your various account statements issued either during the year or in January.

You also may have had tax withheld by an investment company from any gains allocated to you in a mutual fund or other investments. This is tricky, because the gains do not have to be paid out to you to qualify as taxable income. Once they are allocated to your account, they are considered income. You must include in your income any amounts that an investment company (for example, a mutual fund) allocated to you as capital gain distributions, even if you did not actually receive them. If the investment firm paid taxes on your gain, that is your money, and you are entitled to a credit. Generally, the company sends out Form 2439, Notice to Shareholder of Undistributed Long-Term Capital Gains, to acknowledge any undistributed capital gains and any taxes that were paid.

Earned income tax credit: This credit is targeted toward taxpayers with low or moderate incomes. You do not have to be married or have children to claim this credit, which can result in a refund of federal tax withheld, or even extra money. To claim this credit you must be employed. Workers who qualify may also be able to take advantage of an advancement feature, which pays out the tax refund in installments with each paycheck.

Additional child tax credit: This tax credit is separate from the child care tax credit and applies, obviously, if you have more than one child. Unlike the child care tax credit, it is refundable, and therefore requires you to file additional tax forms.

What are the more common non-refundable tax credits?

There are a number of basic tax credits available to individuals, as well as many other specialized credits for various business and other activities. In general, it pays to consult tax professionals who are experienced in handling your specific type of issue, whether it is claiming the alcohol fuel tax credit for your business or taking advantage of the District of Columbia first-time homebuyer tax credit. You also should check your state for local tax credits that may apply, such as the New York State tax credit for preserving historic barns. The more common tax credits for individuals include:

Child and dependent care credit: This tax credit goes toward paying for help with children or other dependents that are unable to care for themselves while you and your spouse are working (or even while one of you is looking for work or is a student). Generally, the credit applies to children younger than thirteen or a spouse or dependent who is physically or mentally unable to care for themselves. The credit is not available to taxpayers who choose the married filing separately status, and you cannot hire another dependent or someone younger than nineteen to provide the care.

The credit goes toward all types of expenses, ranging from daycare to babysitters to summer day camp. The credit allows you to claim a refund up to thirty-five percent of eligible expenses, up to $3,000 for the care of one person and $6,000 for two or more. That yields a maximum credit of $2,100 with two or more eligible children or dependents, half that for just one dependent. As with other credits, the maximum percentage applies only to lower-income taxpayers. If you make more than $15,000, the credit is phased down until it hits twenty percent for taxpayers earning $43,000.

Credit for the elderly or disabled: This credit applies to taxpayers whose income does not exceed certain limits and who, by the end of the tax year, are either age sixty-five or older, or younger than sixty-five but retired on permanent, total disability, receiving taxable disability income or who did not reach mandatory retirement age before the current tax year. If you are younger than sixty-five, you also need either a doctor's note or a Veteran's Administration certificate that proves you are totally and permanently disabled.

Retirement savings contributions credit: This credit, aimed at lower-income taxpayers, provides as much as $1,000 in credit based on ten percent to fifty percent of your contributions to IRAs, 401(k) plans and other qualified retirement plans. The income limit is $25,000 for single filers, $50,000 for married couples filing jointly.

Adoption expenses credit: This provides a credit of up to $10,000 (indexed for inflation after 2002) for the adoption of a child, including foreign-born and special needs children. The credit covers reasonable and necessary adoption fees, attorney's fees and even some travel costs, including transportation, meals and lodging. It begins to phase out for adjusted gross income of $150,000 (also inflation-indexed), and cannot be applied to expenses already reimbursed by government or private adoption programs and agencies, or for expenses where a tax deduction or credit applies. The credit also cannot be claimed for expenses involved in adopting a spouse's child or relating to surrogate parents. The adoption does not have to be completed in the tax year in order to claim this credit if the expenses were paid.

Education tax credits: There are two federal tax credits available to families with students in college, mentioned under Section One, Saving and Investing for College.

Lifetime Learning credit: This credit goes up to $2,000 and can be applied to any student at any time during college, graduate school or even continuing education classes. The amount of the credit is based on twenty percent of paid tuition, up to $10,000, for a maximum credit of $2,000 per tax return for you, a spouse or dependent. You cannot apply for Lifetime Learning and Hope tax credits in the same year, and the same income limits apply as with Hope credits.

Since 2002, the amount of both the Hope and Lifetime Learning credits are indexed for inflation, along with the income limits on eligibility.

Health insurance credit: This credit came about because of an international trade bill. It applies to workers who lose a job because of shifts in imports or exports or when a company moves production to an overseas location. The credit allows for a sixty-five percent subsidy in the form of a tax credit to cover the expense of buying health insurance.

GROSS INCOME ADJUSTMENTS

What are gross income adjustments and how do they work?

Gross income adjustments also are called above the line deductions because they are taken before either the standardized or itemized tax deductions, yielding your adjusted gross income. Like tax credits and regular deductions, they help reduce your overall taxable income and thus reduce your final tax bill. The difference between these above the line deductions and others that you make after computing your adjusted gross income is that the adjustments do not force you to choose between either itemizing or taking the standard deduction. Instead, you can claim any of these adjustments for which you qualify, whether you itemize or not. These adjustments are listed on the first page of your return, just above the line where adjusted gross income is tabulated; hence the name, 'above the line' deductions.

How do I claim these adjustments?

Generally, you have to meet certain eligibility requirements, and may have to submit some tax worksheets. In most cases, though, adjustments are subject to income limits or phase-outs, and you list them on the first page of your return, just above the line where adjusted gross income is tabulated.

What kinds of expenses qualify as adjustments?

Trade and business expenses: What the IRS terms ordinary and necessary expenses of conducting your trade or business during the year can be deducted above the line. In certain cases, such as travel to a trade show or business conference, this can be an opportunity to convert or partly convert some personal expenses to deductible business expenses. This is also where you deduct use of your home office, a personal vehicle for business and many other expenses related to making a living. For specifics, consult a tax specialist or the IRS.

Expenses by teachers and other educators for classroom supplies: Eligible teachers and other educators, including aides, counselors and principals, can deduct up to $250 in qualified, non-reimbursed expenses used for teaching in the classroom. These include books, supplies, computer equipment (including related software and services), other equipment, and supplementary materials. Athletic equipment can be claimed if used in health or physical education classes. There is one catch to this adjustment, however: To be deductible, these expenses must be more than any interest you received during the year on savings bonds that were excluded for educational purposes, as well as any withdrawals from qualified tuition programs and Coverdell Educational Savings Accounts.

Contributions to a traditional Individual Retirement Account: If you are covered by a retirement plan at work and make less than $70,000 for married couples
filing jointly or $50,000 for single filers, you can deduct up to $4,000 in contributions to a traditional individual retirement account ($5,000 if you are fifty or
older). If your company does not offer a pension plan, 401(k) plan or other qualified retirement option, the income limits do not apply. If you are looking for a
last-minute deduction, remember that IRA contributions can be made up until the
tax-filing deadline to qualify as a deduction from your previous year's tax.

Interest paid on a student loan: You can deduct up to $2,500 a year
(adjusted for inflation) over the entire life of your student loans if you qualify. To
receive this deduction, you cannot be claimed as a dependent on someone else's return, you cannot be married filing separately, and the loan has to pay for qualified
expenses at eligible educational institutions. You also have to be pursuing a degree
or certificate and attending school at least half-time. You can, however, claim this
deduction for a spouse or dependent. The loan cannot be from a relative or employer. The deductibility phases out for single filers with incomes between $50,000
and $65,000, and for joint filers between $100,000 and $130,000. This limit is also
adjusted for inflation in future years.

Payment of tuition and fees to an eligible educational institution: This allows
you to claim up to $4,000 for tuition and fees paid, in much the same way as stu-
dent loan interest: You cannot be claimed on someone else's return, must file jointly
if married, and must be pursuing a bona fide degree or certificate at an eligible
institution at least half-time. Non-credit courses do not count, and you cannot
claim this deduction for your children or other dependents. In addition, any money withdrawn from a state tuition plan, a Coverdell educational savings account
or interest on savings bonds claimed for educational purposes has to be deducted
from the expenses you claim. The same income limits apply as with student loan
interest, adjusted for inflation along with the deductible limit.

One final rule: You cannot claim this deduction in the same year that you use
either a Hope or Lifetime Learning credit. In most cases, one of the credits will
reduce your taxes by more than the tuition deduction.

Money contributed to a health savings account: These new accounts replace the
old Medical Savings Accounts and function like an IRA to pay for healthcare expenses. To be eligible, you must have health insurance with a deductible of at least
$1,100 for single filers, $2,200 for joint filers and families. The maximum contribution you can make is $2,650 for singles, $5,250 for families or the amount of your
policy deductible, whichever is less (although you can deposit extra cash if you are

between fifty-five and sixty-five years old). Withdrawals from the accounts can be used tax-free to pay for most uninsured medical expenses, although the money cannot go to pay for your health insurance policy. Interest in the accounts accrues tax-free and balances and interest can roll over each year. Like IRAs, contributions can be made up until the April 15 federal tax filing deadline. The accounts are offered by banks, insurance companies and other financial services firms.

Costs of moving to take a new job: You can deduct the costs to move household goods and personal property, limited storage and insurance fees, utility connection or disconnection charges, some lodging and travel expenses near your new and former homes, shipping costs for your car and even travel arrangements for household pets. You also can claim mileage if you drove yourself to your new location.

The requirements to claim this deduction fall into three categories: First, the move must be work-related. Second, you have to move far enough to qualify. Currently, the distance between your old home and your new job has to be at least fifty miles greater than your old commute. So if you were driving thirty miles a day to work, your new workplace has to be at least eighty miles away from your old home. The last test is length of time in your new work assignment. The expenses must be incurred within one year of starting your new job, and you have to be full time at the new job for at least thirty-nine weeks during your first twelve months in your new residence. The job does not have to be with the same employer, and those thirty-nine required weeks do not have to be consecutive. For the self-employed, the requirement is seventy-eight weeks during the first twenty-four months and meet the same one-year filing deadline.

If you do not make your minimum work requirement, the IRS expects you to file an amended return or list the moving expenses deducted as income on your next return. Finally, do not try to deduct moving expenses paid by your employer, which won't qualify.

Self-employment taxes: If you are self-employed, you will find yourself paying both parts of your Social Security taxes – the employer's half and your own half as an employee. While you formerly paid 6.2 percent of your income in Social Security, and 1.45 for Medicare, you now pay 12.4 percent of your income, up to an annual limit, for Social Security and 2.9 percent on everything you make to Medicare. To ease that burden on the self-employed, you can claim half of the entire 15.3 percent as the self-employment deduction.

Self-employed health insurance: You can deduct all of the cost of medical and qualified long-term care insurance on behalf of you, your spouse and dependents for any month that you are self-employed, as long as you are not eligible for any subsidized health insurance plan maintained by your employer or your spouse's employer. You also cannot deduct more than you earned from your self-employed business activities. However, you can factor any amount that you cannot claim against self-employment earnings as part of your normally itemized medical care expenses.

Contributions to self-employed retirement plans: If you have established a SEP-IRA, Keogh or other qualified retirement plan for the self-employed, you can deduct contributions to those plans as well.

Penalties on early withdrawal of savings: If you liquidated a long-term certificate of deposit or other savings account carrying penalties for early withdrawals, you can claim the amount of forfeited interest against your income.

Alimony payments: These are deductible, but you have to be careful in claiming alimony deductions on your taxes. The IRS is wary of taxpayers who tried to mis-represent property settlements, child support and non-alimony divorce payments in order to claim this deduction. If the alimony ends within six months of some specific event, such as a child leaving school or reaching a certain age, it will be re-classified as child support. 'Excess alimony' also causes problems, so the IRS limits the deduction to payments in the first year of divorce that do not exceed the aver-age of payments in the next two years by $15,000 or more, or alimony payments in the second year of the divorce that exceed payments in the third year by $15,000 or more.

One final catch on this adjustment: You must list the Social Security number of the alimony recipient or the deduction may be disallowed by the IRS. Since alimony received is income, the IRS wants to be sure it can track who is getting your money.

Miscellaneous costs: These include employer-paid business expenses under expense account plans (such as formal per diems), business expenses for performing artists, jury duty pay given to an employer and the purchase of a clean-fuel vehicle, including hybrid gas-electric cars. For more information, check with the IRS or a tax professional.

ITEMIZED DEDUCTIONS

Which is better – taking the itemized or the standard deduction?

The standard deduction is a set amount the IRS allows you to claim to cover all sorts of other expenses and expenditures throughout the year without forcing you to itemize each deduction, fill out schedules and worksheets and retain receipts and other paperwork to back up your claims. It is certainly easier when filing your returns and allows you to use shorter 1040EZ or 1040A returns instead of having to wrangle the standard 1040 form.

Easier, however, is not always better. According to the Government Accounting Office, a 2001 report revealed that more than half a million taxpayers who claimed the standard deduction on their 1998 taxes could have saved an average of $610 by itemizing their returns. Whether it was worth the time and expense to claim their share of the more than $3 million overpaid in taxes is another question, but for some taxpayers with enough deductible itemized expenses, the tax savings is more than worth it. In general, you should scrutinize your personal and business expenses in these categories to find deductible expenses:

- Medical deductions, including everything from acupuncture to X-ray treatments,

- Taxes, which cover real estate, foreign taxes, state and local taxes and some federal taxes in connection with businesses,

- Charitable deductions, including benefit performances, property, artwork and even foster parenting expenses,

- Casualty and theft losses, including accidents, natural disasters and even damages from burst water heaters,

- Miscellaneous deductions, which include union dues, gambling losses (against winnings), bad debts and bar exam costs,

- Miscellaneous employee deductions, which cover many expenses you incur in doing business that are not reimbursed by your employer, including job-hunting expenses, professional journal subscriptions and tools,

- Investor deductions, such as accounting fees, legal expenses, bad debts and many items related to business property.

Check with the IRS or a tax professional to see just how much is covered; it may surprise you. At the same time, going for every penny you can legally deduct has its drawbacks as well, in that claiming too much in itemized deductions can trigger the dreaded Alternative Minimum Tax, which is discussed later.

How do I choose my filing status?

In some cases, there is not much choice, but depending on your circumstances, you might qualify for more than one category. Another point to keep in mind is that your status is defined by where you stand on the last day of the year. If you got married on December 31, for example, both you and your spouse can claim married tax-filing status. It works, the other way, too: If you become divorced by the end of the year, you can claim single status. There are five tax status choices:

Single: If you have never been married, if you are divorced or otherwise unmarried, you can choose this status. If, however, you are claiming a relative as a dependent, you also should review your options for filing as the head of a household.

Married filing jointly: You must be officially married, and report all the income of both you and your spouse together on one tax form. This status offers some tax credits not available to other filers, while the so-called 'marriage penalty' that results in some types of couples paying more tax than if they were filing separately under single status has been reduced or eliminated in many instances.

Married filing separately: In general, most married couples do better filing jointly, but there are situations where married filing separately is a better option, and other situations where you may be required to file separately. In general, it is best to compute your tax return under both filing options and see which gives you the lowest tax bill, an experiment made much easier with sophisticated tax software. Many professional tax preparers, in fact, automatically figure your tax under each status. To file separately, you have to separate all your income, deductions and exemptions as a couple and file individual returns. Also, note that you won't be able to take some tax credits and deductions under this status.

Head of household: This status applies to you if you are unmarried and provide more than half the cost of maintaining a home for at least half a year for you and a relative. The tax rate is generally more favorable than filing under single or married filing separately status, and includes a larger standard deduction than single filers can receive. Married persons who have not lived with their spouses sometimes can qualify for this status.

Widow or widower with a dependent child: If as a surviving spouse you are caring for a dependent child for the entire tax year you can claim this status, which amounts to retaining the filing status for joint married filers. As with the head of household filing status, you must have paid more than half the cost of maintaining a home during the tax year.

What if I am out of the country at tax time?

US taxpayers living outside of the country automatically get a two-month extension to pay taxes and file their annual returns. If you are married and only you or your spouse is abroad, you can still claim the deduction. To claim foreign-filing status, your main place of business or work assignment must be out of the country, or you are serving in the Armed Forces outside of the US or Puerto Rico. You also can exclude your foreign income from federal taxes if you establish your real home in a foreign country for a full tax year (or spend at least 330 days overseas earning your income), or you establish a foreign location as your principal place of business or employment and do not claim any tax exemption there.

What about men and women who are fighting overseas?

Members of the Armed Forces who are assigned to combat zones do not have to file returns or pay taxes for up to 180 days after their last day in an authentic battle region, or their last day of continuous hospitalization for injuries received in a combat zone. In addition to the 180 days, filers also can add to their extensions the number of days until their taxes were due when they entered the combat area.

What are the types of expenses I can claim as itemized deductions?

Once again, the government seeks to give you a break on behavior it wants to encourage, such as going to school or buying a home, or to offset bad circumstances (fire, theft or other casualty losses) or to adjust for income that is not really income, such as taking money out of your own pocket to pay for business expenses even though you are an employee.

Medical expenses: These are deductible as long as they total more than 7.5 percent of your adjusted gross income. While that number can seem rather high, remember that this covers all medical expenses for all your dependents. In some cases, you can claim part of medical expenses paid for your parents, as well. Other often-overlooked medical deductions include:

- Expenses for traveling to and from doctors' offices, clinics, labs and other medical treatments; if you drive, use the standard mileage allowance set each year by the IRS,

- Payments for insurance polices from after-tax income, including some long-term care insurance coverage, depending on your age and up to certain limits,

- All kinds of uninsured medical treatments, such as hearing aids, false teeth, eyeglasses, contact lenses, laser vision correction procedures, eye exams, orthotics and artificial limbs,

- Expenses for drug- and alcohol-abuse treatments,

- Medically necessary costs prescribed by a physician, such as an air purifier, special furniture or other medical equipment, even including the cost of electricity or maintenance,

- Admission and transportation to medical conferences (but not meals or lodging) when these conferences deal with a chronic illness suffered by you, your spouse or a dependent,

- Some medical weight loss programs (in the case of hypertension, for example) and most stop-smoking programs,

- Medical equipment, such as wheelchairs, crutches, close-captioning devices and other equipment for the deaf; also expenses for modifying your automobile with controls for the handicapped or wheelchair lifts and other accessories,

- Seeing-eye dogs or dogs that assist people who are hearing-impaired,

- Home modifications for the disabled, such as adding ramps, widening doorways, moving outlets and fixtures.

Income taxes: You are allowed to deduct any state income tax you pay, usually for the same tax year, from your federal tax return. You can also deduct certain other state and local levies, such as a state intangibles tax on your investments or any tax on interest income that is exempt from federal tax. You can also deduct any mandatory contributions you have to make to some state benefit funds, as well as any city or county income taxes and any commuter taxes you might face.

Foreign taxes: Besides states and local municipalities, you may end up paying foreign taxes or income taxes, or tax in a US possession. These are deductible against your federal tax, with foreign income taxes available either as an itemized deduction or as a credit against your US tax bill.

Property taxes: Any state, local or foreign taxes on your property are deductible from your federal taxes, as well as interest on home equity loans and lines of credit (probably the last remaining consumer loan interest deduction you can find). You can also deduct any local benefit taxes that go toward maintenance, repair or interest payments if you can show how much of the tax goes to pay those charges. You cannot deduct local garbage, water or trash fees, nor any homeowner's association dues and fees that go toward recreation, maintenance of common areas, health or safety.

Personal property taxes: If other property you own is taxed on its value, such as a motor vehicle, you can deduct that tax or portion of tax, as long as the tax is charged every year, even if it is not paid every year, as with multi-year vehicle registrations.

Interest: Your home mortgage interest is deductible, along with some other real estate closing fees, such as points, in some cases. Interest paid on margin accounts that are still in the hands of your broker is also deductible when the interest is posted to the account. You can also deduct interest on business loans, such as loans for rental property and interest on student loans.

Charitable gifts and contributions: These are deductible only if made to qualified charitable organizations (registered with the IRS) and if you do not get anything in return, although anything you pay over the fair market price for an item from a charitable group is deductible. For instance, if you pledged $1,000 at a charity auction for a set of concert tickets with a face price of $200, you could take the $800 difference as a donation.

You can also deduct merchandise at fair market value, or claim mileage expenses incurred for charity work. The IRS is going to want receipts, and if you give particularly generous gifts you have to provide more proof. For contributions of items you value at more than $250, you need a written receipt from the qualified organization. For items worth more than $500, you need to file a tax form listing non-cash charitable contributions as well. If you go over $5,000 on an item, it must be appraised and you need to file the appraisal summary with another tax form.

Another form of charitable giving is donating appreciated assets, such as stocks you have owned for more than one year, to avoid paying the capital gains on the increased value, while still deducting the entire current value of the donation. In some cases, charities also accept cars, trucks, boats and other vehicles, for which you must set a reasonable fair market value, usually based on published guidelines.

If you overdo it with charity, usually fifty percent of your adjusted gross income, you have to carry over the excess amount to future tax returns for five years, although in some cases donations of certain goods to some types of organizations are limited to as little as twenty percent of your adjusted gross. At the other end of the spectrum, there is no minimum amount you need to achieve in order to claim the charitable gifts deduction. To qualify, donations must have been made by December 31, although mailing a check on that date can count.

Casualty losses: If during the year you should suffer damage, destruction or loss of property resulting from a sudden, unexpected or unusual event, including natural or man-made disasters, you can claim the loss on your itemized tax form. The list of qualifying disasters includes, but is not limited to:

- Auto accidents,
- Riots and civil disturbances,
- Drought,
- Flood,
- Earthquakes,
- Explosions,
- Fires,
- Freezing rain,
- Ice and snow,
- Hurricanes,
- Lightning,

- Mine cave-ins,

- Shipwrecks,

- Smog,

- Sonic booms,

- Storms,

- Vandalism,

- Wind, windstorms and tornadoes.

Wear and tear on property and other damage, such as termites and pests, does not count. After determining that you have suffered a qualified loss, it is then subject to two limits: Subtract $100 from your total loss amount (which, in effect, rules out any loss of less than $100) and then determine that the remaining value is more than ten percent of your adjusted gross income and deduct that same ten percent from that remaining value. If you collected any insurance money for the claim, you must also subtract that amount as well.

For losses to personal property and businesses where the area is declared a federal disaster area, you can file an amended return to claim the disaster on your previous year's itemized taxes, and receive any refund right away, rather than waiting to file the tax loss on your next return.

Theft losses: Losses from theft, including robbery, larceny and embezzlement can be deducted, while losses from extortion, kidnapping ransom or blackmail may be deductible, along similar lines as casualty losses. You need to provide proof that the property was stolen and that you were the owner. Your deduction generally is limited to either the amount by which the theft reduced the market value of the property or your cost basis of the property before it was stolen.

Employee business expenses: You can claim these costs as part of your miscellaneous deductions, which must total more than two percent of your adjusted gross income. This deduction covers expenses that you pay yourself but that are normal, required and necessary in the eyes of the IRS, such as a computer or cell phone if – and only if – your employer requires you to have one. Other expenses can include some work clothing, such as uniforms you buy yourself, union dues, dues to bona fide professional organizations, job-search expenses for your current job, license fees, malpractice insurance and more. While some types of travel and transportation are allowed, your commuting expenses cannot be deducted.

Gifts: Gifts given as part of the regular cost of doing business that are ordinary and necessary or, in the words of the IRS, 'reasonable and customary', can be deducted. The total of gifts given to any one individual during the year cannot be more than $25, but that does not include that individual's spouse or children. You cannot deduct promotional items, such as a bunch of paperweights engraved with your name that you give out to clients and potential clients.

Tax preparation costs: This is part of the miscellaneous deduction category and covers tax counseling and advice, fees and expenses for tax litigation, and even the cost of having your tax return prepared.

I have heard something about bunching my deductions – can you explain this?

This is a clever and completely legal way to claim itemized deductions if you find yourself consistently falling just a bit short of the amount needed to beat your standardized deduction each year. Bunching consists of prepaying or rescheduling itemized deductions to move more than one year's worth of expenses into a single tax year, such as taking out a three-year subscription to a professional journal instead of paying annually. After one year of bunching, which can double some of your itemized claims, you simply coast for a year and take the standardized deduction, either using up the prepaid costs you have deducted or postponing others until the next tax year, when you can bunch them all up again.

FILING TAXES

What about getting help with my taxes?

If you have anything beyond a very simple return to file, it can make a lot of sense to get some kind of assistance in planning and filing your tax return. There are several types of help, from books and software designed for do-it-yourselfers to having someone complete your return to arranging for ongoing, year-round tax planning with a certified public account or experienced tax attorney.

What should I look for in a tax preparer?

Selecting the right tax preparer will make a difference in the amount of tax you owe. Several magazines and newspapers conduct annual studies where the same tax information is sent to several preparers, all with different, legal results. This shows that shopping around for a tax professional with the right understanding of your financial situation can pay off.

Like any other profession, you can find many different types of tax preparation professionals with varying levels of experience and education. Since tax preparation is not a government regulated profession, you need to check the credentials and background of whomever you consider to handle your taxes. Here is a rundown of the various types of tax preparers and the questions you should keep in mind to determine just which type of help is right for you.

Franchised or local tax preparation outlets: The people who prepare returns at the national or regional tax preparation chains all received training to some extent, but not necessarily at all levels or at the particular level of help you might need. In many cases, these preparers do not make much more than minimum wage plus some type of commission or incentive, and are often preparing tax returns only as a second job during the height of the pre-April 15 tax season.

If you have a straight forward return without a lot of complicated deductions and income adjustments, help from one of the big tax chains can be a reasonably priced and effective option. Although most of these kinds of preparers will accompany you if you get called in to explain your return to the Internal Revenue Service, you should note that only enrolled agents, licensed attorneys and CPAs are allowed to appear in your place before the IRS.

Enrolled Agents: Typically, an enrolled agent keeps up to date with annual training from the IRS. Enrolled agents are licensed by the federal government and many are former IRS employees. All enrolled agents have passed a comprehensive IRS exam. As mentioned before, an enrolled agent can represent you in a hearing or meeting with the IRS, which is something to keep in mind if you expect to be audited any time soon. Often enrolled agents specialize in one or more specific areas of taxes and tax regulations, so make sure you match your needs to an enrolled agent's area of expertise.

You can locate an enrolled agent through the National Association of Enrolled Agents at 202-822-NAEA (6232), or at the organization's website at *www.naea.org.*

Certified Public Accountants: A CPA has several years of specialized education and has completed their individual state's licensing qualifying exam for accounting, but may or may not be an expert on matters of taxation. The advantage to consulting with a CPA is that he or she can create an overall tax plan for you covering several years and can create strategies and approaches to help you handle complex financial and tax situations.

Financial experts recommend considering consulting with a CPA if you have recently become divorced, gone into retirement, opened, closed, purchased or sold any type of business, or gone through any other significant life changes that are likely to influence your financial situation. When selecting a CPA, though, be sure to find out about his or her practical experience in tax planning and whether they keep up to date with modifications and changes in the tax law. As with an enrolled agent, using a CPA has the advantage that your CPA can represent you in IRS proceedings.

For more information, you can consult the American Institute of Certified Public Accountants on the web at *www.aicpa.org* for more information, or contact your state association of CPAs.

Tax attorney: You should consider working with a tax attorney in situations where you are attempting to shelter part of your income or if your tax situation involves complex corporate matters, trusts and other structural questions for tax planning. A tax attorney may have experience on the latest tax laws, tax court rulings and decisions in tax disputes, but may be less qualified to handle the actual preparation of tax schedules, worksheets and returns.

What about using tax software on my home computer?

The Internal Revenue Service estimates that it takes the average taxpayer more than thirteen hours to complete the typical Form 1040 tax return, including research and compiling records, and more than six hours alone just to fill out all the actual required paperwork.

Not surprisingly, if you do not use a professional tax preparer, you still want to look for some ways to make preparing your own tax return easier and faster. One good solution is commercial tax-preparation software packages that might not only save you time, but may also help find ways to cut your overall tax bill. Not all tax programs are created equal, and there are a number of software selections you can make in this booming sector. That means your first step is to determine your needs so that you can choose the right program for you.

For instance, if your taxes are on the simple side without a lot of deductions and complicated schedules, just about any program might work for you; the simpler the better. On the other hand, if you have income from your own business or other additional considerations, you need a more comprehensive and powerful program that addresses the more sophisticated tax considerations. If you are not exactly sure what you need, look for offerings that include step-by-step help, glossaries and even tutorials that walk you through your tax return line by line. For those who have a good understanding of their tax situation and just want to save time by putting it all in the computer, generating their own clean and tidy tax forms, and taking advantage of software calculators and functions to handle the math and tax computation functions, the best approach is to look for a program that allows flexibility in bypassing some steps and skipping ahead. Finally, do not forget to make sure the software is compatible with your computer's operating system, memory resources and other technical requirements.

If the point of using tax software is to save money on your taxes, do not start by overpaying for your tax software. You should comparison shop not only for the capabilities, but also for cost. You should consider not only at the software's base price, but also charges for any options. For instance, does the software cover your state tax filing, and does it include all the correct forms? Will the software allow you to prepare returns for more than one person? Can you use the software to file your taxes electronically, and is there a charge to do so?

Also, look ahead to next year. With the plethora of annual changes that apply to taxes, you cannot expect that the software you buy this year is going to be accurate and effective next year; that means you should look at the cost and options of upgrading to the next edition. At the same time, if you have an old program around, look at upgrading instead of buying new to save money. In fact, you may have a trial version tucked away in the preloaded programs that came on your computer, or at least a discount offer.

What kind of help can I get with computer tax software?

Before jumping in and whizzing through your tax return, computer experts recommend that you take some time to look at the features of the program, or even the annual updates if you have used it before. This helps you get the most out of the program and avoids frustrating and time-consuming mistakes.

One feature you should definitely search out is any online 'help' connection that puts you in touch with the software provider's technical assistance staff. It is better to find that feature ahead of time and not when you are deep in the middle of the return and suddenly get an unexpected error message. Most packages give you the option of using both online and phone support for any of your specific problems and questions, along with the basic help and trouble-shooting guides that come with the software.

Don't forget to take advantage of all the help your program provides. Before you hit the print button or send your return in electronically, check out the review option that comes with most packages. Sometimes it is an automatic feature that runs as soon as you complete the form, but if it is not, make sure you click on the feature and launch it. The review can point out errors, reminders and suggestions that you could have overlooked in specific line items. Even if most of the suggestions do not apply in your case, it is still helpful when the review feature catches an occasional mistake or missed deduction. Finally, do not forget to save copies of your finished return for your own records, with at least one electronic backup and several printouts for your files.

What about the Free File Alliance?

You might not have to buy tax software at all. In previous years, the IRS has offered the Free File Alliance, a program designed to make online tax preparation and e-filing free for about seventy-eight million filers, according to the IRS. To qualify, you must meet several criteria, including income level, state residence, military service and other considerations. Still, it is worth checking out before you purchase an expensive software package that will be out of date next year.

The annually updated version of Free File usually is available by mid-January. When the new version is operational, the IRS's Free File Wizard page helps point taxpayers to participating software companies, where they can enter some basic personal and tax information to help narrow their choices.

Do not give up if you do not qualify for the free aspects of the program, however. You may still be able to use Free File to get yourself an inexpensive way to file online. Rather than purchasing software, you just visit the software company's website and pay to use the tax program there. Your tax return can then be electronically filed, with your tax information stored online.

What are the most common mistakes I should watch out for with my taxes?

Just as there is no end to the combination of tax deductions, rules, exemptions, classifications and other factors that make filing your federal tax such a complicated and often daunting exercise, there is also an endless litany of mistakes you – or a professional tax preparer – can make in putting your return together. Nonetheless, there are a number of predictable trouble spots you should watch out for and be sure to double-check before you sign and mail (or e-mail) your return.

Math errors: According to the IRS, bad math is the most common mistake on tax returns every year. Mistakes in simple arithmetic or in copying numbers from one schedule to another will prompt the IRS to issue you an immediate correction notice. Checking your math (or getting someone else to do it) is your best defense since, obviously, math errors also can reduce the amount of your refund or cause you to overpay your taxes.

Missing Social Security numbers: For several years, the IRS has halted its practice of printing taxpayer Social Security numbers on tax package labels because of complaints about privacy concerns and the potential for ID theft. While it might make us safer, taxpayers frequently forget to write their identification numbers on their tax returns. The tax ID number (usually your Social Security number) is critical to processing your return because there are so many pieces of information sent to the IRS that are tracked with this number, from tax withholding to bank account interest and retirement plan contributions.

Social Security and other taxpayer ID numbers also are important if you are claiming the child tax and additional child tax credits, as well as credits for educational expenses and dependent care costs, and anything else relating to family members on your return. If the IRS cannot identify and confirm the identities of those individuals, these deductions could be disallowed on your return.

Failing to sign and date your return: Your tax return is a legal document, and the IRS won't touch it if it is not properly dated and signed by you, any co-filers and tax preparers. If you are filing electronically, though, you do not have to sign; instead, you use your own privately selected personal identification number.

Ignoring the preprinted label and envelope from the IRS: Using the preprinted label and envelope that comes with your tax package is the easiest way to be sure your return gets to the right office and processing center of the IRS on time. It is also the best way for the IRS to accurately read your personal information, which can help speed up receiving any refunds or notices relating to your return.

Ignoring or overlooking interest and dividend income: As mentioned before, the IRS uses your Social Security (or other taxpayer ID number) listed on bank and investment accounts to track how much unearned income you have made in the year. Forgetting to include this information on your tax return means the IRS examiners will not only notify you about taxes owed on this income, but the agency could slap you with penalty and interest charges. Besides, now that you can make up to $1,500 before being required to file Schedule B with your return, makes reporting this income much easier.

Overlooking charitable donation claims: It is hard to believe, but every year many taxpayers either forget or choose not to take all the available deductions for donating cash, clothing, vehicles and household items. These valuable deductions only require that you follow a few rules, the first and foremost being that you make your donations to qualified charitable organizations. These groups have official tax-exempt status and are listed with the IRS. In just about all cases you need to have made the actual, physical donation by the end of the calendar year, although checks sent on December 31 are usually honored by the IRS. Remember to retain and file a written record of your donations.

Omitting tax forms: Avoiding this error can be as simple as making sure your W-2 statement of earnings is attached to the front of your return and double-checking any of the additional schedules and worksheets to be included with a more complicated tax return.

Improperly tracking investment basis: Before you can accurately calculate capital gains (or losses) on stocks and other investments you have sold, you need to complete several complicated steps to figure out the original cost basis of your investment or the IRS cannot tell how much you actually made or lost. For example, if any of your investments paid dividends or distributed gains in past years, they probably were reported (and taxed) as income in the year you received that money or reinvested it. In that case, those gains and distributions should be added back to your cost basis, or you will end up being taxed twice on that money. The solution is to keep accurate records, especially if you handle your own trading and investing, or to make sure your broker will handle this task for you.

Overpaying by using the wrong tax form: Using that little 1040EZ form may make filing your taxes quick and simple, but it could also make them more expensive, according to the IRS. If your tax situation is simple enough that you are considering a short form, it would not take that much more time and effort to tackle the long form. While you do not have to complete every line and schedule, you will find that the longer returns present several additional options for reducing your taxable income. If you are using tax preparation software or having your return professionally prepared, you cannot only compare your tax owed using different forms, but also compute your tax under different filing status options, such as a joint return for a married couple versus filing separate returns.

Incorrectly filling out your check: You might dislike signing that check for taxes owed, but you still need to make sure it is properly filled out and signed. Checks to cover your taxes have to be payable to the United States Treasury, not the IRS, for instance. This is a safeguard to prevent thieves from changing the letters 'IRS' into something they can more easily cash.

Another problem the IRS cites comes from taxpayers 'forgetting' to sign their payment checks. This old-fashioned stalling technique might very well prompt the IRS to rule that you missed the filing deadline, causing you to rack up payments for penalties and interest while the IRS returns your check to sign.

Failing to bunch deductions: Many different types of deductions, such as health expenses, are deductible only if you reach a certain amount. If you are a little short of the limit, you can shift, or 'bunch' some of those costs into one tax year to take advantage. This can be as simple as prepaying professional association dues or scheduling some sort of elective medical treatment to take place during a tax year when you know you are going to be close to hitting the threshold for the deductibility requirements.

Not taking all your tax credits: As mentioned before, a tax credit is just about the closest thing you can find to free money when it comes to your taxes. In fact, some types of refundable tax credits are free money if you qualify.

Because there are many credits available, it also can be too easy to overlook some of them, especially when it comes to determining if you qualify for the credit. Still, if you have any expenses relating to education costs, child care, providing dependent care expenses, and other categories discussed before, you should invest a little time to see if you can qualify for one of these big tax breaks.

Using the wrong tax table: This is a common mistake for do-it-yourself tax filers preparing their returns on paper. The fact is, it is not that hard to misread all those tiny tax tables listed in the back of the tax instruction booklets, but it could very well pay to double-check just which figures you take from those pages of small print, especially when it comes to using the correct column for your filing status. Each status means you pay a different percentage of tax in the various taxable income ranges, and using the wrong one can make quite a difference in your tax bill or refund.

Do not stop there – maybe you should not be using any tax table at all. For instance, when figuring your long-term capital gains from mutual fund distributions and other instances, you could report them directly on your form 1040 or 1040a, but you would be overpaying your taxes. Instead, make the extra effort to figure your tax using the worksheet that comes in your return's instruction booklet and claim that income at the lower long-term capital gains rate of fifteen percent; otherwise you end up overpaying your taxes on gains in your higher personal tax bracket.

Missing the extension deadline: When it comes to filing your tax return, there is no such thing as close – you are either late or you are not in the eyes of the IRS, which could mean paying a late filing penalty and interest fees. If your tax paperwork is just piled too high for you to make the April 15 tax deadline, you can request and receive an automatic six-month extension to complete all your paperwork.

To get an extension, submit Form 4868, Application for Automatic Extension of Time to File US Individual Income Tax Return by the tax deadline. Unfortunately, an extension to file your taxes is not an extension to pay your taxes. You should make your best estimate of any tax you owe and make sure that you send that amount in on time.

Putting insufficient postage on your return: The majority of taxpayers in the US still file their returns on paper forms and mail them to an IRS processing center. Unless you have had a very easy time of preparing your return, all those schedules, forms and worksheets probably put your return's mailing weight at more than one ounce, so make sure you have enough extra stamps on the envelope before you drop it in the mailbox. If the post office returns your return for extra postage, you could end up with an unexpected late-filing penalty, and interest if you had tax due, or have to re-mail your return and wait even longer for your refund.

What do I need to know about the dreaded Alternative Minimum Tax?

The Alternative Minimum Tax, or AMT, gets more and more attention each year, mostly because more unsuspecting taxpayers are getting hit with a bigger tax bill than anticipated under AMT. The tax takes effect when your taxable income and deductions meet certain criteria, triggering what critics call Uncle Sam's 'stealth tax'.

Like a lot of troublesome notions, the AMT was created with relatively good intentions, with the goal of ensuring that the wealthy paid their fair share of taxes by disallowing deductions that would reduce their taxes below a certain point. The AMT is a separate approach to figuring your taxes due that works alongside all the normal tax rules. Under the AMT, you pay a flat tax of twenty-six to twenty-eight percent, which is at least lower than the two highest brackets – thirty-three and thirty-five percent – under the regular tax system; however, that tax is computed employing completely different definitions of income and allowing fewer deductions. If you are required to file under the AMT, it results in a higher tax bill than a return prepared under the regular tax rules.

Two more pieces of bad news: Because Congress has failed to adjust and update the AMT, it is not just snagging the very wealthy anymore; it now takes a bigger tax bite for a growing number of middle and upper middle-class taxpayers. Also, because of the AMT's complex and peculiar structure, it is quite difficult to incorporate into normal tax planning strategies.

Where did the AMT come from?

Congress created the alternative tax in 1969 after testimony from the Secretary of the Treasury revealed that 155 high-income US households had paid no taxes at all in 1966. Back in the 1960s, lawmakers were less sensitive to inflation and they failed to index the specific requirements of the AMT for the effects of an ever-increasing cost of living.

As a result, this attempt to close loopholes for the very rich now ends up striking middle-income taxpayers with deductions for a large family, stock options and even high state income taxes.

According to tax experts, just about anyone with four or more children or other dependents, for example, should face up to paying the AMT someday soon. According to one study, the AMT hit about one million taxpayers in 1999 but, if it goes unchanged, will apply to 33 million by 2010 and 46 million filers in 2014, covering nearly any household with income between $100,000 and $500,000.

Overall, married couples and parents are those with the most to fear from the AMT. Since the AMT prohibits deductions for dependents, experts predict that eighty-five percent of married couples with two or more children will end up paying the AMT just because they have children. While efforts have been made to adjust, update or even outright repeal the AMT, the government has been slow to take action because of the additional tax revenue it generates. Currently, the AMT is expected to bring in an additional $28 million in taxes for just one year.

What are the limits on the AMT?

Depending on your tax deductions and income adjustments, it takes a surprisingly low amount of taxable income to trigger the AMT:

- $58,000 if you are married filing a joint return or are a qualified widow or widower,

- $40,250 if you are single or head of household or,

- $29,000 if you are married filing a separate return.

While the AMT wipes out all standard and most itemized deductions on your re-turn, its inclusion also changes other rules, such as those covering employee incentive stock options. Under AMT, they are taxed as soon as you exercise the options, even though you have received no actual income. Under regular tax rules, those options are not taxed until you actually get money from selling the stock provided by the options. The only way around this options problem, experts advise, is to sell your shares in the same tax year that you exercise the options. The AMT also wipes out conventional tax brackets. Instead, you pay a twenty-six percent tax rate on the first $175,000 of gross income and face a twenty-eight percent tax rate on any amount above that limit.

There is not a lot you can do to sidestep the AMT beyond trying to time a big boost to your income, such as an unexpectedly large year-end bonus, or carefully planning how and when you exercise incentive stock options. Alternately, take a good look at deductions such as state tax payments, miscellaneous itemized de-ductions and others, and weigh the cost of claiming them and paying AMT versus skipping them and paying more under regular tax rules. You can also use bunching to try and postpone an AMT hit by pushing some deductions off a year, as well as accelerating income in some cases. To work out the specifics, consult a tax profes-sional with AMT experience.

How long do I need to keep all this paperwork to back up my tax returns?

Obviously you want to hang on to tax-related records that prove your sources of income, document expenses or support the value of property. In general, tax ex-perts advise that you hold all relevant tax records until you are sure you won't be audited, usually about three years, but up to six years if the IRS thinks you have been unrealistic in reporting your income by twenty-five percent or more. To be on the really safe side, most accountants tell their clients to hang on to tax records for six to ten years, just in case.

When it comes to what records to retain, you should hang on to anything you need to do your taxes, including 1040 forms and any accompanying tax worksheets and schedules, and any other supporting documents, such as W-2s, 1099 miscel-laneous income statements, receipts, canceled checks, credit card statements and other paperwork to verify tax-deductible expenses. Unless something backs up a claim on your taxes, you are free to dispose of it.

One exception is any type of asset that you expect to sell that will prompt a taxable event. This includes pension plan statements, retirement account records, investment records and home improvements. You should retain the record until at least three years after you sell the asset.

Investment account statements have data you need as long as you own that particular stock or mutual fund to track splits or reinvested dividends that affect your cost basis when figuring the tax on any gain for years in the future. With retirement accounts, the statements are helpful in determining which contributions were made tax-deferred and which ones were made with already-taxed money.

When it comes to any business ventures you operate, from a small moonlighting operation to something bigger, tax records become even more important. Often the IRS emphasizes reviewing self-employed travel and entertainment expenses, so make sure to hold on to those records. In general, you should retain all business financial account records permanently, along with employment information, tax returns and official documents such as company bylaws and stockholder minutes, for as long as the business is operating.

What if I get hit with a really big tax bill and can't pay it?

Even if you cannot write one single check to pay your tax bill, you still should go ahead and file your return on time so you do not have to face the failure-to-file penalty of five percent per month (up to a maximum of twenty-five percent) of the balance due on your taxes. Instead, you have to pay the monthly failure-to-pay penalty while you have any tax due, which is only 0.5 percent of the amount you owe.

If you have room on your credit cards, you can pay part or your entire bill with plastic. The IRS contracts with independent companies who process credit card payments, from both electronic and paper filers. These firms do charge a processing fee (generally 2.49 percent of your tax bill), but, on the bright side, you get some frequent flyer miles if your credit card offers them.

The IRS can also arrange monthly installments on your tax bill, and even allows you to set your monthly payment and choose the day it will be due. If you have filed and paid taxes on time before and you owe less than $10,000 on your tax bill, the IRS must accept your request, as long as you pay the entire amount due in three years or less. You can apply by attaching the appropriate IRS form to the front of your return.

You have to pay a fee to enroll in the payment plan (billed with your first payment) and both penalties and interest are going to keep getting added to the unpaid portion of your tax bill. Once again, however, filing on time helps. If your return was filed before the deadline and you applied for the payment program before getting an IRS notice, the failure-to-pay penalty is cut in half, from 0.5 percent of the balance due each month to 0.25 percent.

What if my tax bill is just too big to handle?

If the amount you owe is just so large that you cannot foresee ever paying it off, you should approach the IRS about making an Offer in Compromise. This is where you give the Treasury a lump sum payment that is less than what you owe, but which allows the government to receive some of the money right away instead of after years of small payments or attempts at collection.

Whether or not the IRS takes the offer is based on your ability to pay, not just because you want to stall or haggle over your tax bill. There is a $150 application fee with the request, and the IRS reviews your finances to see if your offer is legitimate. The IRS cautions, however, that the Offers in Compromise program is only for desperate cases and that very few taxpayers qualify.

Estate Planning

What is estate planning and does it apply to me?

At its most basic, estate planning consists of figuring out what to do with all your property and possessions before you die. This could consist of nothing more than a simple will, for many people, and maybe a life insurance policy or two.

Estate planning is often assumed to apply only to those with extensive holdings in real estate, a business or farm owners. In reality, most people, even those without large amounts of real property, benefit from some form of estate planning. Estate planning can significantly reduce the government's tax bill for the possessions you leave behind and help ensure that your assets are preserved for others after your death. Equally important, a good, solid estate plan helps avoid family squabbles, allows you to direct that your assets be distributed in the most beneficial manner, and generally ensures that you pass on with your financial affairs in order, so that your family and heirs can avoid the turmoil of sorting it all out in court or on their own.

Like any other type of financial planning, assembling an estate plan is something that is best done well ahead of time rather than at the last minute. This widens your options and allows you to move money, investments and other tangible property out of your estate and into the hands of those you choose in an orderly and tax-free manner using gifting provisions of the tax code, or by establishing trusts and other vehicles for your assets. At the very least, a simple estate plan established after you marry or have children means you have the basics covered and can simply update and modify your plan every few years, rather than leaving everything to chance if your situation changes.

If my finances are simple, does that really qualify as an estate?

There is a lot that can go into your estate if you have acquired even the most basic financial assets during your lifetime. Your estate can be easily defined as 'all your property', which goes far beyond your primary residence and other big ticket items you probably think about as part of your estate.

First, there is the money in your bank and brokerage accounts, including savings, checking, money markets, certificates of deposits, money funds, savings bonds and plain old green backs, including any you may have tucked away in a home safe or bank safety deposit box. Next, count any basic investments, such as mutual funds, stocks and bonds. You also have to include retirement money stashed in your Individual Retirement Account (IRA), 401(k) plan or other specially established retirement accounts, along with any pension plan benefits that may flow to your survivors. There is also life insurance and any annuities or shares in businesses you have purchased or helped establish in which you have an ownership stake.

Beyond financial instruments, you also have your real property, including your home, the contents and any other property. That includes household furniture, clothes, vehicles, jewelry, art, antiques and collectibles.

Add it all up and you see that even in a modest situation you have a number of worldly goods that you need to include in an estate plan if you want them to be preserved and passed on to a surviving spouse, children or other relatives and heirs.

Does my estate include only those items that have a monetary value?

The items discussed above are different types of real property that have some kind of positive worth. An estate also includes all of your debts and outstanding balances at the time of death. These include the outstanding principal on your mortgage and other loans against real estate, your credit card balances, personal debts, unpaid taxes (assuming you do not pass on the day after you file your annual return), outstanding car payments and other items.

The sum of all your debts against your assets results in a net value for your estate, but determining the exact value of some assets can be difficult. If you own part of a small business, the business has to be valued and your portion of it has to be established. That can include the inventory of raw materials sitting in the warehouse and the finished goods waiting to be shipped. Your estate has to establish a cost basis for your investments, too, such as what you paid for 1,000 shares of stock versus whatever gain or loss occurred that could become subject to tax as part of your estate.

In addition to the assets or debts you own now, your estate must also take into account – and value – future payments you expect to receive, such as annual payments on a settlement or loans to friends and relatives that have not been repaid.

Just how involved is planning an estate?

Estate planning has several basic parts that you have to take into account and balance to best serve the needs of you, your family, business partners and other heirs, much like an investment portfolio can have several different components to achieve a number of financial goals.

Typically, a good estate plan starts with your will (and any will substitutes, codicils, revisions or addenda), where you lay out your desires for how your property will be distributed after you are deceased. Your estate plan also may include one or more trusts that allow you to transfer property out of your estate while still maintaining some control and direction over the assets. Taxes are one of the biggest reasons for estate planning, even though only a small percentage of US taxpayers will ever face inheritance taxes, or the so-called 'death tax'. Nonetheless, it is best to make sure that your estate won't owe estate taxes rather than surprising your heirs.

Insurance is another basic tool of estate planning, especially for younger individuals who need to provide for minor children and other dependents, or to cover business partners or even for charitable giving purposes in some instances, such as to a university or other alma mater. Other estate planning necessities can include making allowances for some pre-death situations, such as providing money to pay for health care, nursing or other assistance in later years.

This sounds like an awful lot to handle. How do I get started?

Your first step is to understand everything that the phrase 'your estate' encompasses and to begin planning on what you want to happen to it after you are gone. You need to take into account the different needs and desires that will come up between family members, such as between a husband and wife, especially if there are children from a previous marriage for either spouse. Likewise, you may have to work out differences about estate planning with business partners and others who share your business interests.

Planning an estate also means looking forward and adjusting for changing circumstances. Young couples with children put a heavy emphasis on insurance to provide for their youngsters, as well as choosing guardians and other care issues. On the other hand, an older individual with grown offspring may not include any life insurance in an estate plan, but may have a substantial amount of family property, heirlooms or antiques to be divided among surviving family members, from brothers and sisters to great-grandchildren.

At the same time, tax laws and other rules and regulations applying to your estate may change during your lifetime, requiring an update of your estate plan and a shift in tactics and strategies. The value of your estate may suddenly rise or fall in value, requiring a new approach to handling estate taxes and other issues. Overall, estate planners agree that as your needs and situation evolve with age, so should your estate plan.

What is the difference between real, tangible and intangible property in my estate?

Your estate can be made up of several types of property; Real, intangible and *tangible*. The distinction between them is made because each type requires different considerations under tax laws in estate planning.

Real property refers to real estate. This category includes the home you own, whether your primary residence is a single-family house, condominium, co-op apartment or some other type of dwelling. Real property also includes any second homes you may have, such as vacation property. This also extends to any fragmentary ownership you have in property, such as a timeshare unit or parcel of land. Vacant land, even if it is not for any kind of residence and is held as an investment, is also included, along with any other property or part interest in property you have, such as warehouses, apartment houses and rental and income units.

You should note that the value of any real property includes not just the land and structures, but your share of any improvements on the property, such as wells, roads, sewer lines and other infrastructure.

Tangible personal property is all other personal property that does not exist on paper, such as vehicles, jewelry, the furnishings in your home, art, antiques and other bona fide goods that can be bought and sold.

Intangible personal property is mainly your financial holdings that exist primarily on paper, such as stocks, bonds, mutual funds, bank accounts, retirement accounts and other financial instruments represented by account statements, certificates and other pieces of paper.

How do I determine my property interest?

There are two major types of property interest involved in planning your estate: Legal interest and beneficial interest. Determining your property interest for estate planning purposes is important, because it shapes not only how you arrange the distribution of your three different types of property, but also the way in which you give it to your spouse, children or other heirs. In order to make estate planning decisions, you need to know your interest in each piece of your property, but also what kind of interest you want to assign and who will receive it in your will.

Holding a legal interest in a property means that you have the right to buy, sell or make other important decisions about the property, but that you cannot benefit from the property itself nor any sales, transfers or other transactions. This is the form of interest that a trustee holds for property in administering a trust. He or she is responsible for the property, but does not gain anything from transactions involving the property itself.

If you hold a beneficial interest, this means that you benefit from the property. Gains from sales go to your trust or to you, along with income from the property, interest paid and any other profits (or losses) from activity relating to the assets held in the trust.

For example, if you set up a trust for your grandchild and establish his or her aunt as the trustee, your grandchild holds the beneficial interest, meaning the trust is for his or her good, and the aunt holds the legal interest, meaning she is responsible for all the decisions relating to the trust.

Beneficial trusts also carry other interest definitions. They can be structured as a present beneficial interest or a future beneficial interest, as well as a contingent interest or a vested interest. Present and future refer to the timing – whether the benefit of the trust is derived immediately or is set for some time in the future, such as granting money to a child upon turning twenty-one years old. A vested trust means the benefits are fully granted to the recipient, while a contingent trust means that some specific act or event must take place, such as granting money to a child only after graduation from college.

Why should I worry about estate planning when the 'death tax' is being eliminated anyway?

The value of estates on which the estate tax can be charged is being raised each year and the tax itself, under current law, expires for one year in 2010 before coming back at the $1 million level in 2011. So, yes, the bulk of personal estates, and some estates involving small businesses, are going to be settled without paying any estate tax at all. However, avoiding taxes is never the only reason for making any financial decision, and estate planning is no different. There are many other compelling reasons for you to plan your estate in an organized and timely manner.

The first is to make sure that your family members are cared for, especially if you are their sole support, but for many other reasons as well. In families where there have been several sets of parents, stepparents, multiple grandparents and half siblings, estate planning offers the only way to make sure that your assets are divided according to your wishes, especially when it comes to protecting the interests of your own children from a previous marriage who may be unrelated to your current spouse or other family members. An estate plan also means that your family can go forward without any significant financial interruptions that may force them to alter their lifestyle or living arrangements, and to avoid costly and emotionally draining hearings, legal filings and court procedures.

Secondly, when you are involved in a business, any successful venture may easily trigger the estate tax laws, but more importantly, the business itself can suffer without clear lines of succession within management if financial decisions and assets are tied up during lengthy court proceedings and disagreements with other heirs or business partners.

I am leaving everything to my spouse, so why do I need an estate plan?

While it is true that you can leave everything in your estate tax-free (or at least tax-free at the federal level) to your spouse, you could be leaving him or her with nothing more than a lot more headaches and problems.

Instead of simplifying things for the surviving spouse, your loved one will now be forced to deal with all the estate planning issues that you avoided. It also means that if your spouse has any significant personal holdings, you will have substantially increased the total size of that estate, which may create more tax issues and estate planning headaches than there were before.

Besides, there are more taxes than just federal ones to take into account. Many individual states assess their own estate or inheritance taxes. Staying under the IRS limits helps, but you won't have sidestepped the entire death tax problem without doing at least some basic estate planning.

In addition, there is no guarantee that in leaving your entire estate to a spouse that your spouse will be there to receive it. In that case, your children or other heirs will be faced with handling an estate where no planning was done and which may involve significant tax questions.

What other considerations do I need to take into account when considering my estate planning?

At its most basic, estate planning is how you want to handle any or all of your responsibilities in life after you pass on. Naturally the first consideration is to your immediate family and their financial security, but many other elements come into play.

This material was created to provide accurate and reliable information on the subjects covered. It is not intended to provide specific legal, tax or other professional advice. The services of an appropriate professional should be sought regarding your individual situation.

Your personal situation: Your health, age and financial condition all factor into planning your estate. If your health is questionable or your age is advanced, it is best to start sooner rather than later while you can still make the decisions that suit you best. You also should gauge the complexity of your life, on both personal and financial levels. If you are divorced, separated or living with someone, estate planning allows you to make sure that your stepchildren, domestic partner or ex-spouse is provided for when they might not otherwise be recognized by state laws covering your estate.

Your financial situation: If you have a complex financial situation, you also want to make sure that investment partnerships or future agreements are properly handled and do not damage your partner's interests or those of your heirs. You also need to consider any insurance arrangements (either current policies or new ones you want to buy), particularly risky investments (such as a venture capitalist underwriting a new start-up), and any money that might come to you after your demise, such as insurance or financial settlements or even inheritances from others who have done their estate planning.

Your family situation: Besides your children and their current and future financial status, you may want to provide in some way for grandchildren, including some who may not even be born yet. You also should consider any brothers and sisters, or even parents who may depend on you for some financial support now or are likely to need your help in the future. Others to consider include your extended family, such as cousins, aunts or uncles, that you want to include in your estate planning decisions.

What do I need to do to start planning my estate?

To get started with a basic estate plan, you need to take a look at your personal and financial situation and start to define your own approach to how you want your affairs handled if something dire happened today. You also need to take a longer view, and make sure you are setting up an estate plan that will evolve to handle more complicated, longer-term situations if you should live to a ripe old age.

The first decision, and the one that is most subject to change over the years, is defining your goals for establishing an estate plan. Is your goal to provide for your spouse and current family if you are to suddenly die at this point in your life? To ensure that your children have enough money for college and beyond? To protect business interests, to avoid taxes, to fulfill some charitable goals, or to make sure other family responsibilities are protected? Only you can decide, and those decisions will shape the rest of your estate planning activities.

Your next moves are to assess your current situation, checking any will that you might already have, along with insurance policies, property that you own, and any long-term financial or legal commitments you may have made or have pending. Then you need to consult with the appropriate estate planning professionals, develop a course of action and put it into effect. Part of that course of action includes establishing regular intervals to review and monitor your estate plan so that you can incorporate any changes required as your personal, financial and professional life evolves.

What kinds of professional help will I need with my estate plan?

If your situation is straightforward enough and you have the time and desire, you could handle all the planning for a simple estate yourself, writing a do-it-yourself will, purchasing insurance, assigning a power of attorney and structuring financial accounts so that your heirs can easily access them when required. In most cases, though, you will find the process for anything beyond the most simple estate is easier to navigate with the help of professionals who can present you with several options and help ensure that your heirs won't have to unravel problems or mistakes later.

In general, however, you should consider getting advice and assistance from some kind of financial planner, an insurance agent, an attorney and, if your estate is demanding enough, an accountant as well. In some cases you might not need a team consisting of all these professional advisers, but you should consider how much help they can provide.

Financial planner: Financial planners come in two varieties: Fee-paid and commission-based. Fee-paid planners charge a set hourly rate (anywhere from $100 to $200 per hour) for reviewing your situation and recommending a financial plan.

Many are certified financial planners registered with the Financial Planning Association. Commission-based planners are professionals whose compensation comes not from charging you, but from sales charges on the investments they sell you. Both kinds of planners can be very effective and ethical, although fee-paid planners are considered more objective in recommending investments since they do not have a financial stake in collecting commissions.

Accountant: An accountant or some other type of tax professional is important to estate planning because you need to understand the tax implications of your decisions. An important part of this is gauging what the tax effect on your current plan will be, not just in the immediate future, but ten or twenty years down the road. Knowing how taxes will effect your plan later means you can decide now, how, or at least when, you need to modify your plan to get the most advantageous tax treatment.

Insurance agent: An insurance agent plays a role in just about any plan that involves a spouse, children or any other dependents you want to protect and provide for after you are deceased. This includes not only life insurance, both term and whole life policies, but also disability insurance, liability insurance, 'key man' insurance in a business and many other types of policies and protection.

Lawyer: An experienced estate planning attorney is probably the first person you want to consult in laying out your estate plan. At the most basic, you want an attorney to prepare a will, but you also need a lawyer's help in dealing with questions of guardianship, trusts, legal issues in your business, property deeds and more.

How do I figure out what my estate is worth?

Your first step is to inventory your various personal holdings – real, tangible and intangible property – and what those holdings are worth today. In some cases, you may find yourself with a number of items – home, vacation property, vehicles, art, jewelry and other personal property – for which you need to determine a current value.

To do this you can hire professionals, such as a property appraiser for your real estate, an art appraiser, antiques expert, etc., or you can determine the current market value through other less expensive services. This can include getting a list of 'comparable sales' for homes in your neighborhood, consulting 'blue book' price manuals for cars and other vehicles, and even using sales of similar items at online auction services to see what your possessions are currently worth on the open market. In general, you should value all your real estate, including your home, any second home or vacation properties, vacation time shares and additional real estate investments, such as a partnership in a limited liability company.

Next, you should assess the value of your personal property, including vehicles, boats and other large valuables, but also smaller items such as jewelry, art, antiques, collectibles and other valuables. You may also want to inventory your possessions that are primarily of sentimental value, such as family heirlooms and artifacts, and decide who should receive these items, rather than risking that they will be sold in a garage sale or prompt a series of emotional family squabbles. This can include asking your children or other heirs just what they might be interested in receiving in a kind of family wish list.

Finally, you need to take stock of your intangible property, including bank accounts, retirement accounts, stocks bonds, and other investments and holdings. Valuing your stocks and mutual funds is relatively simple, since these prices are set on a daily basis. For bonds or other interest bearing investments you can check the investment's interest payment schedule, or ask your brokerage firm to compute a current value. For stock options and other complicated instruments, your financial planner can figure a current worth.

What debts should I include in valuing my estate?

The total value of your estate is going to include not only your assets, but also your debts, since your estate will have to settle those accounts. This includes paying off the balance of any mortgage or other real estate loans, including home equity loans and lines of credit, installment payments on time-shares, assessments on condominiums and co-ops.

You also need to tally up any outstanding loans on cars, student loans, credit card balances, personal loans, margin loans with a stockbroker, and any other revolving or installment payments you owe or have coming due. In many cases, auto loans or credit cards already carry credit life insurance to pay off the balance of your account, which means the debt won't have to be paid by your estate, so do not include any such accounts in your overall debt figure.

What else should I consider in figuring my estate's total value?

Once you know your total assets and total debts, you know the current net worth of your estate. Do not forget to include any future debts or income in arriving at your estate's net worth. This can include loans that are not scheduled to be repaid until sometime in the future, pledges to schools and charities, annuity payments, legal settlements and any other commitments you will owe or that others will owe you in the coming years.

What do I need to consider in drafting my will?

Probably the first thing that estate planning professionals emphasize is that a will that is perfect for you and your estate today may be inadequate several years from now. This means that you should consider your first or current will a good starting point that needs to be updated, changed and amended as you go through significant changes in your lifetime.

Basically, a will clarifies your wishes and instructions so that your family, heirs, business partners, charitable causes and the government all understand your intentions and sentiments, and helps ensure that everyone receives what you consider a fair share of the assets you spent a lifetime building.

Despite the common misconception that wills are the place to express emotion, either praising or scolding family members and friends for their actions during your life, estate advisors stress that a will should be a straightforward legal document that clarifies your wishes rather than muddying the legal waters with emotional issues that may also create legal problems and invite someone to contest your will later.

What happens if I die without a will?

If you die without a will you are said to die intestate, which means that a probate court decides how your estate will be handled. This can mean that your estate's value will be reduced by probate and attorney's fees, and that the ultimate distribution of your assets could be delayed by months and even years as a court appointed administrator sorts out your estate.

In addition, dying without a will means that many of the people or institutions you might want to include will be simply cut out. Instead, the laws of your state will determine just who is and who is not an official heir to your estate. This means a domestic partner, close friend or favored charity will have no standing and no claim to any part of your assets.

Typically, the estate goes to any surviving spouse, followed by lineal descendants, such as children, grandchildren and great-grandchildren. After that, the property passes to any surviving parents, then brothers and sisters and their descendants, followed lastly by any other relatives, such as cousins, aunts and uncles.

Besides the cost of probate and the possibility of paying higher taxes, dying in a state of intestacy means that if you do not have legal heirs to receive your estate, all your property becomes escheat in legal parlance, which means it all goes to the state.

So as long as I have a will, is everything okay?

Not necessarily. When you die, your estate fits into one of three categories: Testacy, when your will covers your entire estate; intestacy, as mentioned above, when the state takes over; and partial intestacy, when only some portion of your estate is covered by your will.

When you die in partial intestacy, the portion of your estate not covered by your will passes to your legal heirs under the rules of probate court or, if someone objects and the matter is large enough, they could contest the will, have it declared invalid and render you intestate, with your entire estate now passing into probate court.

One common tool to avoid partial intestacy is the residuary clause of a will, which is where you assign any and all property not specifically mentioned in your will. It can go to one person or be divided among a group of people, but it acts as a kind of safety net for anything that you may have overlooked in writing your will or that you acquired after your latest will was updated.

Are there different types of wills?

There are several different types of wills, depending on what options best fit your estate. In most cases, a simple will is all that you may need. Typically, a simple will identifies you for legal purposes, sets out and identifies your beneficiaries, including people and institutions, and identifies your estate executor, who will oversee the directions in your will. A simple will also directs who is responsible for your minor children or any other dependents and describes how you want your assets distributed.

Another type of will is a joint will, which covers two people, usually a wife and husband. Joint wills are not required for married couples, usually a husband and wife are better served with individual simple wills. One of the problems with a joint will is that it stands as an irrevocable contract after the death of either party, leaving the survivor stuck with a will that he or she is legally unable to change. Still, in certain unique situations, a joint will may be recommended by an attorney.

A mutual will can be used by siblings and others who want to coordinate estate planning for specific purposes. A typical mutual will distributes its assets based on the death of any one party first and then distributes the assets of the survivor after his or her death, regardless of who dies first or second.

There are two other types of wills that are not valid in many states or under many conditions. One is a holographic will, which means a will that is handwritten and signed without an attorney. A nuncupative will is one that is spoken to some witness. Many states limit this to a death-bed set of instructions and place restrictions on what kind of property or amount of assets can be assigned in this kind of verbal will.

Who should get copies of my will?

Whether you want to hand out copies of your will is up to you. The most important consideration is where to keep your signed original will. While many people use a bank safe deposit box, there is a large chance that the box, and therefore your will, may be sealed or have access restricted at your death; the rules vary from state to state. Other recommendations are that your lawyer should keep the original, or that you keep it in a fireproof safe in your home. Whatever choice you make, the signed original of your will should not be left in a desk drawer, file cabinet or other spot where it could become lost or damaged.

An unsigned copy of your will is what you should keep for reference if you run into questions when dealing with your taxes, business affairs or other items addressed in your will. A copy of the will should also go to your executor, also called your personal representative, and to certain family members, such as children and siblings.

You also should consider giving unsigned copies of the will to the people who will be most affected by your estate decisions, such as business partners or those who may be receiving large amounts of property or other assets. This allows them to incorporate your decisions into their own estate planning process and to make appropriate plans.

What do I do if I want to change my will?

You may end up revising your will several times during your life as your personal and financial situation changes, and it is good to review your will on a regular basis. When you need to make a change, you have two options: Drafting an entirely new will that renders your old one void or creating a new document that changes, amends or deletes portions of your original will while leaving the majority of the original document intact.

In most cases, writing your changes into an entirely new will is the easiest and most straightforward approach so everything current is contained in one complete document.

You may alter your will with the addition of a codicil, a document that references specific portions of the will. Codicils should be prepared by your attorney, since they must specifically cite the appropriate portions of the will that you want to have amended.

The benefits of using a codicil come into play if you have a very long and complicated will and want to make only a few simple revisions and updates without reproducing the entire document. A codicil also should be considered if you are making a change that might be contested later, or at a time when your state of mind or health might prompt a challenge to the will. If the codicil is thrown out, the rest of your will remains in force.

What kinds of events in my life require updating my will?

Any kind of significant change in the size of your estate or a change in your personal relationships generally needs to be accommodated in your will. The first and most common reason is your marital status; if it changes, your will should, too. That includes getting married, getting divorced or remarried, as well as if your spouse dies. You need to update your will if any other heir or dependents die, especially if any of these individuals were to receive specific pieces of property or other assets.

If the size or makeup of your estate changes in any notable way, it also needs to be included in your will. This can include a big increase (or decrease) in the value of stocks or other holdings, or a shift in the balance of your holdings. If, for example you wanted to leave one child your beach house and the other your mountain cabin, and the beach house was wiped out by a hurricane, you would want to rework the division of property.

Other major reasons for updating a will include any change in your life that prompts you to reconsider how you want to distribute your assets, such as deciding to support a charity or foundation, or a change in a personal relationship that causes you to want to include or exclude someone from your will, or to increase or decrease what they receive. Estate planning advisors caution, however, that you should take some time and consideration before you 'write out' someone from your will for emotional reasons that might prompt a challenge to your will later.

Can I do anything I want in my will or are there rules?

While it may seem that since it is your estate you ought to be able to distribute it any old way you please in your will, that is not always the case. Certain state laws aim to protect a spouse and minor children from losing their home or being left too little in a will. Other laws in some states cover several issues that you should make sure are addressed in your will, lest the state step in and take over. Some of these issues are:

Abatement: Abatement laws direct what happens if you specify dollar amounts in your estate, but there is not enough money to cover your wishes. This can include a sudden drop in the value of some property, or a situation where you may have spent money or otherwise distributed property mentioned in the will before you updated it. One way around the problem is to divide your property in percentages, rather than in dollar amounts.

Ademption: This is where some specifically mentioned piece of property in your will is gone from your estate, either missing or distributed without your having updated your will. In order to avoid ademption rules, consider assigning backup property in some cases, such as an amount of cash if the specific piece of property is unavailable.

Divorce: If you fail to update your will after a divorce, some states have laws that prevent an ex-spouse from claiming part of an estate that was left to them as a spouse. If you want the property to go to your ex-spouse, make sure it is spelled out in the will to avoid running afoul of this kind of law. Otherwise, make sure to update your will to reflect the change in marital status.

Simultaneous death: These unfortunately grim laws cover what happens to property left to a spouse who dies along with you, or to a spouse or other beneficiary who dies soon after you. The problem is that you do not want your estate passing directly into the estate of someone else who has recently died, where it will complicate matters and possibly be subject to another round of estate taxes and the probate process. This problem is avoided by including a survivor clause in your will, specifying that any beneficiary must remain living for some amount of time after your death to receive your assets, or else those assets pass to someone else.

Community property: These laws in several states specify that anything acquired during marriage is a marital asset jointly shared between you and your spouse. Your will needs to determine what is and is not community property when distributing your assets, and should make sure that it does not mix individual and community property in a way that might void the individual property rights.

Spousal elective shares: In non-community property states, this law gives your spouse the right to choose between what you leave in your will or to claim a specific percentage of your estate. This is to protect a husband or wife from being 'stiffed' in the will of an angry or vindictive spouse. Obviously, receiving a larger share than what is specified in your will is going to create problems with all the other distributions, so make sure this is addressed when dividing property. These laws also can cover certain property even if it is not part of your official estate.

Homestead allowance: Some states have laws covering what happens to your primary residence if you have a spouse or minor children so that they do not lose their home. Again, this needs to be taken in consideration when valuing your estate and distributing property.

Homestead exemption: These laws protect your estate from being forced to sell a primary residence in order to satisfy creditors of your estate, again with the intention of protecting the home of a surviving spouse and minor children. With some state homestead exemptions, certain types of personal property, such as jewelry or cars, may also be exempt. Estate experts advise, however, that you should not depend on such laws as a way to avoid paying creditors after death.

Family allowance: These laws allow your spouse and children to tap your estate for living expenses while your estate is being settled. The amount varies with the size of your estate and the laws of your specific state. Otherwise, you may want to make other arrangements to cover living expenses of your family while your estate is being reviewed.

Omitted heirs: These laws cover a spouse or child who was not present in your life when the will was written. If you failed to update your will but got married or had a child, these laws specify what amount of your estate must go to the family members you overlooked.

What happens with my will and estate when I die?

When it comes to your will, all roads lead to the probate process. If you die intestate or with an otherwise invalid will, then your estate proceeds through probate court and is assigned to an administrator, who makes all decisions about applying the inheritance and estate laws of your state. This can be expensive, time-consuming and result in a distribution of your property that you might not have wanted and without the flexibility that proper estate planning can provide.

However, if your will is valid, the function of the probate court is to ensure that all the required legal steps are taken to execute the will. This starts with the court swearing in your executor, or personal representative, and the executor petitioning the court for the probate of your will, where the court accepts your will as valid. The executor then notifies your heirs, creditors and the public through a published death notice that you have passed away, inventories your property, pays your taxes and debts, and distributes your estate to your beneficiaries.

If your will does not name an executor, or your executor has died or cannot fulfill the job, the court appoints a new executor. The court also appoints the executor if you die without a valid will. In addition to your normal taxes and debts due at the time of your death, your estate also pays administration costs, such as legal advertising bills, property appraisal fees and other expenses, as well as reasonable fees and compensation to your executor (usually about two to five percent of the estate) and to your attorneys (usually the same amount). You should note that these costs come off the top of your estate; that is, they are paid first, followed by any family allowance while your estate is being settled, then your funeral expenses, debts and taxes and any remaining claims. Depending on the size and complexity of the estate, the probate process takes anywhere from six months to twenty-four months.

What if I have out-of-state property?

Depending on what kind of property it is, your estate could end up with two probate processes at once. While tangible and intangible property is always probated in the state where you live, any real property you hold out-of-state must be probated where the property is physically located. For example, if you live in California but maintain a ski lodge in Colorado, most of your probate will take place in California, but the ski lodge must be probated in Colorado under that state's laws.

The second probate process is called an ancillary probate and can be costly, since it can involve travel by your executor and can require your estate to hire an attorney to handle proceedings in the ancillary probate state.

In many states, however, the probate courts recognize the legal authority of your executor to handle your estate and allow your executor to represent your estate in the ancillary state without requiring a second complete probate process.

You should note that while state laws covering probate and inheritance issues can vary widely, many states now subscribe to the Uniform Probate Codes, which can allow for greater flexibility in executing your will and distributing your estate. The biggest factor in states that follow the uniform code is the amount of court supervision required, which can range from complete supervision to partial or no supervision at all. If you live in a uniform code state, take these options into consideration when structuring your estate and selecting an executor.

Does everything mentioned in my will or included in my estate get reviewed during probate?

Not all property in your estate falls under the probate court's purview. In fact, your estate will probably contain a great deal of nonprobate prop-erty and the court will have jurisdiction only over your probate estate.

Probate property generally includes anything that you own by yourself, while nonprobate assets are any items that you own jointly with other people who will receive those assets automatically after your death. Because such assets pass automatically to a specific individual, there is no need for probate to determine where they should go. Nonprobate items include any asset with a named beneficiary, such as insurance policies or retirement accounts.

Other nonprobate property includes living trusts and joint tenancy arrange-ments with right of survivorship. These arrangements are called will substitutes, and they offer a structured way to reduce your estate size and simplify the probate process for your heirs and beneficiaries, as well as including some tax advantages.

Other assets where you may have assigned a beneficiary can include savings bonds, bank and investment accounts, qualified retirement plans and Individual Retirement Accounts (IRAs), and other types of retirement accounts. Be sure to consider all your nonprobate assets when inventorying your estate and writing your will, since these will not have to be distributed through the estate process.

What else do I need to know about the probate process?

In general, probate is designed to ensure that there is a fair and consistent set of rules and procedures in place to protect your wishes and the rights of your heirs and beneficiaries. Fees and expenses must be fair and reasonable, interested parties must be properly notified about your death and the proceedings of your estate, and creditors must prove their claims and deal with your estate rather than harassing family members for payment.

In certain cases, if your estate is in a lower tax bracket than the people re-ceiving your property, probate can help reduce any taxes on your estate. Finally, all costs of probate and administering your estate are tax deductible, further less-ening any tax impact from the estate tax.

On the other hand, there are several significant drawbacks to the probate process. First and foremost is the amount of time involved in following the standardized procedures, notifying the various parties, arranging appraisals, and sometimes going through numerous complicated hearings to settle matters. There is also the cost, which, although tax deductible, can still reduce your estate by a significant amount, depending on the complexity and size of your assets.

Another complaint about the probate process is the lack of privacy. Since it is a state court, all the proceedings and documents become part of the public record, including your estate inventory and inheritance tax returns. Some states do offer some privacy guarantees in probate.

There are programs available in certain states for smaller estates that aim to streamline the probate process. These probate alternatives are called probate affidavits, summary probate or small estate affidavits, among other titles. If your estate qualifies, they are worth checking out to see if they will reduce the time, cost or complexity of handling your estate.

How much work does my executor have to handle?

The executor, or personal representative, for your estate takes care of a great deal of paperwork. It can be a time-consuming and tedious job, especially with a large or complicated estate.

The executor's responsibilities include notifying creditors and others that you have died, collecting and creating a complete inventory of your estate property, managing any estate property, including real estate and businesses, handling and paying creditors, filing tax returns and paying taxes, and distributing your property.

The executor has to contact every financial institution where you have accounts, arrange for a change of address to receive all statements and other communications, collect payments that are due to you, deal with Social Security, hire appraisers to value property if needed, open and maintain a separate account to collect all your cash and pay for administering the estate, etc.

In addition to handling creditors' claims and distributing assets, your executor essentially takes over your financial life during the time your estate is in probate. If the insurance bill is due on the home you are leaving to a spouse, the executor has to pay the bill. If you own other properties, the executor has to make sure they continue to operate, collecting rents, arranging for repairs, etc. If you have a business interest, your executor may end up managing those operations for a time as well.

How do I choose an executor?

Typically the executor is a family member, friend or business associate, but the executor also can be a professional, such as an attorney or trust officer from your bank or some other corporate representative.

Besides being honest, trustworthy and well-organized, an executor should be fair, dependable and located near the probate court and your property in order to operate efficiently. Before designating an executor in your will, you should contact anyone you are considering and make sure they are up to committing the time and effort to directing your estate.

In general, probate attorneys advise against having more than one executor for your estate, especially if they are family members who may have existing disputes or disagreements between themselves or with others in the family. Such co-executor arrangements usually just complicate an already difficult and time-consuming chore.

If your estate includes business operations, you should be sure to consider an executor who will have an understanding and familiarity with the business, its market and operations since he or she will have to oversee the business while your estate is in probate. Otherwise, you may want to set up your estate to provide for other professional business management to keep the operation going.

How can I arrange for my estate to avoid as much of probate as possible?

Avoiding probate offers a way to save time and money in the distribution of your estate, as well as in planning your estate. You can do this through a few arrangements known as will substitutes, which set up distribution of your property outside of your will, with the assets being transferred directly on your death. Instead of being open to interpretation or review by a probate court, will substitutes are established under other laws that take precedence over state inheritance laws.

Joint tenancy: This is where you and others share an undivided ownership of property with both of you having the same rights to its use. The property is divided equally between any number of owners. Joint tenancy also includes the right of survivorship, which simply means that upon the death of any one of the joint tenants, that person's share of the property is divided equally among the surviving owners. For instance, two unmarried people may use a joint tenancy with right of survivorship to protect each other's ability to remain in a home after the death of the other partner.

Joint tenancy is simple to set up and simple to dissolve when necessary. In some cases it can be prepared without an attorney, although that is not recommended. It offers a clear title transfer to the other joint tenants and additional privacy, too, since it is not part of your will and probated estate, although joint property may have to be listed on state inheritance or estate tax returns. In addition, a joint tenancy can protect the property from claims by creditors, since it is not part of your estate, although property moved into a joint tenancy to avoid creditors may still be subject to claims.

The disadvantages of joint tenancy arrangements are mainly those that come with the automatic transfer of ownership. You cannot designate that the property go to someone else, you cannot time the transfer, and once the joint tenancy is down to one surviving owner, that individual has the right to do whatever he or she wishes with the property. A joint tenancy arrangement also may be subject to claims from creditors of your co-owners, which could result in a forced sale.

Finally, a joint tenancy comes with many potential tax disadvantages, while the tax advantages in reducing the size of your estate will not apply to it if the transfer of the tenancy – or any other nonprobate property – results in an inheritance or estate tax. Be sure to explore the potential effects of joint tenancy on your taxes.

Living trusts: Living trusts are more complicated than joint tenancy arrangements, but offer more alternatives and control. You establish the trust during your lifetime (hence the name 'living trust') and you can make it revocable up until the time of your death or some other event specified in your trust documents, such as mental incapacity.

A trust comes with a complete cast of characters. The person establishing the trust is the trustor, or settlor, who also designates a trustee to manage the trust for the income beneficiaries who receive money or some rights to the trust property. Minor beneficiaries must have guardians or custodians appointed in the trust. Trusts also include a remainderman, who receives whatever is left over after the beneficiaries have received their portions of the trust. Since the original trustor may also serve as the trustee, a successor trustee also must be named to take over responsibility after the death of the trustee.

One of the main advantages of living trusts is that you can use them to avoid ancillary probates in other states by putting any out-of-state real estate holding into a trust. A living trust also offers more control and planning since it can direct where property or trust rights go after the death of beneficiaries, an option not available with co-owners of a joint tenancy. A trust also allows you to name alternate beneficiaries and offers more probate protection than joint tenancy or other types of will substitutes.

A living trust also offers a chance to preview how your trust will work before you die. By naming a trustee other than yourself, you can see how the trustee manages the trust and handles distributions to the beneficiaries, as well as how your beneficiaries handle their gains under the trust. If you spot problems, you can alter or revoke the trust. You also can set up a living trust to provide for your needs should you become incapacitated, rather than relying on a court appointed guardian or conservator.

The disadvantages of living trusts are the complexity of establishing them through an attorney and funding them by transferring assets into the trust, including investments, vehicles, real estate and other property. Anything you overlook is subject to probate. Trusts also need to be monitored and can face a longer period of being subject to claims from creditors after you die. Establishing a trust can also be costly, with fees ranging up to a few thousand dollars for just one trust.

What are the other types of will substitutes?

There are several other will substitutes, some obvious and well-known and others more obscure. Not all of these will substitutes are available in every state so, as usual, check your local laws before depending on any of them.

Tenancy-by-the-entirety: Available in many states, but not in most community property states, this allows property to pass to a co-owner spouse as a right of survivorship. Only husbands and wives can exercise this right, and on the death of one the surviving spouse automatically becomes the sole owner. Neither spouse can transfer his or her property interest without the consent and notification of the other. In the event of divorce, the tenancy shifts to another form.

Joint tenancy bank accounts: This is a special type of joint tenancy for bank accounts, and can be useful in making sure that family members or others have access to cash while the rest of your estate is undergoing probate. The risks here are that one party can withdraw money without the consent of the other, and that money placed in a joint tenancy account can be subject to gift taxes.

Savings bonds: The US Treasury gives you two options with savings bonds. Under the alternative payee option, either of two co-owners can cash the bond. You can also designate a beneficiary payee when you buy bonds, giving the bond's proceeds to your named beneficiary after your death.

Payable on death accounts: Called PODs for short, you simply designate a named beneficiary for one or more accounts at your financial institutions. After your death, the beneficiary needs to provide a copy of your death certificate and proof of their identity. Since the beneficiary has no rights to the account before your death, the assets are protected and you can retain control by spending the money, canceling the POD feature or selecting a new beneficiary at any time.

Retirement accounts: Individual retirement accounts (IRAs), 401(k)s, Roth IRAs, 403(b) plans and other retirement investments all allow you to bypass probate and name a beneficiary. The tax effects and procedures differ from account to account.

Deeds: Consult with your attorney for options on writing deeds to real property in such a way that the property transfers under a will substitute after your death. The deed must be a valid legal deed and not just a property transfer instrument to be legal and valid.

What other types of trusts can I consider?

There are many different types of trusts and many different ways you can use them in protecting, controlling and distributing the assets in your estate. In general, the act of putting property into a trust converts the property from being included in your overall estate by giving it new legal standing. This can help your estate avoid taxes in many cases, speed up the transfer of property after your death, insulate the property from some creditors' claims, and increase your control over how the beneficiaries use their inheritances.

No matter what kind of trust you establish and how it is set up, most trusts share some common attributes. They start with the trustor, or person setting up the trust, and that person's objectives and goals for creating the trust in the first place. The trust documents are usually created with the help of an attorney and the property to be placed in the trust needs to be established. The trust also must designate who the beneficiaries will be, whether an individual or an institution, along with a trustee to manage the trust and an outline of rules and limitations governing the trustee's administration of the trust.

Despite the wide variety of trusts and their applications, trusts will fall into one of three categories: Testamentary, living or pour-over.

Living trust: As discussed before, a living trust is one that you establish and fund while you are alive, with the option that you can act as the trustee. Living trusts can offer some tax advantages, keep property out of the probate process and offer a strategy for asset management.

Testamentary trust: This kind of trust is established by your will, where you also appoint the trustee, and is funded with assets from your estate. The advantages are tax avoidance and reduction, and the opportunity to appoint a trustee to manage the trust assets.

Pour-over trust: This type of trust is created while you are alive but is funded after you die, usually with insurance proceeds, pension payouts or any residual property remaining in your estate. The primary goal is tax reduction or avoidance.

What are some general rules when considering trusts?

Even if you are not an expert in all the legal ramifications of establishing and managing trusts, you still want to be knowledgeable and informed when working with your attorney and other advisors in creating any kind of trust.

- In general, you want to look at any pre-packaged trusts very carefully. These trusts are offered by many financial services and investment firms and while they may be useful, these one-size-fits-all approaches may not adequately address the specific needs of your estate or may be more expensive than working individually with an attorney,

- Trust agreements should be in writing, even though there are circumstances where an oral, or nuncupative trust, may be valid, just as with an oral will. In general, planning any estate decision and writing it down is better than word-of-mouth communications. Additionally, real estate and some other forms of trusts are required to be in writing,

- Your trust must be an active trust; that is, it has to define the duties and responsibilities of the trustee and set the obligations of managing the assets, such as paying taxes, managing investments, making payments and other activities. Trusts that fail to set out trustee responsibilities may be declared passive trusts and declared invalid. In that case, the property is distributed directly to the beneficiaries, negating any tax or asset management benefits you had in mind,

- The trust documents must state that you are creating the trust and how you are funding it with specific property now or in the future,

- The trust documents must clearly identify everyone involved, especially beneficiaries, whether individuals or institutions,

- Make sure that whomever you select as your trustee has the experience and ability to handle all the obligations of the trust and is familiar with whatever property or assets he or she is responsible for handling, in addition to considering that person's overall character, judgment and trustworthiness.

What are some specific ways I can use trusts?

We have already outlined the basic advantages of trusts in avoiding probate and reducing or avoiding estate taxes, but trusts are about more than just avoiding these problems. The main advantage of a trust is that you can specify what the property is for, how it is to be used, when and under what conditions it can be distributed, how the trust assets can be managed, who will benefit and who will run things after you are gone. You can even direct what happens with your property after the initial beneficiaries die. Some common uses for trusts include:

Protecting your property: Instead of leaving a lump sum of money or large valuable pieces of property to a son, daughter or other person, you can structure a trust to distribute only interest payments, to make small, incremental payments during a period of time, or to delay a payout until a certain age or other condition has been met, such as graduation, marriage or birth of a child. A trust also preserves the assets until payments are due to be made.

Providing educational money: Another very typical use of trust money is to pay for the college education of children, grandchildren or anyone else, from your favorite nephew to your employees' children. Trusts can be established to restrict the money for certain types of educational purposes or institutions, limit what educational expenses are covered or even withhold payment if the beneficiaries fail to matriculate.

Charitable trusts: These trusts can be structured in a variety of ways to provide for your favorite charities and institutions, with payments spread over time, tied to particular events or designated for specific purposes. Charitable trusts can pay a certain amount of money to the charity with any remainder going back to your estate or some other beneficiary, or they can pay you during your lifetime with any remaining balance going to the charity after your death.

What are the differences between living trusts and those that are created after death?

A living trust, or intervivos trust in legal parlance, is by nature limited to assets you possess and can afford to place in a trust while you are alive. Living trusts also allow you to provide for yourself, or to immediately move assets into the trust and put the property to work for your beneficiaries. Creating a living trust means you can prioritize transferring the necessary assets into the trust and monitor the results during your lifetime.

You will also have a better picture of the value of whatever assets you assign to the trust while you are alive, because after you die the value of the assets may change significantly or even be wiped out. Finally, a living trust is the only way to guarantee that the trust goes into effect while avoiding the potential complications of the probate process, although a living trust can be challenged in probate court in some circumstances.

In turn, a trust created after your death, or a testamentary trust in legal terms, is established in your will, and so becomes subject to the probate process where any mistakes or challenges to the trust will complicate the process. However, a testamentary trust can be established with proceeds received after death, such as insurance payments or residual property left in your estate. You also can establish this kind of trust for time-specific purposes, such as setting aside money for your minor children, and then eliminate the trust later when they are grown, without ever having to fund it. On the other hand, the property funding the trust may have changed in value by the time of your death or be distributed in some other way during probate proceedings.

If I create a living trust, should I make it revocable or irrevocable?

With a revocable trust, you can reclaim property you have put into that trust or even eliminate the trust altogether at just about any point up to your death. With an irrevocable trust, once you transfer the property it becomes a permanent asset of the trust and you cannot get it back.

The biggest difference between the two types of living trusts is their treatment under estate tax rules. Only an irrevocable trust allows you to exclude the property from your estate, since you no longer exercise any control over those assets. While that allows you to lower the value of your holdings to avoid estate or inheritance taxes, assets put into an irrevocable trust are likely to be subject to gift tax rules, so consult with a tax specialist or accountant when deciding on how to structure trusts. In addition to considering IRS rules on estate and gift taxes, you also have to navigate the particular laws of your state that govern estates and inheritances.

There are situations where revocable trusts can convert to irrevocable status. The most obvious situation is at your death, but the terms of your trust also may provide for the trust to become irrevocable in case you become incapacitated or incompetent.

What is a marital deduction trust?

As the name implies, a marital deduction trust is available only to married couples and has some great advantages. Property goes into the trust with your spouse as the beneficiary with the right to use any property in the trust after your death.

The biggest advantage here is that no matter how valuable the property you place in the trust, the surviving spouse will not have to pay any federal estate tax. Your spouse can designate a beneficiary for any property remaining in the trust at the time of his or her death. In this way, you both can delay the decision to choose a secondary beneficiary as long as possible, which may or may not be a benefit to you.

If, however, you do not want your spouse choosing a beneficiary for the remaining property, you can choose a similar type of trust, called Qualified Terminable Interest Property trust, or QTIP trust for short. This kind of trust operates much like a marital deduction trust except that you can designate the recipient of the trust's remaining property when your spouse dies.

With a QTIP trust, you are essentially preserving the property and assets in the trust for the use of your surviving spouse during his or her lifetime, but still retaining control over where the remaining property goes after you both die. However, if that kind of decision is not clear, you can trust your surviving spouse to make that determination later by using a marital deduction trust.

What is a bypass trust?

This is another type of trust that married couples may want to consider since it offers another way for them to sidestep estate taxes. Instead of property in the trust going directly to the surviving spouse, it bypasses him or her and goes to another individual, such as one of your children. While the property is held in trust for your child or other beneficiary, your spouse retains the right to benefit from the estate assets. This is different from simply making a direct gift of property to a child or someone else and relying on them to provide for your spouse, and avoids triggering any gift tax consequences.

Because the property is never transferred to the ownership of your spouse, he or she will not have to include it in their own taxable estate. The trust documents need to specifically spell out just how the property is to be managed and what kinds of payments, benefits or other kinds of distributions go to your spouse.

The downside to using a bypass trust is that there are many types of IRS restrictions and rules applying to estate taxes in bypass trusts. You and your estate planners have to figure in the value of your estate, exemption amounts, your spouse's potential estate and many other factors in choosing and structuring a bypass trust, as well as in utilizing a QTIP or marital deduction trust.

What about setting up charitable trusts?

While you can use gifts and the charitable deduction to assign property to a charity during your lifetime, a trust offers the ability to structure the disbursement of property over time or to place conditions and restrictions on your donations. There are two types of charitable trusts: The charitable lead trust and the charitable remainder trust.

A charitable lead trust is an irrevocable trust you can use to make a series of payments to a charitable institution. After a number of years, property remaining in the trust either reverts to you or transfers to some other specified individual.

Under a charitable remainder trust, you select a beneficiary to receive a series of payments over time, whether a predetermined number of years or another period, such as their lifetime. After the beneficiary dies, whatever remains passes to the designated charity.

In using the charitable trusts, remember that if the beneficiary is your spouse, you are adding to his or her estate; take that into account when planning. If the beneficiary is someone other than your spouse, any payments they receive are considered gifts by the IRS, and they are subject to gift taxes on any amount over the annual $13,000 gift limit.

Another type of charitable giving trust is a pooled interest trust, often promoted by colleges, universities and large cultural institutions as part of a 'planned giving' strategy for fund raising. Typically such arrangements allow you to make a donation and receive some interest back on that amount until you reach a certain age or for some other fixed period of time. What happens is that your money is combined with contributions from other alumni or interested benefactors. While none of you have to go to the trouble or expense of establishing a separate trust for the charity, pooled trusts also limit your options and are created by the institution itself.

How do grantor-retained trusts work?

Grantor-retained trusts allow you to receive some form of payment for use of property in the trust until your death, when the assets of the trust go to named beneficiaries, usually a relative. These trusts are irrevocable and similar in structure to a charitable remainder trust, but without giving anything to charity. There are several types of these trusts, with the difference being how the amount of property is allocated to you.

In a grantor-retained annuity trust, called a GRAT, the trust pays you a fixed amount of money at regular intervals. A grantor-retained unit trust, or GRUT, pays you a specific fixed percentage rather than a set dollar amount. There is also a grantor-retained income trust, or GRIT, which allows you to put property in the trust but still continue to receive income from it or retain the right to use the property. Another form of a GRIT is something called a qualified personal residence trust, which allows you to put your home into a trust and continue living there. In this kind of trust, income is partly defined as your right to continue using the home.

The tax laws and implications of any one of these grantor-retained trusts can be quite complicated, involving questions of gift and estate taxes, but some tax advantages may also occur depending on how the value of the property in the trust changes over time. As with most complicated trust questions, these decisions should involve not only an attorney to make sure the trust is properly structured, but an accountant who can project the tax impact on the estates of both you and your beneficiaries.

Can I put my life insurance proceeds into a trust?

Tax laws require that the death benefits paid out by your life insurance be counted as part of your estate, which can raise the value of your estate to the point where it triggers the estate tax or, in the case of larger estates, simply increase the amount of estate taxes that have to be paid.

You can get around this issue by creating an irrevocable life insurance trust (ILIT). By transferring your insurance policies into the trust, you change ownership and shift the death benefits outside of your estate.

There are some limitations on these kinds of trusts. First, since they must be irrevocable to avoid being hit with estate taxes, you won't be able to change the policy itself in any way after it goes into the trust. You also cannot act as the trustee of a trust that involves your own life insurance policy. Finally, you need to stay alive for at least several years after creating the trust. According to the IRS, if you die within three years of establishing an irrevocable life insurance trust, the trust is declared invalid and the death benefits are treated as part of your estate.

In establishing this kind of trust, you should ask your estate planner whether it should be established as a Crummey trust. This kind of trust allows you to add up to the annual gift exclusion in cash or other assets to an irrevocable trust, making it possible for you to pay any insurance premiums due on policies placed in the trust.

What kind of tax issues do I have to deal with in setting up my estate?

Besides the federal estate tax, or death tax, as it is called, you need to look at several other tax issues when arranging and structuring your estate. You need to take the gift tax into account when establishing trusts or distributing property before you die, as well as watching out for something called the generation skipping transfer tax, any inheritance taxes in your home state, and something called the Estate Recovery Act.

You have mentioned the estate tax several times, but just what is it exactly and how does it work?

If your estate is large enough – over $2.0 million as of 2008 – the federal government can charge an estate tax of up to forty-six percent on your estate. Typically the tax applies to only one to two percent of all estates in the country; still, in the 2003 tax year, the estate tax raised $22 billion in tax revenue for the US Treasury.

Estate taxes have been implemented three times before the turn of the twentieth century, largely to help finance wars. The taxes were usually quickly abolished after hostilities ended. In 1916 the estate tax was again implemented to help finance World War I and the tax has remained in effect since then.

Motivations behind the estate tax are that the tax reduces the inequity between the rich and poor in the country and that it helps avoid the creation of a 'spoiled' inheritor class that hasn't earned its wealth. Other arguments for the estate tax say that it encourages large amounts of charitable giving by individuals and estates who give away assets to avoid the tax, and that it is a necessary way of raising revenue for the government. Critics of the tax argue that it is ineffective on all those grounds, while penalizing citizens for their success in work, savings and investment. They also claim that the tax prompts many small and family-owned businesses to be dissolved or sold and that it reduces stock in the country's capital economy.

The results of those arguments in Washington have resulted in some adjustments to the estate tax law that might help your estate, but which require significant attention – and maybe a little luck – on your part. Between now and 2009 the estate tax limit is being raised as high as $3.5 million and the tax rate is being lowered down to as little as forty-five percent until the tax is completely phased out in 2010. The tax comes back, however, in 2011 when it is supposed to impose a tax rate of fifty-five percent on any estate worth $1 million or more.

Whether or not US lawmakers will adjust the rates, make them permanent, repeal the estate tax or make more modifications is unknown. Unless you can arrange to die sometime during 2010, the estate tax is something you have to consider when planning your estate.

What are all the ways to get around the estate tax?

There are only two ways to completely avoid the estate tax: Giving your entire estate to your spouse under the marital deduction, as long as he or she is a US citizen, or making sure the size of your estate stays under the current exemption threshold to avoid triggering the tax at all.

As mentioned before, the appropriate use of trusts is one way to reduce the size of your estate, and even the estate of your heirs and beneficiaries. Other ways to reduce your estate size are by giving annual gifts to others, up to the $13,000 inflation-adjusted individual yearly limit to avoid gift taxes. Another way is through the use of donations that allow you to use the charitable giving deduction. Since all these estate-reduction strategies require planning and time, you can see why estate planning usually requires professional help and is not something to be left until the last years of life.

Can you explain how the gift tax works?

The gift tax is designed to keep you from transferring large portions of your estate before you die by just giving it away to avoid estate taxes. Instead, any gift of more than a certain amount to any one individual in a year is subject to a federal gift tax. The basic limit was set at $13,000 in 2009 that you can give to any one person in a single year.

By 'gift' the tax laws mean not only cash and property, but also selling property to someone for significantly less than its fair market value and making a reduced-interest or no-interest loan. To be considered a bona fide gift, though, you have to give up all control of the property and receive nothing of equal value in return. Items not covered by the gift law include anything you give to your US citizen spouse, most charitable donations, political donations, tuition payments and medical expenses you pay.

By combining these annual allowances and exclusions over a period of time, you still can plan to significantly reduce the size of your estate by giving away or donating cash and property and prepaying tuition for grandchildren or some of your own medical expenses. Estate experts also point out that even if some gifts are subject to the gift tax, you may not have to actually pay them. Instead, gift taxes can be credited against any taxes your estate ends up owing after your death.

Just what is the generation skipping transfer tax?

This very complex – and somewhat hefty – tax was created to close an estate tax loophole used by the very wealthy. In families where both the parents and children were already very well off, any money inherited by the children might not be spent during their lifetimes. It would then become subject to a second generation of estate taxes when the children died and passed the property on to their own children. To avoid one of these tax rounds, the original parents would transfer property directly to grandchildren or even great-grandchildren to skip as many rounds of estate tax as possible while keeping their family fortune intact for future generations.

What the generation skipping transfer tax does is to close that loophole by imposing taxes on those types of property transfers that more or less make up for the tax that would have been collected on the property had it stayed in the original estate. Still, there are significant exemptions under the transfer tax rules. As with the estate tax, recent changes to the law have raised the transfer tax limits, and the tax itself disappears in 2010 but is set to return in 2011. Between now and 2009 the exemption limit on transfers rises to as much as $3.5 million before dropping to $1 million in 2011.

There are a number of rules and regulations governing transfers that define how many generations are involved for a transfer to be taxable, the age difference between the person giving the property and person receiving it, whether the transfer was direct or indirect and many other considerations. In most cases, navigating these tax rules on transfers will require you to sit down and plan with an attorney or other advisor.

What about estate and other taxes at the state level?

Depending on where you live, there may be a local estate tax, an inheritance tax or something called a soak-up or pick-up tax. What's more, you do not necessarily have to live in a state to be subject to one of these taxes. If you own real estate in a state with these kinds of taxes, that property is usually subject to the local estate or inheritance tax as well.

Local estate taxes function more or less like the federal estate tax, but may have different exemption limits, rates and other rules that you will want to take into account when planning your estate. While many states have been phasing out estate taxes, others have been postponing or bringing back estate taxes to help with state revenue shortfalls. Some more bad news: Local estate taxes are no longer deductible from federal tax your estate pays.

State inheritance taxes do not take anything out of your estate, but instead treat the property that goes to your beneficiaries as income. You want to take this into account when planning on what and how much to leave to individuals. In general, the executor of the estate has to file and pay state inheritance taxes. Some states maintain separate inheritance tax rates depending on the relationship of the inheritor to the deceased.

A pick-up or soak-up tax is something you have to plan for but will not have to pay, even though you need to file an estate tax return. In the case of these taxes, the state receives a portion of the estate tax that normally goes to the IRS.

Do I need to worry about the Estate Recovery Act?

While not really a tax, the Estate Recovery Act is something about which to be very concerned if it applies to you. The act requires your state to recover from your estate money to repay certain types of Medicaid benefits provided to people older than age fifty-five who received payments during a specified period of time.

The specific rules and regulations of your state's particular Estate Recovery Act will vary, and some states protect your house with a marital or other kind of homestead exemption, while others may not go after property that does not pass through probate. At any rate, if you expect to receive and use Medicaid payments and benefits, consult with your attorney on the guidelines in your state and options for avoiding or minimizing the effect of this act on your estate.

What kind of insurance issues do I have to deal with in setting up my estate?

Insurance planning is just as big a part of structuring your estate as tax, financial and legal planning. For one thing, you want insurance to protect your assets during your life so that you actually have an estate to leave to your family, friends and favorite charities, as well as any property already within your estate. In addition, insurance proceeds, such as death benefits, may constitute a significant part of your estate for one or more of your beneficiaries.

In general, you want to consider insurance to provide for the very expensive and often unexpected costs of medical bills, in-home care or long-term nursing home care that might eat away or even wipe out your estate if you should become seriously ill or infirmed. You also want to look to insurance to provide income for your family members or charities that depend on you for their support, and to provide for yourself and your loved ones if you become disabled. Finally, you want to make sure your personal liability is protected against lawsuits arising from auto accidents or injuries that might occur on your property and sap part of the assets that will make up your estate.

What should I do about life insurance?

No matter what other insurance matters are included in your estate plan, life insurance almost always is front and center. Life insurance is most important when you are younger and have a spouse, domestic partner and any dependents who count on you to pay some or all of the bills and support them now and later in life. In this case, your life insurance benefits are designed to replace lost income and protect the standard of living for your loved ones.

Beyond family responsibilities, though, life insurance can play several other roles in your estate. Once you understand the size of your estate and its net value, you may want to use life insurance to cover any debts your estate may owe when you pass on, as well as generating cash from death benefits to cover your estate taxes, rather than forcing your family to liquidate a business or sell off pieces of real estate or family treasures.

Life insurance payments can also add to the overall liquidity of your estate. If, for example, most of your wealth is tied up in property and other extensive non-cash holdings, your executor might be forced to sell some of the property in order to pay the costs of appraisals, court costs and other expenses involved in settling your estate.

Finally, even if you do not have dependents or family who need the income, you may have charitable organizations, religious or educational institutions that have received regular financial support form you. You can use insurance to continue this support and further the work of these organizations.

What should I do about health insurance?

Part of protecting your estate involves making sure you avoid the kinds of devastatingly high medical bills that can accompany any prolonged or serious illness. If your health insurance leaves you to pick up even part of these bills, you could end up liquidating assets, draining cash reserves, going into debt and generally wiping out much of your plans for your estate.

While many people have health insurance from their jobs, business or through some sort of professional association, they tend to think of these benefits in terms of being healthy; that is, the amount of co-payments that come out of their pockets for visits to the doctor or the occasional prescription at the pharmacy.

Instead, estate experts advise, you need to look at your health plan coverage from a worst-case scenario, such as battling a major illness like cancer or suffering a medical emergency such as a heart attack or a major auto accident. In these cases you could undergo weeks or even months of expensive treatments, visits to specialists, prolonged hospital stays and follow-up care. Review your health plan from this perspective and see how the medical bills that would follow would affect your assets and your estate.

You should pay special attention to maximum benefit allowances for any particular health episode, as well as any lifetime maximum for certain benefits. Also look at the amount of coverage for hospitalization expenses and medical procedures to see just when your benefits might run out and how much of the bill you have to bear. Every dollar you end up paying could well be coming out of your estate.

Should I also consider disability income insurance?

If you are still working you probably should, even though it is one of the most overlooked forms of insurance and is especially important for younger people who depend primarily on income from working to support themselves and their families. Disability insurance provides money to cover your living expenses when you become too ill or injured to work for longer than a week or two.

Disability insurance can often be purchased through payroll deductions at your place of work. It comes in two different forms: Short-term and long-term.

Short-term disability often is paid by your employer and included as a benefit in combination with your vacation and sick leave, sometimes 'borrowing' against your future earned leave time. Typically it covers about three months of missed income, although it can be longer.

Long-term disability insurance can cover from several months to several years and is designed to replace at least half of your income or more. There are many variations on long-term disability, with some covering only total disability, adjusting for partial disability, or even coming into effect if you have to change your career or line of work due to an injury. Also check to see if your policy is inflation-adjusted, especially if it is going to cover you for many years to come.

In general, most disability policies will cover you up to age sixty-five, when you become eligible for various government benefit programs. When figuring the amount of disability coverage you need, check to see what Social Security disability benefits would come to you if you were injured.

Like life insurance, disability insurance is important to your estate to provide for your own future income and to avoid having to liquidate or sell property from your estate.

What about long-term care insurance?

This type of coverage is similar to long-term disability coverage except that instead of covering your missed income, long-term care insurance covers the cost of your medical care, such as a stay in a nursing home. As with other forms of insurance, it is not just for the later years in life, so consider what kind of coverage you would need in the case of some debilitating accident or illness today, not just when you are ninety years old.

You need to work with an insurance agent to coordinate the various types of coverage between your health insurance, long-term care and long-term disability policies. There can be instances when gaps can occur, such as your health insurance benefits maxing out before long-term care benefits are due. Balancing the cost and benefits of all three types of coverage means that you can continue to be covered without becoming over- or underinsured.

Are there other types of insurance I should consider in estate planning?

All these types of insurance are usually just part of a sound personal financial plan, but they need to be viewed through the lens of estate planning to make sure you do not have any holes that could derail your well-considered estate plans.

In addition to health, life and disability, review any auto insurance, home-owner's policies and renter's insurance to make sure you are adequately protected, especially in cases of liability. To give yourself more liability protection, consider additional umbrella liability insurance that can cover you in all aspects of your life.

How do I incorporate retirement planning into my estate plan?

While your retirement goals and estate plan may seem like completely different concerns, your retirement savings and investments should be coordinated with your estate plan.

If, for example, leaving a large estate behind is not important to you, then you probably plan to finance your retirement with a combination of retirement savings, and other assets and property, with any remainder left when you die constituting your estate.

On the other hand, you may want to have a more specific plan for your estate and feel it is important to leave assets to future generations or charities. In that case, you need to look at the various estate strategies and tax implications and decide whether to pass on retirement accounts to a spouse or other persons while spending down your estate in retirement, or whether it will work out better to preserve your non-retirement assets and live primarily off your retirement account withdrawals and pension income.

What do I do about my IRA and 401(k) plans?

These retirement accounts and other special deposit retirement accounts all have a significant estate planning advantage – you can pass income in these accounts on to a beneficiary without having them go through the probate process. On the other hand, the beneficiaries will owe the tax you would have paid on your unused retirement benefits, depending on what gains and contributions to the accounts were not taxed when they were put into the account. You can select anyone you choose to be the beneficiary of an IRA account, and you may want to designate a contingent beneficiary in case something happens to your primary beneficiary. With a 401(k) account, you are required to name your spouse as the beneficiary if you are married, unless he or she signs a waiver allowing you to designate someone else.

How do Social Security payments factor in?

While many financial planners recommend against counting on Social Security for retirement, especially if you are fairly young, you should at least consider Social Security along with your retirement and pension benefits in planning your estate.

Again, the point is to figure out what assets and money to spend in retirement, what to leave in the estate, how to provide for a spouse and family, and how to minimize the tax expense.

Do not forget that with Social Security you not only receive your retirement benefits, but that you can also receive disability benefits that can help protect your estate. In addition, surviving family members – spouses, children, dependent parents and even divorced spouses in some cases – can receive survivor's benefits.

What other parts are there to an estate plan?

In addition to your will, insurance and any trusts or other vehicles you establish, any good basic estate plan also includes a durable power of attorney for someone you trust and a living will if you are so inclined.

A durable power of attorney is a document that allows someone to act on your behalf in legal, personal and financial matters if you become incapacitated or incompetent. You select your own representative, usually a spouse or other family member, and limit their powers or give them authority to handle all your affairs. A power of attorney usually takes the form of either a general or business power, allowing the representative to pay your bills and handle other necessary day-to-day affairs, or a healthcare power, which gives the representative the ability to make decisions about your healthcare and treatment. You can assign both types of powers to the same agent.

The importance of having a durable power of attorney executed when you are healthy and competent is that it means that should you become incapacitated a court will not have to appoint a guardian to handle your affairs, which can be costly, intrusive and difficult to handle.

A living will also seeks to protect your wishes when you become too ill or incapacitated to make them known. A living will sets out your directions to doctors, hospitals and other healthcare providers to stop certain life-sustaining medical procedures and treatments that prolong and extend the dying process if you suffer from a terminal illness or are near death. Living wills are usually coordinated with the durable power of attorney, so that you have a representative who can carry out the instructions contained in the living will. Your durable power of attorney also should name a contingent agent in case the first person you select is unable to handle the required responsibilities.

Retirement Planning and Social Security

How do I get started with a retirement plan?

With retirement planning, perhaps the best advice to keep in mind comes from author and satirist John Sladek, who once wrote: "The future, according to some scientists, will be exactly like the past, only far more expensive".

Retirement planning must focus on the present and the future at the same time. Like all other types of financial planning, you will be much better off the sooner you start. Also like all other types of financial planning, it is never too late to start. Even if you only have a few years until retirement, it is better to retire with some kind of realistic plan than to retire with no plan at all. Naturally, financial planning is a big part of retirement. This involves calculating your expected expenses in retirement, your expected lifespan, and factoring in the effects of inflation not only between now and when you retire, but also during the twenty years, thirty years or even longer that you live as a retiree. Another financial planning consideration is health care as you age, including consideration of different types of care and medical insurance.

> The authors of this book are not associated nor endorsed by the Social Security Administration or the Department of Health and Human Services.

Once you establish financial goals, you can begin to look at the investing and saving tools available to help you get there. This includes several types of tax-advantaged retirement accounts you can set up on your own, employer-sponsored retirement savings plans, and other types of savings and investments that help you build your retirement nest egg.

At the same time, you also should factor in any employer pension benefits you might receive, along with any Social Security payments. For those who are near retirement age now, planners say you can depend on collecting all or most of these benefits, while much younger workers with several decades before retirement should make their plans without depending on employer pensions or Social Security income.

Are there non-financial considerations I should consider for retirement?

As important as the financial aspects of retirement planning are, also important is planning what kind of retirement you want to have, including where you want to live and how you want to spend your time. Are you the kind of person who can quit working entirely, or will you want to pursue a new part-time career or business?

Do you want to stay near family members or become a world traveler? How does your spouse envision your retirement together? You may need to coordinate your plans and expectations about life after work. If you have been a two-career couple, then you need to get ready for a two-career retirement.

As the country's seventy-eight million Baby Boomers head into retirement, it is important to remember that nearly forty million of them are women who are not likely to be ready to leave work at the exact same time as their husbands. Many of their careers paused for children, while others postponed joining the workforce or launched their careers later in life; many others are simply younger – or older – than their husbands.

In some cases, women are just entering their peak earning years and want to set aside as much money as possible for the longer retirements that come with their generation's greater life expectancy. Women who took time off from working find they need to make up lost ground to save for retirement or to qualify for pension and Social Security benefits.

Sometimes it is the husband who retires early after decades of work, either in a corporate buyout, layoff, or for health reasons. In other cases, some women in the workforce are not yet ready to give up jobs they find enjoyable and fulfilling, and others simply can't afford to join their husbands in retirement until they are old enough to qualify for retirement benefits or to start withdrawing money from retirement accounts.

Whatever the reasons, retirement and financial planners say there's a good chance that one half of a working couple – frequently the husband – retires years before his wife. If you are one of those couples, you need to decide sooner than later how you are going to balance the situation when one spouse is home and the other is working. This requires more than just careful planning for finances and health benefits. Several aspects of the marriage must be reviewed as well, including not just who will do the cooking and where to live, but also exploring the expectations you and your spouse harbor for your golden years.

Whether it is a retired husband adjusting his expectations to his working wife's career or the other way around, planners say these lifestyle considerations need to be factored into the financial aspects of your retirement planning.

How early should I start saving for my retirement?

Financial planners warn that less than five percent of people in the US are financially independent when they retire. Being one of the lucky ones in that minority depends on how much planning, saving, and investing you do throughout your working life. The key is to imagine what kind of life you want when you are seventy and what steps will get you there, rather than working at Wal-Mart or McDonald's to pay the rent in your golden years.

As with other types of savings and investing, it is best to think of retirement planning as a marathon. It's better to take your first steps now rather than later, because no matter when you start, you still have to go the full distance. One reason many young (and not-so-young) workers give for postponing retirement planning is that they think they can't afford to start a regular savings plan, whether that's a bank account, Individual Retirement Account (IRA), or employer-sponsored 401(k) plan. Unfortunately, the longer they wait, the harder it is to compile enough money for a comfortable retirement. Financial planners say the answer to this dilemma is simple: Start saving.

What is the best way to get started with retirement savings?

If you are young enough, the easiest and most painless way to save for retirement is with some kind of automated savings plan. This can be a 401(k) plan if your employer offers one, which has several other benefits that are discussed later. If you work for a public school system or other tax-exempt organization, you may qualify for a 403(b) plan, which is similar to a 401(k) but has some important differences. Likewise, state and municipal government employees may qualify for Section 457 plans, which also have some important differences. Otherwise, establishing either a traditional IRA or a Roth IRA is a good option.

Even if all you do is establish a simple bank savings account, you create a situation where some portion of your income is automatically directed toward retirement savings on a regular schedule. In a 401(k) plan, your company payroll department takes care of this, while any type of IRA can be established to automatically transfer money from a savings or checking account.

Planners note that for young people just starting a first job, saving as little as two percent of your paycheck can be a good start. That almost undetectable pinch allows a young worker to start saving for retirement while also paying off college loans, saving for a home and handling other financial obligations. At two percent, someone making $500 a week would be contributing $10 to a savings account, certainly an almost imperceptible amount no matter what your other financial obligations may be. That is enough to make a good start, compounded over time, especially if a young worker increases the savings amount with each raise. What is most important, planners say, is to get in the habit of saving and investing early.

By automatically taking your retirement savings off the top of each paycheck, you do not have to make retirement savings part of your monthly budgeting and spending decisions. Instead, you are free to spend or otherwise invest your entire paycheck, knowing you have already taken care of at least part of your retirement savings.

This practice follows the most basic – and effective – financial planning advice any advisor will give you: Pay yourself first and learn to live on the rest. As you get raises or move to better paying jobs, you should take as much as possible – at least half – of any increase in income and dedicate that to retirement savings as well until you've hit a level of putting at least ten percent of your pre-tax income aside for retirement savings.

Why is it so important to start saving early?

The first and best reason is that it makes financing your retirement relatively painless, since the younger you are, the more time you have to save and invest. No matter what your job, if you are in your early twenties there is no reason that you cannot accumulate well over $1 million by the time you retire.

Saving and investing young also gives you the most time to have your investments compound and the longest window of time for investing in stocks. Your investments have more time to recover from any down markets, recessions, or other negative financial environments, rather than waiting until your middle-aged years when you need to take a safer, more conservative approach to investing. Young workers also tend to have fewer family responsibilities and debts, making it easier to set aside an adequate amount for their retirement accounts.

Are there other advantages to starting early?

In addition to fully leveraging the effects of time and compounding on your savings and investments, putting aside money for retirement when you start working has the added benefit of keeping your lifestyle in check with another key financial planning tool – delayed gratification.

By starting modestly and increasing your retirement investments in small increments out of any raises, early savers do not sacrifice big chunks of each paycheck for a retirement that may be decades away. Otherwise, the temptation to spend each paycheck while directing any savings toward a new car, vacation, or home can make it seem impossible to start a retirement account. Overall, planners say the biggest challenge for workers in their twenties and thirties is to avoid elevating their lifestyles through the use of excessive credit card debt.

What if I am not a young worker?

The older you are, the less time you have to take advantage of compounding in your investments and growth in your salary and other sources of income. If you are getting a late start on saving for retirement, the only solution may be to make sure you max out retirement plan contributions, boost your other savings efforts, reduce debt, and cut spending.

You should also invest the time and money to meet with a qualified financial planner who helps you determine your situation, including what income you can expect from any pension or Social Security benefits, and find ways to get the most out of what you do have to save and invest. In general, the best solution is to dramatically cut on spending right away.

What is the big danger in waiting a few years before I start saving for retirement?

In many cases, especially when it comes to younger workers, the feeling is that they cannot afford it now, but can always start saving for retirement later. The problem is that later might come too late for some savers. A delay of a few years means missing out on the powerful leverage of compounding as the account gathers interest on top of interest for years to come.

For instance, if at age twenty-five you put $50 (ten percent of a $500 weekly paycheck) into an account that yielded an eight percent annual return (compounded monthly), after ten years, you would end up with a balance of $39,637. If you deposited no more money until retirement, but simply left that sum to compound at the same interest rate for another thirty years until retirement, your initial investment of $26,000 would produce a total of $433,461 at age sixty-five.

On the other hand, if you waited twenty years and then deposited $100 a week at the same rate of return for the next twenty years, you would end up with only $255,240 at retirement, despite investing a total of $104,000 – four times as much as in the first case.

In the first case, you not only end up with more money produced by compounding, but you have the other $78,000 of principal to either invest or spend.

I am confused by all the decisions I have to make about retirement investing!

Another stumbling block that scares people away from getting started with retirement planning and savings is the notion that they will confront a confusing array of complicated investing decisions.

Instead of becoming overwhelmed with choices, planners advise investors to start with index funds that match a market index, such as the Dow Jones Index or Standard & Poors 500, or opt for 'balanced' or 'aged-based funds'. These funds allocate investments for your account based on the length of time until you retire, automatically adjusting risk and investment vehicles as you get older.

Once you have money flowing into the plan, take some time to educate yourself about investing. Start with the educational materials from the plan sponsor, including online worksheets and calculators. If you want more personalized help, experts advise meeting with a qualified financial planner, such as those found through the Financial Planning Association *www.fpanet.org*; National Association of Personal Financial Advisors *www.napfa.org*; or the Certified Financial Planner Board *www.cfpboard.org*.

How do I factor inflation into my planning?

Inflation may seem like a little number – historically, it is just a little more than three percent on average each year – but it is a big cause for concern when it comes to planning your retirement, whether you're twenty-five or fifty-five.

That little number – an average three percent rise in the cost of living each year for the last seventy-eight years – is like the constant drip of water eroding stone. In the case of retirement planning, though, that sneaky little number is eroding your purchasing power, the return on your investments, and quite possibly your quality of life in your golden years.

For instance, if you are fifty today and plan to retire at age seventy, a constant three percent inflation rate means that today's $3 gallon of milk will cost you $5.42 at retirement. Apply that to a $50,000 annual household budget, and it means your yearly expenses will climb to more than $90,000 by the time you stop working in 2024. If you are twenty-five today and plan to retire at age sixty-five, a constant three percent inflation rate means that a $3 gallon of milk will cost you $9.79 at retirement. That means your $30,000 annual household budget will climb to more than $97,860 by the time you stop working in 2044. Inflation never stops; it continues to put cracks in your nest egg for the rest of your retirement.

Although these numbers can be a bit shocking the first time you see them, they are real numbers. On the plus side, inflation does not just affect your costs, but your income as well, so that when milk is $9 a gallon the same thing is true for your salary.

Experts say the key to whipping inflation is a combination of regular disciplined savings at any age, some realistic budgeting to free up savings, and balancing your investments to beat inflation before and during retirement.

What kind of retirement investments will I need to beat inflation?

When it comes to outdistancing inflation, individual stocks and stock mutual funds have outpaced inflation over long-periods of time.

Another inflation-beating investment over long periods of time is real estate, but also other income-producing real estate such as rental properties, warehouses, or land. In addition, investors can look at other types of real estate-based investments, such as Real Estate Investment Trusts (REITS) as well as the stocks of real estate firms or real estate-based mutual funds.

How can I increase my investment when the market drops?

The downside of stocks is that they can be volatile, as recent years have proven. Previously, many financial planners advised aging investors to be completely out of stocks and safely into bonds by retirement, in case of a market downturn. That safe advice has changed today, when many workers by retirement age are in good health and need to support themselves for thirty years or more. Many retirement advisors routinely suggest a life expectancy of one hundred – and then some – for planning.

Experts advise that at retirement you have your first five years of retirement expenses in bonds, CDs or money market accounts, and keep the rest in high-performing stocks and stock funds. The recommended plan is to have enough cash flow for five years of living expenses, leaving your other investments, at least partly in stocks, in a position to continue growing.

As each year passes, move some of your new gains out of stocks to keep a constant five year supply of living expenses in fixed-rate CDs or bonds. If the stock market hits a bump, that five year cushion is enough to allow for a recovery without hurting your income.

As you get closer to age fifty, move into a mixed portfolio of bonds, equities, and cash. How you allocate these assets in your portfolio depends on what rate of return – after inflation – you need to reach and how much risk you can tolerate. Once you choose an allocation, do not just set it and forget it: Review your investments at least every year and adjust them for performance and to rebalance the portfolio after you move some of your money out of stocks. When stocks rise, their increased value means that they suddenly make up a larger proportion of your portfolio. Rebalance by moving money out of stocks and into other investments. Besides rebalancing your investments, this helps to lock in a portion of your stock market gains.

How do I coordinate my retirement plans with the rest of my financial planning?

Even though you may be a diligent and disciplined saver and investor with a practical, realistic plan for your retirement, remember that many things can happen between the time you start working and when you retire forty or more years down the road. You could encounter health problems, job layoffs and buyouts, or find yourself forced into an early retirement for business or health reasons. When you hit that kind of bump in the road, you want to keep as much of your retirement savings intact as possible, since no matter what happens you know you will have to stop working someday.

For that reason, do not become so focused on retirement that you put other financial areas of your life at risk. Remember to keep yourself well insured for healthcare and disability and to establish and maintain an emergency or 'rainy day' fund, as well as other assets such as home equity, that can be tapped in an emergency without upsetting your nest egg.

What are all the elements I need to incorporate into a basic retirement plan?

A good, effective retirement plan is really nothing more than matching your expenses to your income. The key to making it all work is putting your hands on the right information about your living costs, taxes, and the amount of retirement income you can realistically expect. Working by yourself or with a financial adviser, collect the following information.

Your current expenses: This includes monthly budget items such as your mortgage or rent, food, transportation, and utilities, as well as a list of annual or sporadic expenses such as medical bills, insurance, travel, and education. Look over the list and determine which expenses increase or decrease after you retire.

A sense of your retirement lifestyle: This includes where you want to live, if you are going to work part-time or go back to school, along with more basic questions as how often you expect to eat out, go to ball games, or take a trip. Try to foresee any new expenses that might come with retirement.

Your Social Security statement: You probably receive an annual statement estimating the size of any benefit you can expect if you retire at age sixty-two, normal retirement age (sixty-five – sixty-seven), or at age seventy. To order a copy of your current statement, call 800-772-1213 or go to *www.ssa.gov*.

A list of employee retirement benefits: This includes any payments or lump sum payout you expect to receive under a traditional pension, as well as the balances of your 401(k), 403(b), 457 or other retirement accounts. If you do not have recent statements on hand, ask your current and past employers for an individual benefit statement. If you have questions about what information employers must provide, see the Department of Labor's online publication, Protect Your Pension.

Statements for your IRAs: Your next step is to list all of your IRAs and their current values.

To start figuring your retirement plan, use the following table to compile your retirement planning information.

- Your current expenses,
- Estimated new expenses in retirement (hobbies, travel, etc.),
- Social Security Income – early (age sixty-two),
- Social Security Income – normal (age sixty-five–sixty-seven),
- Social Security Income – late (age seventy),
- Estimated employee retirement benefits,
- IRA or other dedicated retirement account balances,

- Other savings and investments,

- Projected additions to retirement savings and investments,

- Your estimated lifespan.

Other savings and investment accounts: This covers anything stashed away in banks, brokerage accounts, credit unions, or other financial institutions. If you need to track down a bank account, a local or state government pension account, or other financial assets you can't locate, you can conduct a search on the website of the National Association of Unclaimed Property Administrators.

Projections of future retirement savings and investments: You need to figure how much money you will continue to contribute to an IRA, 401(k), and any other savings accounts, especially if you continue working, even part-time.

Estimate your lifespan: In an era of modern healthcare, do not sell yourself short and end up outliving your money. Make a reasonable estimate based on hereditary factors and your current health. In many cases, financial planners are telling retirees in good health to plan on a lifespan of one hundred years and then some, just to be on the safe side.

Once all your data is compiled, you have everything you need to either start planning out your retirement plan or to consult with a qualified financial advisor to make sure you meet your retirement goals.

What are the most common retirement planning mistakes?

According to the American Association of Retired Persons (AARP), the five most typical misperceptions about retirement are:

"I don't have to start planning until a year or so before I actually retire." You may have been saving for your retirement for many years, but have you really been planning? Research suggests that people who take the time to plan ahead end up with more resources when they are ready to retire. Once you know your basic goals – your retirement age, the type of lifestyle you want, and how much income you need – you can plot a path to achieve these goals. If you wait until the last minute, you won't have time to fill the potential gap between expenses and retirement income.

"Once I retire, the money only has to last a few years". As life expectancies grow, financial planners now recommend that you ensure your retirement income is sufficient through age ninety or even one hundred. If you work even a year or two longer than you have planned, you can improve your situation by saving more, probably increasing your Social Security benefit, and reducing the number of years in retirement.

"The human resources office at work will give me all the information I need to plan for retirement." Your employer is required by federal law to provide basic information about your pension, 401(k), or other retirement account at work – such as the date when you become eligible to receive a pension, what the amount is if you retire on different dates, and the options for drawing money out of your 401(k) or similar retirement account. Your employer, however, has no obligation to educate you about other important retirement topics such as Social Security, Medicare, long-term care, and tax planning. To develop a complete picture, you either need to spend time reading to become self informed, or locate and work with a financial advisor you can trust.

"I can count on consistent, strong investment returns to pay the bills when I retire." The recent market shocks show, however, that if you happen to retire when the market is down, you could end up with much less income than you expected. This experience suggests some basic lessons:

- Diversify your investments in different industries and different forms, such as stocks, bonds, mutual funds, and real estate.

- When you make your financial plan for retirement, assume a conservative rate of return on investments (currently, planners suggest around four to eight percent per year), and don't forget to account for inflation (currently, planners suggest three per year).

"Medicare will cover the cost of my long-term care." About thirty-one percent of older Americans mistakenly believe they have insurance (perhaps Medicare) that covers long-term care, according to a recent AARP survey. The reality is, Medicare does not cover long-term nursing home stays. The average monthly cost of a nursing home stay is $4,654 – meaning that an unprepared retiree will burn through savings quickly.

What are some useful retirement planning resources?

The American Savings Education Council website at *www.asec.org* features 'Savings Tools' with a variety of worksheets to help with retirement planning and saving. You can write for brochures and worksheets, enclosing a self-addressed business-sized envelope, to ASEC Savings Education Brochures, American Savings Education Council, Suite 600, 2121 K Street NW, Washington, DC 20037-1896.

Savings Fitness: A Guide to Your Money and Your Financial Future, by the US Department of Labor and the Certified Financial Planner Board of Standards, is available at no cost by calling 800-998-7542.

Get a Financial Planning Resource Kit from the Certified Financial Planner Board of Standards by calling 888-237-6275.

The Cooperative Extension System, an affiliate of the US Department of Agriculture, teaches you to monitor spending and increase savings, or use their guidelines and interactive calculator to create a budget at *www.money2000.org.* AARP offers a wide variety of information on many financial issues at *www.aarp.org*; click on 'Money & Work'.

What do I need to do after retirement to keep my plan on track?

In years past, workers who retired at sixty-five were lucky to spend a decade in their golden years before passing on, but with today's improved fitness, healthcare and extended life spans, you could live for thirty or even forty years after you retire.

Even though you may have been smart and diligent enough to save a good amount of money for your retirement, you may find after a few years that your situation has changed. Inflation might soar, you could change your lifestyle, shift priorities or discover new interest in retirement – such as travel – for which you might not have budgeted.

For these and many more reasons, it makes sense to keep a close eye on your money after you retire. You need to continue to save when your investments are making money to properly balance your investment allocations and to keep an eye on expenses. In essence, the way you manage your financial life after retirement won't be all that different from the attitudes, approaches, and habits you formed during your working years, except that you will not have to worry about getting fired. So, as you go through retirement, keep the following financial tips in mind.

Create and maintain a financial plan: You should be sure to know exactly where your money is coming from, whether it's investment income (interest or principal), retirement plans, Social Security payments or withdrawals from your savings. For as long as possible, try to keep your money in tax-deferred vehicles without incurring penalties, and focus instead on using money from sources that are not tax-deferred, such as payments from Social Security, traditional pensions and savings from non-retirement accounts.

If you are worried about how fast you can afford to draw down your savings and other financial assets, planners recommend that taking out about four percent a year is a good general guideline. If your budget works out so that you spend only four percent of the cash you have on hand, you should not run out of money. Of course, any number of online financial calculators can help you figure out just how much of your nest egg you can spend from year to year, or you can develop a more comprehensive plan with a financial counselor. The key is to know what you have, where it comes from, and how long it is going to last.

Remember to keep a budget so that you can have enough cash coming in to support your lifestyle while protecting yourself against inflation. Generally planners recommend keeping a certain percentage of your savings in cash or cash equivalents for immediate use or access, with other money in bonds paying off in a year or two and the rest of your nest egg in stocks to promote long-term growth and offset inflation.

Rent instead of buying: If you are considering spending most of the year sailing the Caribbean, fishing from that seaside cottage, or roaming this great land of ours in a six-figure recreational vehicle, try it out before making any kind of financial commitment. You might find that you get seasick and cannot tell port from starboard, end up hating the sound of the pounding surf after a few weeks or can't stand being on the road all day. You will be a lot happier if you test out any big lifestyle change or radical relocation, before making a major (and expensive) commitment.

Be a smart shopper: Just because you are retired from work is no excuse to let your guard down as a consumer. Take a good look at any fees, charges or other expenses that might be depleting your savings and investments. Look over your bank and brokerage statements and review any monthly, annual or per-item fees or commissions to see if you can get the charges waived by restructuring your accounts. If not, go shopping and try to find the same service from another institution for less.

Do not stop with your financial accounts, either. You can join AARP at fifty and take advantage of that group's offers, as well as taking advantage of any senior discount you find at your local dry cleaners, movie theater or other business. Do not be shy about it either – chances are that as a retiree you will be a good and loyal customer, so do not feel guilty about letting a local restaurant or drug store show that they appreciate your business.

Shop around financially: If you are planning on buying a certificate of deposit, opening a money market account or taking out a loan, use your local newspaper or the Internet to research and find the best rates. Opening an out-of-state bank account is easy and allows you to get the best rate on your savings deposits while still keeping ready access to your cash. Banks want to fight for your business, so let them.

Re-evaluate your insurance needs: Insurance should not be a 'set it and forget it' financial situation. You may find you no longer need certain types of policies, or can get by with less coverage. Your life insurance and disability policies may not be needed once you've stopped working or no longer have a family to support. You might switch from being a two-car family to owning just one vehicle. At the same time, you may find new uses for insurance in your estate planning, either life insurance or long-term care policies of some kind. Look over your homeowner's and auto policies to see if you are eligible for discounts, and don't be afraid to shop around.

On the other hand, do not make the mistake of hurting your finances with too much insurance. Financial planners advise that you shouldn't buy insurance if the payments will take money away from basic living expenses. It is a waste of money to buy a policy unless you know you can keep up the payments. Otherwise you might sacrifice to buy a policy, pay the premiums for years, and then cancel the policy later when you realize you can't afford it.

Consider long-term-care insurance: This can be a tough call to make, even for financial planning experts. Some argue that today's boundless medical advances and healthcare technology make it a necessity, especially if you have limited funds. Other planners advise retirees that their best bet is to bank the money they would spend on long-term care premiums and make their own plans.

In either case, it is up to you to consider the options given your personal and family medical history, as well as any care arrangements other family members can offer. If you are relatively healthy and have assets to protect, you may want to consider long-term-care insurance. Retirees who have suffered a stroke, heart attack, or Alzheimer's most often benefit from this insurance.

Watch out for fraud: It is sad to say, but con artists often go after retirees. Do not buy any investment you do not understand, that does not fit in your financial plan, or is sold by someone pressuring you into handing money over right away. Chances are, if it sounds too good to be true, it is.

Do not forget your financial planner: If you have used a financial planner to get to retirement, do not stop now. Conversely, if you find yourself faced with more concerns than you expected, make this the time to start using professional help. The world financial situation – and your financial needs – will continue to change even after you retire. A review of your investments, tax situation, and other financial needs can help ensure that your savings are safe and available to meet your needs. Even if you don't use a planner, review your insurance and investment accounts on a regular basis, at least annually. Stop to see where you are financially and what you want to do. Besides protecting your money, make sure that you are spending it in a way that allows you to enjoy the retired life you've earned.

Do not quit working: Well, at least keep working part-time, if you enjoy the job and you are still up to it. This is a good financial move because whatever money you make isn't being drawn from retirement accounts, which keeps that cash safe for later.

Be careful if you begin collecting Social Security between sixty-two and your 'year of normal retirement' set by the Social Security Administration, based on your birth year. If your job pays over a certain amount (it varies by year), you could end up forfeiting a big portion of your Social Security benefits – as much as $1 for every $2 you bring in over the limit. You must decide whether to keep your income below that limit or put off receiving Social Security until later in your retirement after you have completely finished working or otherwise reduced your earned income.

Like a lot of things in retirement, do not make this a purely financial decision, either. If you like the social contact, enjoy using your skills and keeping up to date with your profession, you may decide that any tax penalty is well worth the cost.

Keep funding retirement plans: If you do continue to work part-time in retirement, you may still be able to put some of your earnings into a company 401(k) or your own IRA. More employers are not requiring full-time status to be eligible for 401(k) benefits because they want to attract experienced, older workers. Besides extending and adding to your retirement savings, putting money into these accounts also reduces your taxable income.

Do not forget about taxes: As you stop working and reduce your income steam, your tax situation changes, especially as you start to tap IRAs and other retirement accounts. You may find yourself in a lower bracket or facing the prospect of paying deferred taxes on retirement plan contributions. Just as other aspects of your life continue to shift during retirement, so will your taxes, along with any financial decisions you have made to help lessen their bite over the years.

INDIVIDUAL RETIREMENT ACCOUNTS

What do I need to know about Individual Retirement Accounts?

An Individual Retirement Account, or IRA, is an investment account that you open in your own name through a bank, brokerage firm, mutual fund. You can put just about any type of investment into an IRA, including stocks, bonds, and mutual fund shares.

The biggest key to an IRA is that it gives you significant tax advantages. In a traditional IRA you may qualify for a tax deduction on the money you contribute. More importantly, your investments can grow without paying taxes while you maintain an IRA, allowing you to build a sizable nest egg before you retire. When you start withdrawing money from the IRA, you pay tax on any untaxed contributions and gains at your normal tax rate. In many cases, retirees who had high-paying jobs find themselves in lower tax brackets after they stop working, which means they pay less tax on their IRA money than if they had simply put it in a taxable account while they were working.

In a Roth IRA, contributions to the account are made with after-tax money. Your gains are not taxed at all, as long as you follow the IRS rules for withdrawals. Roth IRAs are recommended by some financial planners who believe that tax rates will rise as the Baby Boomers retire and by those who value paying the taxes now and being able to withdraw money tax free later. There are income limits on qualifying for establishing a Roth IRA.

How do I go about setting up an IRA?

Opening an IRA is a matter of filling out some simple paperwork for the IRS and making an opening deposit with a brokerage house, bank, savings and loan, credit union, or mutual fund. While you should hang on to your IRA paperwork, the financial institution that administers your IRA tracks the contributions.

Up until 2001 you could contribute only $2,000 each year to an IRA, but since then Congress has approved new IRA contribution limits for all taxpayers through

2010. This is especially important to workers older than fifty, who are allowed to make additional 'catch-up' contributions to build their IRAs in the last few years before their retirement.

Currently, the maximum contribution to IRAs for those younger than fifty is $5,000 per year and $6,000 for workers older than fifty. In 2009, the normal contribution was indexed for inflation, and older workers will be allowed to make additional catch-up contributions of $1,000 more than the normal maximum.

You do not have to make regular IRA deposits or even contribute the same amount of money, if any, to your IRA each year. You can establish more than one IRA; for instance, you can keep part of your IRA in bank deposits such as CDs and money market accounts, and other money in stocks or bonds at a brokerage firm. However, your total contributions to all your IRAs cannot go above the maximum limit in any one year.

Whatever amount you put into your IRA, it does not affect contributions from your spouse. If both you and your spouse work, you each can put the maximum amount into your own separate IRAs each year. You can also establish a spousal account for a non-working spouse; however, joint IRAs in more than one name are not allowed.

What are the differences in the various types of IRAs?

Besides the two types of IRAs mentioned before, you also have the option of opening an Education IRA. As the name indicates, this account is created to pay for certain types of qualifying educational costs, but is structured much like the retirement accounts. Each type of IRA has differing rules and tax advantages, so look over your financial situation and retirement plan to determine which offers the best options for your situation.

Traditional IRA: This was established by Congress in 1974. In this type of IRA, your investments are allowed to grow tax free until you withdraw money when you retire. While anyone can open up a traditional IRA, some taxpayers are allowed to deduct their annual IRA contributions from their taxable income each year. Whether you qualify for the contribution deduction depends on if you are already enrolled in a qualified pension plan – including a 401(k) or a regular defined benefit plan through your employer – as well as how much income you have during the year.

The rules on traditional IRAs include:

- You cannot make withdrawals from the account until you reach age 59 ½. If you must withdraw money before that time, you pay a tax penalty on top of regular taxes on any tax-deferred money in the account,

- The IRS rules require you to start withdrawing money from your account when you turn 70 ½, although you do not have to take all the money out at once and face a big tax bill; you can spread out withdrawals over many years,

- If you do not make withdrawals on time or take out a minimum amount of money, you face a tax penalty,

- Once you reach age 70 ½, you cannot make new contributions to your IRA.

Roth IRA: This type of IRA was established in 1997 and has two major differences to the traditional IRA. The first is that your annual income must be below a certain level to open a Roth IRA. If your adjusted gross income is $166,000 or more (for married couples filing jointly) or $105,000 (for all others), the amount of money you can contribute decreases until your income is more than $176,000 (married filing jointly) or $120,000 (all others), at which point no contributions to a Roth account are allowed. Any contributions you make over the allowed amount are subject to a 6 percent penalty. Refer to IRS Publication 590: Individual Retirement Arrangements, for more information about contribution limits.

The second big difference with a Roth IRA is that while there is no tax deduction on your contributions, you will not have to pay any taxes at all on the gains earned from your IRA investments. This is one reason that financial planners recommend Roth IRAs for younger workers, who will see their earnings grow tax free over many years, as long as your withdrawals comply with IRS rules. Another unique benefit is that, since your contributions are already taxed, you can withdraw that money (but not any earnings) tax free after five years if you face an emergency or other sudden need for the money. This is another feature that makes it more attractive for younger workers to commit to establishing a Roth IRA.

Even though you can't touch your Roth earnings until you turn 59 ½ without paying penalties, you don't have to withdraw any money by the time you turn 70 ½ and the IRS allows you to continue making contributions as long as you continue to earn income, regardless of your age.

Education IRA: These accounts used to be known as Education IRAs, but now are called Coverdell Education Savings Accounts, or ESA for short. You can set up a Coverdell account for any named beneficiary younger than eighteen as long as you meet IRS income limits. Contributions are not tax-deductible, but earnings are tax free as long as they are used for qualified educational expenses. The accounts can be invested in stocks, bonds, mutual funds, and other vehicles, just like an IRA. ESAs don't have to be used for college, either; they can also pay for pre-college educational expenses, including elementary and high school tuition, books, and even computers.

Anyone can set up an ESA for a qualified beneficiary, which means several accounts can be established for one student. No matter how many accounts there are for an individual beneficiary, however, the annual total contribution limit to accounts set up for that person is $2,000. Any amount above this is subject to a six percent 'excess contribution tax,' which means you need to coordinate contributions with parents, grandparents or any one else putting money into an ESA for the same student.

Which should I choose – traditional or Roth IRA?

At first glance, the Roth IRA offers many advantages, especially with its completely tax free investment growth and wider withdrawal policies. While this is the case for many investors, the traditional IRA offers significant tax advantages if you expect to be in a lower tax bracket at retirement. Traditional IRAs also can offer advantages in other situations, such as in estate planning. The best way to decide is to compare both accounts with your tax advisor.

How do I handle my annual contributions to my IRA?

The easiest way to deposit money into your IRA is to simply write a check for your maximum annual contribution. You also can make deposits throughout the year, either as you have the money or with automated regular transfers from a bank account to your IRA investment account. In addition, contributions to a traditional IRA are deductible (if you qualify) from your previous year's taxes as long as you make the deposit before the April 15th tax deadline.

Can I transfer other retirement money into an IRA?

IRAs are a very convenient vehicle for consolidating or restructuring your other retirement accounts. You can, for example, transfer money from an employer's

401(k) account into a traditional IRA. This is particularly recommended when you leave an employer and don't want to leave your 401(k) money behind in that plan. You can also move money out of a 401(k) into a traditional IRA if you want to have more control over the investment options.

You can transfer money from a defined benefit pension plan into a traditional IRA when you retire or leave the company offering the plan. Pension money transferred to an IRA is not subject to the annual contribution limit, which means you can transfer all your pension money in one year if, for example, you receive a lump sum payout from your pension plan. To move your pension money into a Roth IRA, you first have to transfer it into a traditional IRA and then convert it to a Roth IRA account. However, starting in 2008, you were able to convert directly from a 401(k) to a Roth IRA.

Can I move money between IRAs?

You can transfer your money between IRAs directly at any time, as often as you want, to either consolidate accounts or select new investment options, or for any other reason, without facing taxes or penalties.

You can elect to receive the money personally before re-depositing it, although the IRS will allow only one transfer like that during a twelve month period. In that case, you have sixty days to reinvest the funds in another IRA or face the prospect of paying taxes on your withdrawal along with an additional early withdrawal penalty. There are times when it may make sense to take advantage of this sixty day window to put your hands on some tax free working capital in an emergency, but be sure you have the ability to repay your retirement account or you are subject to taxes and penalties.

What about converting my traditional IRA to a Roth IRA account?

You can do this, as long as your MAGI does not exceed $100,000. But you will have to pay taxes on any tax-deferred money in the traditional IRA. After withdrawing that money and paying taxes, you simply deposit what is left in a new Roth IRA. Doing this depends mostly on the tax consequences. If you temporarily find yourself in a low tax bracket, you might want to consider such a move and avoid having to pay taxes on any IRA gains when you retire. At other times, you may find that your traditional IRA investments are in a loss position and that withdrawing the money won't result in as much of a tax bill.

How do I handle withdrawing money after I retire?

Your first consideration is how much money you need to live on and your annual cash flow requirements. Obviously, the longer you can leave money to grow in any type of IRA investment, the more money you will have to see you through retirement.

With Roth IRAs, you do not have to take taxes into consideration, but with traditional IRAs you will want to limit the size of your distributions to only what is necessary in order to keep as much money as possible compounding tax free in your account. You have to pay taxes only on the actual amount you withdraw during any given tax year.

Another consideration with traditional IRAs is the requirement to make required minimum withdrawals (there is no such requirement on Roth IRAs). To calculate your minimum required withdrawal from a traditional IRA in a specific tax year, simply divide the value of your account at the end of the previous year by the number of remaining years of your life expectancy. If, for example, you have a life expectancy of ten years and ended last year with $75,000 in your traditional IRA account, you need to withdraw $7,500 this year to avoid penalties. Your minimum withdrawal changes from year to year as you adjust your life expectancy and the value of your IRA changes.

How do I determine my life expectancy for IRA withdrawals?

The IRS allows you to calculate your life expectancy two ways. Under the first, easier method, you simply refer to the IRS life expectancy charts each year and use that figure. In the second method, you determine your life expectancy at 70 ½ and subtract one year from that figure every year for the rest of your life. Note that you aren't allowed to switch the methods of figuring life expectancy after you start making withdrawals; whichever method you start using is the method you have to use in future years. Because these life expectancy calculations are going to affect your future tax payments, you should consider consulting with an experienced tax or retirement advisor who can balance your tax situation against your required withdrawal amounts.

What if I need to withdraw some of my IRA money early?

If you withdraw any money from a traditional IRA before you reach 59 ½ you have to pay taxes and a 10 percent early withdrawal penalty. In the case of a Roth account, you can withdraw your contributions at any time, but if you take out earnings less than five years after opening the account and before you turn 59 ½ you also face a penalty and taxes. Taking money out under these circumstances is called an unqualified withdrawal.

There are exceptions to the rules, though, that allow you to take money out without paying the penalty (although you still have to pay taxes). The circumstances are:

- You have unreimbursed medical expenses that are more than 7.5 percent of your adjusted gross income,

- The distributions are not more than the cost of your medical insurance,

- You are disabled,

- You are the beneficiary of a deceased IRA owner,

- You are receiving distributions in the form of an annuity,

- The distributions are not more than your qualified higher education expenses,

- You use the distributions to buy, build or rebuild a first home,

- The distribution is due to an IRS levy of the qualified plan.

What about making a late withdrawal?

Once you reach 70 ½, the IRS requires that you take a minimum withdrawal from a traditional IRA each year, mostly so that taxpayers do not use IRAs to shelter money that would normally end up in their taxable estates. If you do not take distributions on time, you face a very steep fifty percent tax on the amount that you should have withdrawn. Of course, with a Roth IRA, you don't have to take any distribution at any time.

Can I borrow from my IRA?

Unfortunately, you can't borrow against any of your IRAs, as you can in many 401(k) or 403(b) employer-sponsored plans. As mentioned before, you can withdraw IRA money for a short period, Then you have sixty days to redeposit the money back in your IRA or another qualified retirement plan. The sixty day limit starts with the day you receive the money; if you keep it longer than that, or don't redeposit it into a qualified account, you'll be hit with taxes and penalties.

Can I put real estate in my IRA?

You can buy real estate with your IRA, as well as a number of other types of investments. While IRAs run by banks and financial services firms are generally limited to the traditional stocks, bonds, and mutual funds, investors who open so-called self-directed IRAs can choose their own investments, which can include not only real estate but business loans and airplane leases. Certain investments are prohibited by Congress, among them alcohol, artwork, and antiques, but warehouses and apartment buildings are fine.

These alternate investments are treated just like stocks, bonds, or certificates of deposit with the income remaining in the account, tax-deferred until it is withdrawn as IRA distributions in retirement or, in a Roth IRA which is completely tax free after retirement.

There are a number of rules to remember when making unusual IRA investments. First, the investment must be an 'arm's-length' transaction, meaning the account holder or certain family members and associates cannot live in a property or be involved in an investment that is held by an IRA. Other challenges include making sure the account has enough of a cash cushion to handle emergencies and cover mandatory distributions when you reach age 70 ½. Violating these and other rules can result in the entire IRA being declared invalid by the IRS, subjecting the investor to taxes and penalties that can more than wipe out the entire account.

Setting up a self-directed IRA is not as easy as stopping by your bank. First, you will need an independent IRA custodian. This kind of firm acts as the trustee for the account, but you are on your own to choose the investments, manage the properties, and handles all paperwork. If you want more help, you can hire an independent IRA administrator, who sets up the account and handles all transactions such as collecting rents and paying bills. The account can be a traditional IRA, or a Roth IRA if the investor meets the adjusted gross income limit. You also may want to hire an IRA advisor, who works with IRA administrators. The advisor actually finds investments and makes the deals. Both IRA administrators and advisors work with custodians.

Experts say that approach is only for investors experienced in the unusual investments they want for their IRA. Unprepared investors could find themselves running into headaches. Talk to advisors and professionals to make sure you will not run into the Unrelated Business Income Tax, a complicated rule that relates to profits of more than $1,000 in commercial activity in your IRA, and that the account is structured and funded to handle all expenses related to the investments, as well as being able to make mandatory distributions.

Where can I get more information on IRAs?

The best source is the Internal Revenue Service regulations covering both traditional and Roth IRAs. You can order IRS Publication 590: Individual Retirement Arrangements by calling the IRS at 800-829-3676 or read it online at the IRS website, *www.irs.gov.*

401(K) ACCOUNTS

What do I need to know about 401(k) accounts?

More than seventy percent of working Americans participate in a company-sponsored 401(k) plan. These accounts allow you to set aside as much a percentage of your annual salary, tax free, in a program of investments selected by your employer.

Most companies match part of your contribution to a 401(k), usually fifty percent of the first six percent you deposit. In that case, you are getting another three percent of your salary as free money for retirement from your employer. Financial advisors stress that you should always contribute up to the level of your company match, since you are essentially giving yourself a raise just by signing up.

If your employer has a 401(k) plan, you are eligible to start contributing after one year of service, according to the law, although many employers will make you eligible in as little as thirty days or after your probationary period expires.

Financial planners are unanimous in praising 401(k)s as the first step in retirement planning for most working Americans. The combination of an immediate income tax break on contributions, regular automatic contributions in up and down markets, tax deferred compounding of earnings over time, and the additional money contributed through an employer match make these accounts almost unbeatable for retirement savings.

What kind of tax break do I get with my 401(k) contributions?

Because the money deposited into your 401(k) plan is deducted from your paycheck before taxes are taken out, putting money into your account serves to lower the amount of income you pay tax on.

For example, if you make $50,000 a year and contributed the full fifteen percent of your pay allowed by law, the amount of your income subject to taxation falls by $7,500 since, in the eyes of the IRS, your take-home pay was only $42,500.

During this time when you're lowering your income tax bill, the remaining $7,500 is growing and compounding in your account, tax free, until the money is withdrawn.

Is it worth enrolling in the plan if I cannot contribute the whole fifteen percent?

Financial planners advise that the best thing you can do is to just start saving in a 401(k), even if it is only a small percentage of your salary. For young workers just starting out, a contribution of as little as two percent of each paycheck is enough to get started without leaving you strapped for cash each week. As you receive raises, put at least some of that new money into your 401(k) until you have reached the maximum contribution limit, or at the very least the maximum level of your employer's match.

How should I select my 401(k) investments?

The typical 401(k) plan offers a mix of different mutual funds ranging from low risk, low yielding bond funds to more aggressive, higher paying stock funds. You should review all the choices and settle on a mix of investments that fit with your degree of risk tolerance, age and investment goals.

In general, workers in their twenties or thirties should concentrate on stocks, including index funds, since they have many years until retirement to ride out the ups and downs of the stock market while reaping the higher gains from equities. For older workers nearing retirement, a more conservative mix of choices is usually recommended in order to protect their investments.

Ask your company's 401(k) plan coordinator for information on selecting the investments that suit your needs, or sit down with a financial advisor to review your mutual fund selections.

What should I look for in evaluating my 401(k) account's performance?

It is easy to 'set and forget' the investment selections for your 401(k) plan, choosing a few mutual funds when you open the account and then watching as automatic deductions from your paycheck and matching contributions from your company continue to bolster your account. As your investments rise and fall, along with changes in your personal financial situation and retirement outlook, you can very well lose track of your account. Your asset allocations may end up out of balance, and you can easily overlook administrative costs or errors. For that reason, take the time to examine these areas whenever you receive your monthly or quarterly account statement.

Investment choices: Check to see that your 401(k) mutual fund selections match your retirement goals, especially if you are still using the same selections as when you first opened the fund. Be sure you are reallocating or rebalancing your portfolio annually, either on your own or working with a financial planner. Take time to gauge the progress of your retirement savings, too. Think about when and where you want to retire, the kind of lifestyle you want and how you think your health will hold up. Then refocus your savings goal as needed, making sure that your investment choices are the right ones to help you achieve those goals.

Do not overinvest in any one company: First and foremost, make sure you are not putting too much into your own company's stock. You already depend on the firm for your entire paycheck, and the employer match in many firms is made up of company stock, so don't bet a lot more of your retirement money on your employer.

Financial planners say you should limit your investment in any single company to no more than ten – twenty percent of your 401(k) plan. This is even more important as you get nearer retirement, because you don't have a lot of time to regain money lost on a single company's stock.

Do not overinvest in any one sector: Limit your investment in any one business category – healthcare, technology, financial services, and so on – to a maximum of twenty percent of your 401(k) plan. This means you should not rush in to load up on stocks from some currently 'hot' sector. Once you have heard that it is hot, it is quite likely too late for an individual investor to make any money.

Keep an eye on plan costs: Administrative fees silently erode your investment returns, no matter how well your funds are doing. The individual funds within many plans assess small fees to cover marketing and overhead costs. As a general rule of thumb, you should not be paying anything higher than one percent of your portfolio's value in costs each year. If your account statement does not disclose these fees and other costs, call the plan administrator or check the plan website to find out.

Double-check where your money is going: Mistakes are part of life, but that does not mean you should pay for them. Make sure your paycheck deductions are all there and that they are going into the right investments. If you have taken a loan against your 401(k), make sure the balance is correct and your payments are properly credited. In past years, the Department of Labor has found a few employers who took advantage of employee contributions by either using the money for company expenses or holding contributions too long before putting them into the accounts.

What do I do with my 401(k) account when I change jobs?

When you leave an employer, you have several options for handling any existing 401(k) account. You can transfer the money to a new employer's 401(k) plan, roll it over into an IRA account, or, in some cases, leave the money right where it is in your existing plan. Whatever you do, remember this: Basically, your money should never touch your hands. Mishandling a 401(k) transfer or rollover is a sure way to get yourself hit with a tax penalty.

In general, financial planners recommend that you take control of the account rather than leaving it with the former employer, where you might pay less attention to your account performance, or even forget about it in several years. Instead, move the money into a new employer's 401(k) or into your own IRA. If you are going to move the money into an IRA but want to have the option of later moving the money into another employer's 401(k) plan at some later date, choose something called a rollover IRA. In most cases, this allows you to move the money out of your IRA and into a new 401(k) account later, allowing you to take advantage of 401(k) plan loan provisions. If you use a regular IRA, tax laws require that your money stay locked into the account until retirement, unless you want to pay taxes and penalties.

The worst thing you can do, however, is to withdraw money from your 401(k) account with no plan on how to handle it. If you don't redeposit the money within sixty days into a qualified retirement plan, you'll have to pay income tax on the entire amount as well as a ten percent early withdrawal penalty. You also face the temptation to spend the money, effectively wiping out your retirement savings.

Is it a good idea to borrow from my 401(k) account?

Under most 401(k) programs, you may borrow up to fifty percent of your vested balance, as long as it is not more than $50,000. You pay the money back – with interest – during a period of up to five years, although it can be longer if you are using the money to buy a house.

Being able to loan yourself money and pay it back to your retirement account has been a selling point with 401(k) programs in years past. If you are paying twenty-three percent credit card interest and can borrow from your retirement plan to pay the debt off at eight percent, that seems like a good deal, with a guaranteed return of fifteen percent. While it is better to have interest payments go toward your golden years instead of a finance or mortgage firm, a 401(k) loan can be expensive in many ways.

First, while all the money that went into your plan was from pretax paycheck deductions, you have to repay the loan with after-tax dollars. If you are in the thirty-three percent marginal federal income tax bracket, for example, that means you are spending $1.49 from your wages to replace each dollar you borrowed, plus your interest payments. In the case of paying off credit card debt, that's not a problem, since you were paying your cards off with after-tax dollars anyway.

Another drawback to 401(k) loans is that your interest payments are not deductible as 401(k) contributions. The interest you pay yourself also counts as profit on your investment, which means it will be taxed as earnings when you retire and start taking withdrawals from the account. That means you pay taxes on that money twice – once as part of your regular paycheck, and again as earnings in your retirement account. In addition, if you fail to repay the loan, you have to pay income tax and the ten percent early withdrawal penalty, so make sure you can repay the loan without trouble. Finally, most plans require that you repay the loan immediately if you leave the company, which means you have to either come up with the entire sum owed or face those taxes and penalties again.

Financial planners cite several concerns in opposition to 401(k) loans. Rather than restructuring your personal finances to avoid credit card debt, you may continue to run up your credit card balances while paying off the loan and get even further into debt. You might stop making new contributions to your account while you're paying off the loan, which hurts your chances to increase your savings for retirement. To be safe, address your debt issues first and get your spending under control before taking a 401(k) loan, and by all means continue making new contributions.

With all those concerns, there still are times when a 401(k) loan may make sense. Consult online calculators to figure you how much interest you are paying now on your debt versus what it would cost to repay your 401(k) loan. You may find your monthly payments are lower under a 401(k) loan, too, creating more breathing room in your family budget as well. At the same time, project what your 401(k) would earn on the borrowed money if you left it in your account during the five years you would have the loan, versus what your loan payments to the account would make as you repay them and the money is reinvested for the same amount of time.

Take your interest savings with the loan and subtract or add the difference between your account's earnings on the reinvested loan payments and what that money would make if you left it in place. If you see a substantial savings, and do not foresee a risk of default on the payments or leaving the company, a 401(k) loan can make sense, as long as you also find a way to spend less than you make to keep your future debt under control.

When I retire, what is the best way for me to get the money from my 401(k)?

The options for withdrawals, also called distributions, from your 401(k) account depend on the rules governing your company's plan. In general, though, you usually have the following choices:

Leaving your money in the plan: You can retire and simply leave your money in the 401(k) plan until you want to start making withdrawals. You have until the time you turn 70 ½ to start taking money out, or else the IRS can hit you with a stiff penalty. If you do not need the money right away, this option allows you to continue increasing your money with your 401(k) plan investments, avoiding taxes, and ensuring the money passes directly to a beneficiary instead of into your estate if you should die before distributions begin. The drawbacks to this approach are that your investments remain limited to what is offered in your plan, usually a mix of a dozen or so mutual funds. You may need more options as you move into retirement. Also, if your company ends up in financial trouble, you could lose some or all of your account or face a long delay in getting it.

Cash out in a lump sum: A lump sum distribution gives you all of your account balance at once in cash, meaning you can use the money for some big retirement expense, such as buying a new home, an RV for traveling the country, launching your own business, or any other use. The downside, besides the temptation to go on a retirement spending spree, is that you have to pay income tax on all the money you withdraw for that tax year. In addition, the IRS makes your employer withhold twenty percent of the lump sum toward your taxes due, so that even if you do not owe that much in taxes, you have to wait until you file your next return to the get the balance back.

Rolling over a lump sum into an IRA: Just like the option available if you leave the company before retirement, you could roll over your entire 401(k) balance into a traditional IRA at a stock brokerage firm, bank, credit union or other financial institution. This gives you much more flexibility in your investment choices, as well as the option to sell them or move money around within your investments at any time. You have to make the transfer within sixty days of the withdrawal from your plan. In addition, you should consider how any sales commissions or management fees for the new IRA account compare with fees in the current 401(k) plan.

Convert to an annuity: In some plans, your employer offers the option to convert some or all of your 401(k) money into an annuity offering regular, fixed payments. Annuities can be structured to give you income for the rest of your life and take away any worry about how to manage your investments. Buying an annuity however, can be confusing and expensive, so study all the options as well as your needs. You have to decide whether to receive lifetime payments or payments over a specified number of years, as well as whether you want to cover a surviving spouse. You can give yourself some extra time to weigh annuity options by rolling the money from your 401(k) into an IRA, and then purchasing the annuity on your own later, when you can find a wider choice of annuities than your 401(k) plan may offer.

Receive your money in installments: Under some 401(k) plans, you can structure your withdrawals to distribute a percentage of your money in installments, usually during a span of five, ten or fifteen years, in monthly installments. Again, you should make sure you are comfortable leaving your account in your employer's plan, but this option offers a steady source of income without the expense or commitment of locking you into an annuity. You are still limited to the dozen or so investment options in your employer's 401(k) plan, and, unlike an annuity, you are still responsible for managing your investments and bearing any losses in the account.

Combine options: Under some plans, you can mix and match several of these options, giving you a chance to customize an approach just for your specific needs. Still, planners say you should remember a few basics. Make sure you provide enough guaranteed income (from your plan, as well as Social Security and other sources of income) to cover your living expenses for several years. This gives you the option to either cut out luxuries or enough time to change your investment strategy to recover from a down market.

What does it mean when I get a notice that I am in a blackout period?

A blackout period is a window of time when 401(k) participants and beneficiaries are not allowed to trade or make any other changes in their accounts. Blackout periods can happen for many reasons, but usually it is because the company is switching to a new provider for the plan or because of a change in investment options. If you were planning to make any withdrawals, take a loan against the account, adjust your asset allocation or make any other changes to the account, you have to wait until the blackout period ends.

Under the recently passed Sarbanes-Oxley Act, which was approved in response to corporate scandals such as the Enron affair, 401(k) plan administrators now must give at least thirty days notice of any blackout period. The notice must be in writing and stated in a way that the average plan participant can understand, not legal boilerplate.

Financial planners advise that while you should not ignore blackout notices, they do not mean you have to take any action about your account. In fact, if it has been several years since you established the account, receiving a blackout notice can be a good reminder to review your 401(k) investments, look at the performance and fees, and to make sure your portfolio has the right mix of equities, bonds, and cash.

PENSION PLANS

Although they may seem more like relics from the past, do not forget to include defined benefit pension plans in your retirement outlook. Unlike IRAs or employer-sponsored 401(k) and 403(b) savings plans, defined benefit pension plans mean your employer guarantees you specific monthly payments when you reach the qualifying retirement age.

How much money you get from your pension benefits depends on how long you work for the employer and how much you are paid during that time. Pensions are insured and monitored by the federal government so that retirees get their pension payments even if the employer ends the pension plan or goes out of business.

How do defined benefit pension plans work?

In most cases, any defined benefits plan pension starts paying benefits after you reach retirement age and stop working. The payments are usually monthly checks that continue for as long as you are alive, although some pension plans let you choose instead to receive a lump sum payment upon retirement.

Another decision to make about your pension plan is whether you want your pension benefits to cover just you or if you want the pension extended to cover both you and your spouse. If it is you alone, then your pension payments are larger, but they also end when you die. If you elect to have your pension cover your spouse, the payments are smaller but your spouse continues to receive benefit payments after your death. If you decide you want to have the pension cover just you, you must get your spouse's agreement in writing.

Do Social Security benefits factor into my pension payments?

In many plans, your Social Security benefits payments lower the actual amount of money you receive from your employer's pension plan, so be sure to account for this when creating your retirement plan. Otherwise, you could be disappointed when you start receiving less retirement income than you expected.

Because employers pay into the Social Security system for each employee, pension laws allow them to reduce your pension payments by as much as half of your projected Social Security benefit. The concept is that your employer already paid the government for half of your Social Security taxes, and so is allowed to deduct some of that already paid retirement benefit from your pension payout. In most cases, if you retire before you're eligible for Social Security payments, the pension pays you the full amount from the plan until you begin receiving Social Security payments from the government.

What does it mean when I become 'vested' in my pension plan?

'Vesting' means that you have earned a legal guarantee to receive your pension benefits. Vesting is designed to provide workers with an incentive to stay with an employer for more than a few years, since, if you quit before becoming fully vested, you receive no pension benefits or only partial payment when you retire.

There are two formulas used in calculating whether you are vested in a plan. The first is called the 'cliff' formula, which allows you to claim 100 percent of your pension benefit as long as you have participated in the plan for at least five years. Under this formula, if you quit any time after the five year vesting requirement, you can receive all of your pension money at retirement.

The second vesting approach is a system called 'graded vesting', which awards you a percentage of your pension benefit gradually over the years. At bare minimum, most graded vesting plans award you twenty percent of your pension benefits after three years of participation, and then give you an additional twenty percent every year thereafter. While some plans offer more accelerated vesting, pension laws bar employers from offering anything less than this formula.

What are cash balance pensions?

Many companies convert their traditional defined benefit pension plans to new cash balance pensions that offer vested employees a certain 'account balance' when they retire. Under cash balance plans, you can choose to receive the money as a lump sum when you retire or as an annuity offering regular monthly payments. Cash balance plans pay only a limited amount of money earned by the employee during the years, while defined benefit plans continue to pay retirees for the rest of their lifetime.

In a typical cash balance plans, your pension account is credited each year with a pay credit (such as five percent of compensation from your employer) and an interest credit (either a fixed rate or a variable rate that is linked to an index such as the one-year Treasury Bill rate). Increases and decreases in the value of the plan's investments don't directly affect your benefit amount.

When you retire and become eligible to receive benefits, the amount of money you receive is determined by your account balance. Say, for example, you have an account balance of $100,000 when your reach sixty-five. If you retire at that time, you have the right to an annuity, which might pay about $10,000 per year for life. In many cash balance plans, however, you (with consent of your spouse) could take a lump sum benefit equal to the $100,000 account balance.

In addition, some cash balance plans will let you (again, with consent of your spouse) choose to receive your accrued benefits in a lump sum if you quit before reaching retirement age. If you get this kind of early lump sum distribution, it can be rolled over into an IRA or to another employer's plan, if that plan accepts rollovers.

With so much media coverage of pension plan problems, how do I check whether my pension is safe?

It is not surprising that you want to keep an eye on the financial health of your company's pension plan. While millions of workers are depending on employer-paid pensions for their retirement, it seems that hardly a month goes by without another large corporation declaring that its pension is seriously underfunded. In recent years, General Motors, Ford, IBM, and Boeing have been among the hundreds of employers struggling to come up with more cash to support their underfunded pension plans.

Typically, a pension plan is not officially underfunded until its assets are worth less than ninety percent of the plan's current liabilities. Being labeled as underfunded does not mean your pension plan is in trouble, since stock market losses and low interest rates on bonds and other fixed income have lowered the performance of most pension investments. Most financially healthy companies can make up the shortfall once pension investments pick up, but if the firm is running into other financial trouble, your full pension could be at risk.

Most defined benefit plans are insured by the Pension Benefit Guaranty Corporation (PBGC), a federal government corporation that makes sure you and your fellow employees get at least minimal benefits if your company goes bankrupt or stops supporting your pension plan. Even with that protection, you could still end up getting much less than you expected from a healthy pension plan. If your employer is in financial trouble, compare your expected monthly pension benefit with what the PBGC would guarantee if the plan goes into default. If that difference is big enough, you could end up with a smaller pension benefit than you expected. For example, the maximum current benefit in 2009 that PBGC would pay someone who is sixty-five years old at retirement is $4,500.00 per month or $54,000 a year. For additional information please visit *www.pbgc.gov.*.

How do I stay informed about my pension plan's condition?

Your pension plan administrator is required to give you a copy of the summary plan description (SPD) of your pension benefits within ninety days of the time you become a plan participant, or at any time when you ask for a copy of the summary. The plan description explains when you begin to participate in the plan; how and when your benefits under the plan vest; what calculations are used in determining your service and benefits; when you can expect to receive payments; and how to file for benefits when you leave the company.

Companies with pension plans have to file financial statements, described in the plan's summary annual report (SAR). Your company is required to make the annual summary available to you. In addition, you can write and request your individual benefit statement every year, which outlines what benefits you have accrued and vested.

Finally, do not just automatically trash any mail you get about your pension, it could be valuable information. For instance, most pensions pay premiums for their PBGC insurance, and if the plan is underfunded the company pays an additional premium. You and other plan participants have to be notified if your company starts paying the under funding premium, which alerts you that the plan is struggling.

If you hear or see indications of cutbacks, layoffs, or other financial woes at your workplace, don't be shy about asking the pension plan administrator if your benefits are going to be affected.

What are my options if I think my pension plan is in trouble?

Sometimes the best you can do is to keep aware of the situation and adjust your retirement plan to the fact that you may not receive the full value of your pension if the PBGC takes over. If your plan allows a lump sum withdrawal, and you think things are headed for trouble, you can exercise that option and put the payout into an IRA or other retirement account. In this case, it is best to consult with a financial advisor who can offer pension plan guidance. Remember, bankruptcy or otherwise defaulting on your pension plan are not your only employer concerns. You should weigh your pension options whenever there is a significant change of control at your employment, such as in a merger or acquisition, when you can't be sure what the future holds for your pension.

Where else can I go for pension information?

The Department of Labor provides lots of pension information on its website at *www.dol.gov*, as well as offering the publication, What You Should Know About Your Pension Rights. You can call advisors at the Employee Benefits Security Administration division of the Department of Labor at 866-444-3272, or contact local offices of the department to get help with obtaining written copies of your pension's summary plan description, summary annual report or other paperwork if you can't get this from your plan administrator.

Another source of help and information is the Pension Benefit Guaranty Corporation. You can visit the PBGC website at *www.pbgc.gov* for information about defined benefit pensions or for help in tracking down a pension when the company has gone out of business, merged, or closed its pension plan.

I have worked at a lot of different places over the years – how do I find out if any of these old employers owe me a pension?

It might sound unbelievable, but quite a number of workers in this country actually lose track of pensions they have earned. All in all, there are literally thousands of people who are entitled to their share of the millions in pension money that continues to go unclaimed in this country.

It is not all that hard to let an old pension slip your mind when you consider that the workforce is more mobile now and that people change jobs more frequently, making it relatively easy to forget about some small vested pension benefits that they earned early in their careers. If you left the company before retirement, if the company has merged, changed names, moved, gone bankrupt and re-emerged under a different name, figuring out what you can collect and where to go can be a bit of a search.

To track down an old pension, your first stop should be the Pension Benefit Guaranty Corporation. Since 1974, any company with more than twenty-five employees enrolled in a defined benefit plan must register with PBGC. When any company terminates a pension plan that is not fully funded, PBGC becomes the trustee of the plan and guarantees payment of the basic benefits.

As well as dealing with underfunded or bankrupt pension plans, PBGC also keeps track of benefits for employees who cannot be located. Unclaimed pension money from the plans go to the PBGC along with the names of the individuals. When, for example, a company wants to end its defined benefit plan it terminates the pension fund, pays all the benefits, and gives the names of any former workers who cannot be found to PBGC. This agency then works to find them through publicly available databases, such as the postal service and telephone directories.

Any worker the PBGC cannot find goes into a database that you can search on the agency's website at no charge. To date, PBGC's search program has found more than 14,000 people who were owed more than $34 million dollars. Still, the database includes another 13,000 names of people entitled to $43 million in benefits, with more 'lost' workers being added all the time.

There are also nonprofit groups that work to help reunite workers with lost pensions. These groups are often financed by the US Administration on Aging and private foundations, and there is no charge for their services.

If you believe you are entitled to a private pension and you cannot contact your former employer, visit the PBGC website. Even if you do not find your name there, do not give up. The PBGC gives step-by-step advice on what to do if you cannot find your name in its database.

You also can contact the Pension Rights Center in Washington, DC, an independent consumer organization dedicated to protecting and promoting pension rights for workers and their families. The center has several specific pension projects working in specific states and maintains a list of pension resources and places you can get help on its website, *www. pensionrights.org*, or you can call 202-296-3776.

If you worked for a state or local government, or as a public school teacher, you should first try to contact the agency or school system that hired you. If you cannot find information on your pension that way, contact the National Association of Unclaimed Property Administrators, P.O. Box 7156, Bismarck, ND 58507. You can also search under your name at the Missing Money website, *www.missingmoney. com*.

What should I do if I leave an employer who offers a pension plan before I'm eligible to retire?

Your first and most important step is to keep good records. Make sure you keep any pension-related paperwork the company gives you in a safe deposit box or other secure place. If you quit after becoming vested in a pension plan, the company should give you a notice of deferred vested benefits, which also should be kept in a safe place. If you move after leaving, remember to contact the pension plan administrator with your new address.

What are the important documents I need to keep on hand to deal with my pension?

As with anything that involves money, rules, and the government, there is plenty of paperwork relating to your pension plan. If you write and request any of this information, your plan administrator must respond within thirty days, although you might have to pay copying costs for some documents.

Pension plan document: This lists the requirements you must meet to receive a benefit from the pension plan. Ask the person in charge of your plan for a copy, or look at this document in the main office of your plan administrator or employer.

Pension plan summary: Also called the 'Summary Plan Description' or SPD, this is designed to summarize your plan in language that you can understand. A foreign language version may be required if enough plan participants speak a language other than English. Your plan must give this summary to you automatically. You should receive it within ninety days after you become a plan member.

Individual benefit statement: This tells you whether you have a right to a pension. If you do, the statement should tell you how much you could receive at retirement age if you stopped working on the date of the statement. Some plans distribute these statements automatically every year. If your plan does not do this, write to the person administering the plan and ask for this statement. If you leave the plan after you are vested, you should receive a statement when you leave.

Widows' and Widowers' benefit statement: This explains how much your benefit will be reduced to provide protection for your spouse. You should receive this statement automatically if you are married at the time you become a plan member and are at least thirty-five years old.

Summary annual report: This one- or two-page document provides a yearly report on your pension plan's investments. Your plan is required to give you this report once a year. The plan files a detailed financial report with the government every year. For more detailed information, ask your pension plan administrator to send you a copy of this report.

Over the years I have ended up with an entire menagerie of retirement accounts – pensions, IRAs, 401(k)s, and more. Is there any way I can combine them?

More than half of all US workers have two or more different types of retirement accounts, financial planners say, while almost one-fifth of workers have five accounts or more. Depending on your situation, you may not be able to get them all into one account, but you certainly can combine a few to reduce the complexity of your financial planning. The advantages are that you pay less in fees and spend less time sorting through paperwork, tax forms, and account statements. You simplify the overall management of your accounts while getting a better picture of just how your retirement savings are shaping up. When you review your accounts each year to check on asset balance, investment performance and fees, take some time to see if it also makes sense to consolidate at least some of them.

In addition, it makes it more unlikely that you will forget or overlook an account, especially with companies changing names, selling divisions, merging, and going bankrupt through the years. Another advantage is that combining accounts gives you a better picture of exactly where your money is invested. The problem in maintaining many separate and different types of accounts is that it can skew your investing perspective and leave you holding several similar mutual funds, all with the same risks and return profiles, or with large holdings in the same few stocks.

Finally, combining several small accounts into one with a hefty balance means you may be able to qualify for discounts, personalized advice, and other perks from financial services companies. For instance, some larger investment planning firms require certain account minimums before they will accept you as a customer. Financial planning fees may be lower, too, since your account is larger.

To consolidate accounts, choose those you wish to keep, and then contact the plan administrator or financial services firm for the necessary paperwork to close and transfer accounts. The manager of any account into which you are moving money should be glad to help you with the arrangements. Not everyone will be happy; the companies you are leaving may charge fees to close your accounts, so ask about these expenses up front.

In deciding how many accounts and which type to retain, compare the options. For example, 401(k) accounts offer loan provisions, while IRAs do not. On the other hand, you have many more investment options with IRAs than with most 401(k)s. You also may want to keep more than one account just so you can designate different beneficiaries when you plan your estate.

SOCIAL SECURITY

How does Social Security work?

The Social Security system was created in 1935 under the administration of President Franklin D. Roosevelt, designed to provide an old age pension for the elderly poor, and started paying out retirement benefits in 1940. Besides paying retirement benefits to nearly all working US citizens, the program also pays disability benefits and survivor benefits to widows, widowers and surviving children. The program has been amended and expanded, and now provides these programs administered by the Social Security Administration (SSA):

- Retirement insurance,

- Survivor's insurance,

- Disability insurance,

- Hospital and medical insurance for the aged and disabled,

- Black lung benefits,

- Supplemental security income (SSI),

- Administration for children and families,

- Unemployment insurance,

- Medical assistance,

- Food stamp supplements,

- Child support enforcement and establishment of paternity,

- Services for maternal and child health and child welfare,

- Workers' compensation,

- Railroad retirement, sickness and unemployment insurance,

- Veterans' benefits, and

- Federal, state and local government employees' retirement systems.

How is Social Security financed?

Even though Social Security is often discussed as a kind of trust operation for all US workers and employers, Social Security is simply a special tax collected to pay retirement and disability benefits to US workers and their families. There are no individual accounts and, experts point out, most retirees collect far more in Social Security benefits than they have paid in during their working lifetimes.

Your Social Security tax is listed on your pay stub under FICA taxes (Federal Insurance Contributions Act), which covers your payments for Social Security as well as Medicare. On your pay stub, you may find these taxes notated as OASDI (which stands for 'old-age, survivor and disability insurance') and HI (for Medicare 'hospital insurance').

Under the law, 12.4 percent of your salary, up to an annual limit, goes toward financing the Social Security system. If you are a salaried employee you pay only half, and your employer picks up the other portion. If you are self-employed you pay the full load, although you can deduct half of the amount – called self-employment tax – as a business expense.

Is it possible to overpay your Social Security tax?

While this is not a common problem, it can happen if you are making a high salary and switch employers once or more during the year, and consequently wind up having too much Social Security tax withheld. While the amount of income taxed is capped at $97,500 for 2007, a new employer is likely to tax your earnings until they reach the ceiling, even though you may already have maxed-out for the year at your previous job. If this happens, be sure to claim the Excess Social Security tax credit when you file your income taxes for that year. In fact, you can claim this tax credit even if you owe no tax for the year.

Is everyone eligible for Social Security benefits?

No. Social Security benefits are earned by working for a minimum number of years and making a minimum amount of money. These are awarded as credits under the

Social Security system. Children younger than age twenty-one who do household chores for a parent (except a child age eighteen or older who works in the parent's business do not participate in Social Security).

Do I have to report these credits in order to qualify?

You do not have to report them, but you do need to make sure they are properly recorded. Each year your employer sends a copy of your W-2 (Wage and Tax Statement) to the Social Security Administration, which then enters the earnings shown on your W-2 on your lifelong earnings record. To have this happen correctly, the name and number on your Social Security card must match your employer's payroll records and W-2; if not, your employer is likely to get a letter asking for a correction. If your Social Security card is not correct, contact any Social Security office. Tell your employer if your name and Social Security number are incorrect on the employer's record.

This can be especially important for women who change their names when getting married or divorced, for example, in order to be sure they receive all the Social Security credit due for their work. In fact, whenever you change the name you use in employment, report it to Social Security by filling out the form Application for a Social Security Number Card (Form SS-5). You need to have proof of identity under your old name as well as your new name. If you were born outside the US, you also may need to show evidence of US citizenship or lawful alien status. You can get the form from any Social Security office or by calling Social Security's toll-free number, 800-772-1213.

Even if you do not work, you should report any name change so that your earnings record shows the correct name and credits when you apply for any type of Social Security benefits.

Are there any other special situations where I need to make sure I'm getting proper credit for Social Security?

Another important area where you should make sure you are getting the Social Security credit due is if you are running a business with your spouse. If a married couple own and operate a business together, and you expect to share in the profits and losses, you may be entitled to receive Social Security credits as a partner even, in most cases, if you and your spouse do not have any formal partnership agreement.

To make sure you receive all the credit due for your share of the family business income, you must file a self-employment return (Schedule SE), even though you and your husband or wife files a joint income tax return. If you do not file a separate Schedule SE, all the earnings from the business could be reported under your one spouse's Social Security number, which means you won't receive any Social Security credits for them.

You also need to be careful about checking your Social Security credits if you served in the military. If you were on active duty or on inactive duty for training since 1957, you have paid into Social Security, while soldiers, sailors and airmen on inactive duty in the Armed Forces Reserves and National Guard weekend drills have been covered by Social Security since 1988. If you served in the military before 1957, you did not pay into Social Security, but you still may be credited with special earnings for Social Security purposes. Even if you are receiving a military pension, you may still be eligible for Social Security benefits, too.

What about paying Social Security taxes for my household help?

If you hire a household worker, such as a cleaning person, a cook, a gardener or a babysitter, you are responsible for seeing that wages you pay him or her are reported properly. You must deduct Social Security taxes from the wages if you pay the person $1,400 or more during the year (this amount is indexed for inflation and will be adjusted in future years). Besides deducting the employee portion of the tax, you must pay an equal amount in your role as the employer and send the combined taxes to the Internal Revenue Service. You can report the earnings and pay the taxes when you file your federal income tax return. By the way, that $1,400 total includes reporting any cash you pay to cover the cost of the employee's transportation, meals or housing. If you do not report the wages on time, usually quarterly, you may have to pay a penalty in addition to the overdue taxes.

There are a few exceptions to this rule, and a few surprises. For instance, you do not have to pay Social Security taxes for household workers (such as babysitters) who are younger than age eighteen, unless household employment is the worker's primary occupation. Even family members may be covered by this tax. If you hire your children to perform household work for you, and they are twenty-one or older, the Social Security Administration says you have to pay Social Security tax on their wages. In fact, the SSA rules even state that, 'household work performed by your parent may require taxes be paid in certain situations'.

How do I handle reporting wages for my nanny, gardener and other household workers?

In general, you can check with the Internal Revenue Service for forms and instructions, along with the filing schedule for your particular situation, but the following general guidelines will help.

Keep complete records: For Social Security purposes, you need the names, addresses and Social Security numbers of all household workers and the amount of wages you paid them. To be accurate and make sure that the worker receives proper credit, copy the Social Security number and use the name listed on each worker's Social Security card. If one of your employees does not have a card, he or she should apply for one at any Social Security office.

Deduct the right amount: Currently the Social Security tax rate, for both employees and employers, is 6.2 percent on wages up to $97,500. The Medicare tax rate is 1.45 percent of all wages. You can check with the IRS each year for the appropriate rate.

File your report: Surprisingly, you do not have to use a whole batch of special forms for all this. In fact, you can report wages of $1,500 or more that you paid a household worker right on your own federal income tax return (IRS form 1040). As the employer, you pay your share of the Social Security and Medicare taxes, along with the taxes you withheld from the employee's wages, when you file your return.

Submit W-2 reports on time: Since you are the boss, you also have to give your household employee copies B, C and 2 of IRS form W-2 (Wage and Tax Statement) by the end of January after the year the wages were paid. Then you send copy A to the Social Security Administration by the last day of February. You can get this form and the instructions for completing it from the IRS.

How do I incorporate Social Security benefits into my retirement planning?

In general, the closer to retirement you are now, the more you can depend on current calculations of your Social Security benefits for planning purposes. While there is much talk about changes to the program as the Baby Boomers start to strain the country's treasury for retirement payments, along with discussions of benefit reductions, privatization plans and other reforms to Social Security, such changes are at least several years away. In some cases, financial planners advise younger workers that they should plan to be completely self-supporting in retirement without Social Security, and to consider any benefits they do receive as an added retirement windfall.

In general, you want to factor in Social Security benefit payments with your other retirement benefits, including required distributions from IRAs, 401(k) accounts, pension plans and other sources of income.

When can I start collecting Social Security benefits?

You can start collecting Social Security payments before you reach your official 'full retirement' age; as early as age sixty-two, in many cases. However, the amount of money you receive will be reduced.

When you take early retirement, your monthly benefits are permanently reduced by a percentage based on the number of months you receive benefits before you reach full retirement age. This does not mean you receive less money during your entire retirement, however. In general, early retirement gives you about the same total Social Security benefits over your lifetime, but in smaller amounts to take into account the longer period you will receive them.

For example, if your full retirement age is sixty-five and two months, the reduction for starting your Social Security at age sixty-two is about 20.8 percent; at age sixty-three it is about 14.4 percent; and at age sixty-four it is about 7.8 percent.

Even if your full retirement age is older than sixty-five (meaning you were born after 1937), you can still take early retirement at age sixty-two, but the reduction in your benefit amount is even greater than for workers whose full retirement age is age sixty-five. For example, say your full retirement age is sixty-seven. In that case, the reduction for starting your benefits at age sixty-two is around thirty percent; at age sixty-three, it is about twenty-five percent; at age sixty-four, about twenty percent; at age sixty-five, about 13.3 percent; and at age sixty-six, about 6.6 percent.

How can I determine what my full retirement age is?

While the full retirement age has traditionally been age sixty-five, because of longer life expectancies the Social Security law was changed in 1983 to increase the full retirement age in gradual steps until it reaches age sixty-seven. This change began in the year 2003 and affects people born in 1938 and later.

Year of Birth	Full Retirement Age
1937 or earlier	65
1938	65 and 2 months
1939	65 and 4 months
1940	65 and 6 months
1941	65 and 8 months
1942	65 and 10 months
1943–1954	66
1955	66 and 2 months
1956	66 and 4 months
1957	66 and 6 months
1958	66 and 8 months
1959	66 and 10 months
1960 and later	67

Can I take early retirement at age sixty-two even if my full retirement age is not until age sixty-five?

If you were born after 1937, your full retirement age is older than sixty-five. Nonetheless, you can still begin to take your retirement benefits at age sixty-two, but the reduction in your benefit amount will be even more than it is for people retiring now.

For example, if your full retirement age is sixty-seven, the reduction for starting your benefits at sixty-two is about thirty percent; at age sixty-three it is about twenty-five percent; at age sixty-four about twenty percent; at age sixty-five, about 13.3 percent; and at age sixty-six, about 6.6 percent.

What happens if I decide – or am forced – to stop working before I reach age sixty-two?

If you stop working before you reach age sixty-two, remember that during years with no earnings you miss the opportunity to increase your benefit amount by replacing lower earning years with higher earning years. That's because your retirement benefit calculations are based, for most retirees, on an average of your thirty-five highest years of earnings. Years in which you have low earnings or no earnings are counted – even if you made no money – to bring the total years of earnings up to thirty-five. So, the more years you work, the more opportunity you have to raise your lifetime average, especially if you are making more money as you get older. Once you stop working, you add more of those zero-earning years to your lifetime average. One caveat: If you stop working because of health problems, do not wait until you hit age sixty-two to think about Social Security. Instead, consider applying for Social Security disability benefits as soon as you are forced to stop working. The amount of the disability benefit is the same as a full, unreduced retirement benefit. If you are receiving Social Security disability benefits when you reach full retirement age, those benefits are converted to retirement benefits.

What happens to my benefits if I continue working and delay my retirement beyond my full retirement date?

If you decide to continue working full time beyond sixty-five or whatever your full retirement age, you will find that your continued work will increase your Social Security benefit in two ways. According to the Social Security Administration:

- Each additional year you work adds another year of earnings to your Social Security record. Higher lifetime earnings may result in higher benefits when you retire,

- In addition, your benefit will be increased by a certain percentage if you choose to delay receiving retirement benefits. These increases will be added in automatically from the time you reach your full retirement age until you start taking your benefits, or you reach age seventy. The percentage varies depending on your year of birth. See the chart below for the increase that will apply to you,

- For example, if you were born in 1943 or later, eight percent per year (2/3 of 1 percent per month) is added to your benefit for each year you delay signing up for Social Security beyond your full retirement age.

The rate of actual increases by year is:

Increases for Delayed Retirement

Year of Birth	Yearly Rate of Increase
1917—1924	3.0 percent
1925—1926	3.5 percent
1927—1928	4.0 percent
1929—1930	4.5 percent
1931—1932	5.0 percent
1933—1934	5.5 percent
1935—1936	6.0 percent
1937—1938	6.5 percent
1939—1940	7.0 percent
1941—1942	7.5 percent
1943 or later	8.0 percent

Experts at the Social Security Administration stress one very important point if you decide to delay retirement beyond your full retirement age. Even if you continue working, be sure to sign up for Medicare at age sixty-five. In some circumstances, medical insurance costs more if you delay applying for it.

How do I determine how much money I will get at my different retirement dates?

As explained before, the amount of your total Social Security benefit is figured on your earnings averaged over most of your working lifetime. Higher average earnings mean you will get higher benefits. If you have some years of no earnings or low earnings, then this lowers the average and your benefit amount may be less than if you had worked steadily.

In addition, you have seen how the amount of your benefits also is affected by how old you are when you elect to begin receiving benefits. If you start your Social Security retirement benefits at age sixty-two, your benefit is lower than if you wait until a later age. So, how do you weigh all these factors when figuring the actual amount of your monthly benefits?

About three months before your birthday every year, you receive a Social Security Statement that provides you a record of your earnings, estimates of your Social Security benefits for early retirement, full retirement and retirement at age seventy. It also provides an estimate of the disability benefits you could receive if you become severely disabled before you are eligible for full retirement, as well as estimates of the amount of benefits paid to your spouse and other eligible family members due to your retirement, disability or death.

If you need to request a current statement, you can fill out and mail in the Social Security Statement request form (SSA-7004), available on the Internet or from the Social Security Administration, or request a statement online at *www.ssa.gov*. The Social Security Administration website *www.socialsecurity.gov* also has a number of online planning calculators for retirement, disability and other benefits. These online tools can be used to figure out various benefit scenarios.

Is it important what date I choose to officially start my retirement?

Yes. According to the Social Security Administration, your choice of a retirement month could mean additional benefits for you and your family. The SSA advises that if you plan to start your retirement benefits after age sixty-two, you should contact Social Security beforehand to determine which month will be the best for you to claim benefits.

For instance, under current federal rules, many workers can receive the most benefits possible with an application that is effective in January, meaning you start collecting benefits in January, even if you do not plan to retire until later in the year. Depending on your earnings and your benefit amount, it may be possible for you to start collecting benefits even though you continue to work.

If you are not working or your annual earnings are under certain earning limits, or you plan to start collecting your Social Security when you turn sixty-two, you should apply for benefits three months before the date you want your benefits to start. These rules can be complicated and confusing and the specific income limits can change from year to year, so in most cases it is best to discuss your plans with a Social Security claims representative sometime during the year before the one in which you plan to retire.

If I am already receiving benefits as a surviving spouse, when should I start receiving my own full benefits?

Widows and widowers can begin receiving benefits at age sixty (or age fifty if disabled), including divorced widows or widowers. If you are receiving widow's or widower's benefits, you can switch to your own retirement benefits as early as age sixty-two, assuming you are eligible and that the amount of benefits you will get in retirement will be higher than your rate as a widow or widower. In many cases you can begin receiving one benefit at a reduced rate and then switch to the other benefit at an unreduced rate after you have reached your applicable full retirement age. The rules vary depending on each individual's situation, so you should contact a Social Security benefits representative to discuss your options.

What about benefits for other members of my family?

If you are receiving retirement benefits, some members of your family can also receive benefits. According to the Social Security Administration, those who may be eligible include:

- your wife or husband age sixty-two or older,
- your wife or husband younger than age sixty-two, if she or he is taking care of your child who is younger than age sixteen or disabled,
- your ex-wife or ex-husband age sixty-two or older,
- children up to age eighteen,
- children between the ages of eighteen and nineteen if they are full-time students through grade twelve, or
- children older than age eighteen if they are disabled.

What kind of benefit's can a wife or husband expect to receive?

A husband or wife can get one half of the retired worker's full benefit. However, if the spouse begins collecting benefits before reaching full retirement age, the amount of the spouse's benefit is permanently reduced by a percentage based on the number of months before she or he reaches full retirement age.

For example, if your spouse starts collecting benefits at sixty-four, the benefit amount would be about forty-six percent of your full benefit. At age sixty-three it would be about forty-five percent and 37.5 percent at age sixty-two. However, if your spouse is taking care of a child who is under age sixteen or disabled and receiving Social Security benefits, your spouse gets full benefits, regardless of age.

If you are eligible for both your own retirement benefits and for benefits as a spouse, you always receive your own benefit first. If your benefit as a spouse is higher than your own retirement benefit, you receive a combination of benefits equaling the higher benefit you would receive as a spouse only. If, however, the spouse starts taking retirement benefits at any time before reaching full retirement age, both the full personal benefit and the spousal benefit amounts are reduced.

Do the benefit amounts for my family members have any effect on how much I receive from Social Security?

If you have children eligible for Social Security, each will receive up to half of your full benefit, but there is a limit to the amount of money that can be paid to a family. The limit varies, but is generally equal to about 150 to 180 percent of the wage earner's basic benefit rate. If the total benefits due your spouse and children exceed this limit, their benefits will be reduced proportionately. Your benefit will not be affected.

What about after a divorce?

A divorced spouse can get benefits on their former spouse's Social Security record as long as they were legally married for at least ten years. The divorced spouse must be sixty-two or older and unmarried, and can get benefits even if his or her ex-spouse has not retired yet. However, the worker must have enough credits to qualify for benefits and be age sixty-two or older. The amount of benefits a divorced spouse gets has no effect on the amount of benefits a current spouse can get.

What is the maximum Social Security retirement benefit paid out?

The maximum benefit depends on how old you are when you retire, as discussed before, and the amount can vary from year to year as it is adjusted for inflation. The current benefits range goes from a maximum payment of $1,444 a month for a person retiring at age sixty-two to a maximum of $2,643 a month for a person retiring at age seventy. These figures are based on earnings at the maximum taxable amount for every year after age twenty-one. You can check the maximum amount of taxable earnings for each year on the Social Security website, as well as finding a listing of historical rates.

Does my spouse's benefit affect how much money I can expect to receive?

If a husband and wife retire, each receives his or her own benefit amount. Social Security imposes no 'marriage penalty' when two members of a couple are each entitled on their own earnings record.

How do I sign up to start receiving Social Security benefits?

You can call the Social Security Administration's toll-free number, 800-772-1213, to apply for benefits, or to make an appointment to visit any Social Security office to apply in person. You can call to find the office nearest you, check your local phone book, or use the office locator online at the Social Security website. You also can apply for benefits online at *www.socialsecurity.gov*, although only for retirement, disability or spouse's benefits.

To complete your application, you need some or all of the documents listed below. If you do not have all of this paperwork, though, Social Security encourages you to go ahead and apply for benefits and the agency may be able to help you get all the documents you need. The information needed includes:

- your Social Security number,

- your birth certificate,

- your W-2 forms or self-employment tax return for last year,

- your military discharge papers if you had military service,

- your spouse's birth certificate and Social Security number if he or she is applying for benefits,

- children's birth certificates and Social Security numbers, if applying for children's benefits,

- proof of US citizenship or lawful alien status if you (or a spouse or child is applying for benefits) were not born in the US, and

- the name of your bank and your account number so your benefits can be directly deposited into your account.

When applying, you need to submit either original documents or certified copies, which can be mailed to Social Security or brought to your local office. In either case, the documents will be copied and returned to you.

What happens to my benefits if I work and receive Social Security payments simultaneously?

This can be an area of much confusion to workers who are still on the job and eligible for Social Security benefits, or for retirees who want to go back to work.

Yes, you can continue to work and still receive retirement benefits. Beginning in the month that you reach your full retirement age, your earnings will not affect your Social Security benefits. That is the simple part. The confusion arises, however, with the Social Security rules that require that your benefits be reduced if your earnings exceed certain limits for the months before you reach your full retirement age. These rules are:

- If you're under full retirement age, $1 in benefits will be deducted for each $2 in earnings you have above the annual limit,

- In the year you reach your full retirement age, your benefits will be reduced $1 for every $3 you earn over a different annual limit until the month you reach full retirement age. Then your earnings no longer affect the amount of your monthly benefits, no matter how much you earn.

To check these annual limits, call SSA or visit the social website at *www.security.gov.*

To further complicate this question, if other family members receive benefits on your Social Security record, the total family benefits will be affected by your earnings. This means your earnings will offset not only your benefits, but those payable to your family as well. If a family member works, however, the family member's earnings affect only his or her benefits.

To further complicate matters, there is a 'Special Monthly Rule' that you want to take advantage of when possible. This rule applies to your earnings for one year, usually the first year of your retirement. It allows you to receive a full Social Security check for any month you are considered retired, regardless of how much money you make in the year. Your earnings must be under a monthly limit. If you are self-employed, the services you perform in your business are taken into consideration as well. While this may seem slightly confusing, it is worth getting more information. You can request the leaflet *How Work Affects Your Benefits* (Publication No. 05-10069), which has the figures for the current annual and monthly earnings limits.

Do I have to pay taxes on the money I get from Social Security?

Maybe, maybe not. On average, twenty percent of people who get Social Security end up paying taxes on their benefits, although this category includes only people who have substantial income from sources in addition to their Social Security.

Each year you receive a Social Security Benefit Statement in the mail showing the amount of benefits you received. You can use this statement when you are completing your federal income tax return to find out if any of your benefits are subject to tax. If you meet certain limits, you may owe tax on your benefits. To get the current limits, contact either the IRS or the Social Security Administration.

If I think I will have to pay tax on my benefits, can I have federal tax withheld from my Social Security payments?

This is not a requirement of the IRS, unlike when you are working, but you may find it easier than paying quarterly estimated tax payments every three months.

To have federal taxes withheld, you need to file form W-4V from the Internal Revenue Service, which you can obtain by calling the IRS at 800-829-3676 or by visiting the SSA website. After completing and signing the form, return it to your local Social Security office by mail or in person (to get the address of your local Social Security office, call 800-772-1213). Every time you need to change or halt the withholding, you need to complete a new form and submit it.

For more information, call the IRS at 800-829-3676 and ask for *Tax Information for Older Americans* (Publication 554), and also request *Social Security Benefits and Equivalent Railroad Retirement Benefits* (Publication 915).

Can I arrange to have my state payroll tax automatically deducted from my Social Security benefit?

The Social Security Administration cannot withhold state taxes from your monthly benefits check. Before assuming you have to pay state tax on your benefits, however, call and check with your state's taxing authority. You might be pleased to find that you live in one of the several states that do not tax Social Security benefits at all.

If I am receiving Social Security benefits and continue to work, will I still have to pay Social Security and Medicare tax on my earnings?

Yes, you will, as long as you continue to work in any kind of job covered by Social Security. Your employer must go on deducting your Social Security and Medicare taxes from your salary and must pay the equal employer's share of the taxes. Your earnings will be reported to SSA every year just like any other worker's earnings.

If you are self-employed while getting benefits and your net profit from your business is more than $400, you, too, will have to continue paying your Social Security and Medicare taxes when you file your personal income tax return for the year. On the plus side, these extra earnings could end up increasing the amount of your benefits.

How does my pension affect the benefit payments I receive from Social Security?

If you get a pension from work where you paid Social Security taxes, it will not affect your Social Security benefits.

However, if you get a pension from the federal civil service, some state or local government employment or work in a foreign country or some other workplace that was not covered by Social Security, your benefit payment may be lowered.

To sort that out, contact Social Security to ask for the fact sheets entitled *Government Pension Offset*, which is designed for government workers who may be eligible for Social Security benefits on the record of a husband or wife (Publication No. 05-10007) and *The Windfall Elimination Provision*, which is aimed at people who worked in another country or government workers who also are eligible for their own Social Security benefits (Publication No. 05-10045).

What happens if I spend a lot of time overseas, or even move out of the country?

As long as you are a US citizen, you are free to travel or even choose to live in most foreign countries without hurting your eligibility for Social Security benefits. However, there are a few countries – Cambodia, Cuba, North Korea, Vietnam and many of the former USSR republics (not including Russia) – where the SSA cannot send Social Security checks.

However, if you work outside the US, then different rules apply in determining whether you can get your benefit checks. In addition, if you are not a US resident or US citizen, you probably will have 25.5 percent of your benefits withheld for federal income tax.

For more information, call and ask for a copy of the booklet *Your Social Security Payments While You Are Outside the United States* (Publication No. 05-10137).

How can I appeal decisions about my Social Security benefits?

You have the right to appeal any decision made on your claims regarding Social Security. Not surprisingly, there is a fact sheet you can request: *The Appeals Process* (Publication No. 05-10041). In addition, you also can be represented by an attorney or other qualified person in appealing decisions as outlined in another fact sheet, *Your Right to Representation* (Publication No. 05-10075). Both are available from Social Security.

Where can I go for more information about Social Security benefits?

Your first stop, if you have access to a computer, should be the main Social Security website at *www.socialsecurity.gov*. The site also offers an online office locator so that you can find the nearest local Social Security office to handle your questions in person. If you have a touch-tone phone, you can get recorded information and some services 24 hours a day, including weekends and holidays, from some offices.

If you need an appointment or to speak to a service representative, call Social Security's toll-free number, 800-772-1213, Monday through Friday between 7 a.m. and 7 p.m. If you are deaf or hard of hearing, call the toll-free TTY number, 800-325-0778, between 7 a.m. and 7 p.m. Monday through Friday.

Insurance and Risk Management

How do I incorporate insurance into my financial planning?

Insurance of any kind is primarily designed to help you protect your assets and provide money after accidents and catastrophes, whether it is an auto collision, natural disaster or death. For a predictable, regular premium, you can make sure that your pocketbook is safe from a huge bill to repair your car after a crash or to rebuild your home after a hurricane, for instance, while disability or life insurance protects your family and estate from the loss of your income in the event of a serious accident or death. In fact, you can insure almost any kind of property or event, from special riders to cover jewelry and computers to unique policies that pay off if your pet gets sick or when something goes wrong with a vacation trip. In addition to this kind of financial protection, life insurance can also be used in estate planning and to provide cash accumulation, wealth transfer and estate tax liquidity.

Do I really need to buy life insurance?

There are two reasons to purchase life insurance. The first is to protect your family, business partners, charities or other dependents from financial loss in the event of your untimely death. The second is to utilize life insurance as a tax advantaged accumulation vehicle. For example, if you reach retirement age and no longer need the policy as protection, you may utilize withdrawals and loans as a retirement income plan. Obviously, this is dependent on the type of policy you have, and the returns on the cash value within it.

Insurance experts explain that the reasons for buying or not buying life insurance are different from person to person, and vary at different times of life, according to your age, financial situation, health and other considerations. Here is how various personal and financial scenarios affect your need for life insurance.

Single with no dependents: Your estate needs only enough money to cover your funeral expenses, remaining medical bills and any outstanding debts, such as loans, installment debt, credit cards and so on. But you also should consider whether you may have elderly parents or other relatives depending on you later in life for support. If so, remember that buying life insurance when you are younger is cheaper than signing up later in life when you might have a health problem and find insurance to be more expensive or harder to buy.

Single with dependents: Now things get a little more complex. In addition to funeral expenses, remaining medical bills and any outstanding debts, you also want to consider any financial care for surviving parents, relatives or other dependents, as well as education costs for children you might have, along with replacing your income to support a spouse and family and provide for a surviving spouse's retirement.

Married couple with no children: First, the basics: Funeral expenses, remaining medical bills and any outstanding debts, especially a mortgage, home equity loan or any significant car payments. You also need to determine your spouse's ability to be self-supportive, including the number of years left in employment, any difference between the income you provided and your spouse's ability to make a living, and how much he or she will be able to provide for his or her own retirement.

Couple with children: Once your survivors get past any funeral expenses, remaining medical bills and any outstanding debts, you need to consider how they will handle mortgage payments, childcare expenses and education costs, including college. Do not overlook the fact that even if one person is a stay-at-home parent, he or she might have to work and will need money for childcare or other services they could handle at no cost when you were alive.

Retired or nearly retired couple: Besides funeral expenses, remaining medical bills and any outstanding debts, you need to consider income replacement for the surviving spouse, as well as any necessary retirement expenses, such as a new home, vacation home, long-term health plans and the effect on any money or other assets you plan to leave for your children or grandchildren.

What are the basics I need to consider when buying life insurance?

According to insurance experts and regulators, you should make sure to answer these questions for yourself before buying any life insurance policy.

What kind of assets do you have now, and what standard of living do you want to maintain for your survivors?

Besides funeral costs and medical bills, what would happen to your family members after you are gone? Would they have to move or seriously change their lifestyles? Would there be enough money for current and future educational expenses, living expenses, housing and other financial needs?

Have you had major life changes since buying your last policy, or do you anticipate any in the near future?

Experts all advise that you should be sure to reevaluate your life insurance policies annually or any time you face a major event in your life, such as marriage, divorce, the birth or adoption of a child, or purchase of a major item such as a house or business.

What kind of insurance do I need?

There are two basic categories of insurance – *term* and *permanent* – with several different forms of coverage in each category. No matter which type of life insurance you buy, most insurers want you to provide a medical history and probably take a physical to make sure you are in line with their medical criteria.

Term life insurance pays a death benefit during a specified period of time, such as under a twenty year policy. Term insurance is a good choice if you need coverage for a specific period of time, such as while you are paying off a mortgage or supporting children before they finish college. Term insurance can cover periods as short as a year and as long as several decades. If you are interested in using your life insurance policy as a form of savings, consider a permanent life insurance policy.

Non-guaranteed term life: Non-guaranteed term life gives you coverage only for a fixed, short period of time, typically a year in most policies. This is a pure death benefit coverage, which has its advantages, but which also carries the risk that if your health changed and you developed a medical problem or other condition you would be unable to renew the policy or get another one after your initial term policy expires. Another drawback to non-guaranteed term policies is that the premiums you pay can increase dramatically as you age. That does not mean term life insurance does not have a place in your financial plan. This kind of term coverage can be a very good choice for young people who do not want the higher costs of permanent insurance, but especially for people with financial obligations that will disappear in time, such as a car loan, college savings for youngsters or a mortgage.

Renewable and convertible term: Term policies have the feature of covering a span of years, usually ten, twenty or thirty years. This allows you to extend the cost of the policy over several years and sidestep annual increases.

Annual renewable term policies increase in price each year, but may allow you to renew without additional health underwriting when you renew.

Convertible term is a type of policy that works like renewable term, but offers you the chance to convert your insurance to a permanent policy. The main advantage is that when your regular term premiums start to go up because of your age or health, you can exercise the option to convert to permanent life without having to go and buy a new policy. Convertible term can be a good choice for young people who want to eventually move into permanent life but who cannot afford the higher cost at this point in their lives.

Whole life or ordinary permanent life: This is insurance for WHEN you die, as opposed to term insurance which is for IF you die. This insurance lasts for your entire lifetime, unlike term insurance which concludes at some point, when you must reapply and qualify to continue the coverage. Another difference is that whole life policies spread the cost over your entire lifetime. Whole life policies generally have higher premiums because a portion of the premium is invested to grow cash value in future years. Because whole life is an investment managed by the insurance company, you should be careful and thorough in your choice of companies. Evaluate whole life policies as not just insurance paying a death benefit, but also as an investment that has to fit in with the rest of your financial plan. Insurance experts also warn that the required premiums can be a heavy burden later if your financial situation changes.

Universal life: It differs from whole life because premium payments are flexible in the payment dates and the amount of the premiums. However, the policy must have established cash value at all times to continue to pay insurance premiums. This allows you to manage the investment aspect of the policy as your financial situation changes, although some policies limit how much extra you can pay into the policy. Although the insurance level is flexible, you will probably have to provide some kind of medical information if you increase the insurance benefit. With this type of policy, you need to pay attention to keep it fully funded, especially since some charges may be increased by the insurance company.

Variable life: This type of permanent insurance offers, as the name implies, variable investment performance. The insurance company invests your premiums into a variety of funds that you choose. The cash value of your policy is determined by the investment performance of your premiums.

You need to remember with most variable and some universal life insurance policies that the cash value of the policies rises and falls with the performance of the investments, although some policies do guarantee to pay a minimum death benefit. You are allowed to take loans against the cash value of your policy, but any unpaid loan balance is deducted from your death benefit. You also have the option to surrender, or cash in, a permanent policy, or you can convert it to an annuity.

Because variable life policies are going to function as an investment and insurance, compare the costs, benefits, coverage and investment choices against your separate options for term insurance and independent investments.

How do I decide whether a life insurance policy fits into my financial plan?

That is going to depend not only on your current financial situation, your family situation and your future financial goals and plans, but also on the costs, structure and benefits of each individual policy. The insurance industry advises consulting an insurance expert, usually a qualified and reputable insurance agent who should be able to recommend policies that fit your individual needs.

As with any financial decision, especially if you are using insurance as an investment, study all the options, ask lots of questions and do not purchase anything you do not fully understand.

The American Council of Life Insurance has these recommendations to consider when you are weighing the costs and benefits of different types of insurance policies:

For term policies: How long can I keep this policy? What are the renewal terms and limits? Do the premiums increase? If so when, how, and on what schedule? Is this policy convertible to a permanent policy? Do I need a medical exam to make a conversion?

For permanent policies: What are the premiums? Do they fit into my budget? What is the surrender value of the policy? Are these premiums stable over the long term? What are the loan provisions? What is the range of investment options?

When should I buy term insurance?

For many years, term insurance has had an appeal to people who want to keep their insurance coverage simple and to keep it separate from their investment d ecisions.

Term life insurance is simple insurance coverage that includes none of the cash value benefits you find in whole life policies. Term life insurance coverage can vary from one year to as many as thirty years, or the term can cover you until you reach a certain age, usually sixty-five or seventy, but also older. Whatever the provisions, term insurance policies all expire at a specific time set out in the policy.

Because they expire after a fixed time, you should purchase term life policies if you want to protect a spouse, children or other loved ones from losing your income stream or from accumulated debts. For instance, a married couple would choose term so that, if one of them died suddenly, the surviving spouse would not have to bear the burden of paying the entire mortgage alone. Instead, the term life death benefit could be used to pay off the mortgage.

Another use for term insurance is to replace lost income and protect the financial future of the surviving family members by providing money for college and living expenses if the children are still at home, especially if only one spouse works.

In most cases the insurance company will require that you get a basic medical exam when applying for the policy, although some insurers require exams only for policies with larger benefits. The insurer will also want a medical history and other basic facts. Combined with the results of the medical exam, these could affect your premium or result in your not being issued a policy at all. For instance, smokers generally pay more for most policies, although several firms have different approaches to dealing with applicants who smoke cigars.

As you get older and get closer to the day when you will pass on, the premiums for term policies go up. You can find term policies that allow you to renew the policy without having to take another medical exam. You also should consider *level premium* policies, which allow you to retain low premiums for a specific time period, such as ten or twenty years. Of course, once that term expires, you would have to get a new policy and face the likelihood of paying higher premiums.

What if I get turned down for a policy?

If you have a significant medical condition, ongoing illness or problematic medical history, look for a type of guaranteed-issue life policy called *quick issue* or *simplified issue* insurance. These policies do not require that you take a medical exam, but charge a higher premium to get coverage, since the insurer is accepting greater risk in insuring people when it does not have proof of their medical condition. A life insurance broker usually is the best source to find available guaranteed-issue policies. You also may have to undergo a waiting period before your coverage takes effect, and may face some required yearly fees. These features obviously make guaranteed-issue policies insurance a last resort for most people.

How long should the term be on my life insurance, and how much coverage do I need?

The basic approach to take when weighing what length of term you need is to consider your income, short-term and long-term debts, and financial obligations to dependents and other family members. You also need to look ahead and see that these needs will be covered at future points when they might change. Consider how long it will be until your children or other dependents reach financial independence, when the mortgage on the family home will be retired, whether your spouse works and other family financial matters, today and several years down the road.

What about the cash value benefits of whole life insurance?

Variable universal life insurance, a form of permanent whole life insurance discussed earlier, gives you a chance to build up cash value, a pool of money that earns interest on a selection of stocks, bonds and mutual funds you choose. So, besides buying a lifetime of insurance protection, part of your premium payment is contributed to a separate cash account invested to ideally grow over time.

Some financial planners like variable universal policies for clients who may lack the discipline to regularly save and invest because these policies ultimately force customers to save as they pay their insurance premiums. Other planners recommend term insurance because of its cheaper premium, and advise clients to invest the money left over in other investments, such as mutual funds; which best depends on your individual situation. Variable universal policies also give you the flexibility to alter your death benefit, as well as the corresponding premiums required over the course of the policy.

Of course, cash value in any kind of life insurance has one big difference to other types of investments, in that any money you withdraw or borrow from the cash value of the policy reduces the death benefit that will be paid out. Some withdrawals or loans can also trigger a tax bill if the amount exceeds your paid premiums. Finally, the amount of your premium going towards investments lessens each year you own the policy, with more of the premium going to fund your death benefit.

Is building up cash value worth the extra money I will pay for a permanent life policy?

In many cases, the best recommendation when it comes to buying life insurance is to choose a mix of cash value and term policies. In the case of someone who has covered short-term financial obligations and wants a policy that won't expire and can help build their estate, permanent insurance with a cash value option can be a good choice.

Experts recommend that when shopping for a cash value policy you consider the rating of the company issuing the policies, as well as fees and any internal costs. Also ask your insurance agent or broker if the insurer is a mutual or stock company and what its record is in paying above any policy guarantees.

How does the cash value portion of the policy work?

Take the example of a young person who signs a $100,000 universal life insurance policy with $800 premium payments a year. About $150 of the premium goes toward *mortality expense*, which is actual insurance. Another $50 goes to cover administrative costs and the remaining $600 goes to your cash value.

While this kind of deal is appealing in your younger years, the chances of your dying increase each year, and so does the amount of your premium that purchases your insurance. That leaves a decreasing amount each year to add to your cash value. With universal life the cash value typically accumulates quickly at the beginning and then slows down as the insurer's mortality expense doubles about every ten years. Your $150 initial mortality expense at age twenty-five turns into $300 at age thirty-five, $600 at age forty-five and so on, leaving that much less money to be added to your cash value.

Even while the cost of insuring you has steadily increased, your premiums remain level and fixed, since your life expectancy is already figured into the policy. Just note that your premiums can go up in a universal life policy, where you can increase or decrease your payments. If you underpay the premium in the early years of the policy, you may face higher premiums later to make up any shortfall in your mortality expense.

While all this is going on, the cash value of your policy is increasing each year as the investments in which it is placed gain interest. Insurance experts say a traditional whole or universal life insurance policy can earn around six percent per year, and many companies guarantee a return of at least four percent. Variable life insurance can earn more, since your money is tied to the performance of stocks, bonds or mutual funds, but can also lose cash value if those investments fail.

At your death, your beneficiaries receive the death benefit, but not the remaining cash value. This is called an option A death benefit. With an option B death benefit, you can arrange to have the cash value added to the death benefit.

How do I access money in my cash value account?

You take out a loan against your policy and pay it back with interest, depending on current interest rates. This has the advantage of paying yourself back with interest, which adds to your cash value, although you are not required to repay the loan. However, any unpaid balance on the loan will eventually be deducted from your death benefit.

Besides taking a loan, you can simply withdraw money from your cash value. Like an unpaid loan, this reduces your death benefit by a corresponding amount; exactly how much varies by policy. Make sure you know before you take the money out. In some cases, withdrawing part of your cash value could just about wipe out any death benefit from the policy. Under some whole life policies, the death benefit is lowered by twice the value of what you withdraw or more.

Even though you can use the money in your policy, it is not without some cost to you, your beneficiaries and your estate. Talk to your advisor and check your policy documents to find the cost of loans and withdrawals.

Are there any tax consequences with cash value policies?

Gains in the cash value portion of your policy are taxable when they are withdrawn and are tax-deferred as long as they remain untouched. If you withdraw less than the total amount of premiums you have paid into the policy, you do not face any taxes. Typically, the cash value will not exceed total paid-in premiums for at least ten years with the average whole life insurance policy, and at least fifteen years with the typical universal life, depending on the amount of premium payments you have made.

Another tax consequence you could face is if you take a loan against your cash value, but surrender the policy or allow it to lapse before the loan is completely repaid. You would then have to pay taxes on the difference between the outstanding loan amount and the total of premiums you have paid into the policy.

Cash value policies can give you the option of providing insurance protection for your family at a predictable, level premium during your lifetime, with some financial flexibility you can utilize the cash value when financial opportunities or emergencies arise.

What kinds of situations are best suited to cash value policies?

Cash value policies are worth considering for individuals who have high incomes and the need for insurance throughout their lives. While the cash value is not as completely accessible as in a savings account and may not perform as well as other individual investments, the combination of level premiums, tax deferral and the flexibility of accessing the cash value through loans or withdrawals needs to be considered as a total package.

In other instances, if you have a large estate and grown children, you can take a whole life policy and use the cash value to pay for policy premiums after you retire. While that reduces the death benefit, it still provides money your beneficiaries can use to pay estate taxes.

What about credit life insurance?

Credit life insurance covers some specific loan or line of credit and is designed to pay off the balance to the creditor if you die. In general, you should not buy a separate credit life policy when getting an auto loan, for instance, but instead factor the loan amount into your current liabilities when determining your overall coverage. Credit life policies tend to be expensive for the coverage they provide. You should never be forced to buy credit life insurance in order to get a loan and should report any lenders who do so to your state insurance commissioner.

Many of your credit cards may be issued with a type of credit life insurance already in effect. Check your card agreements. If they provide coverage, make sure you do not include those charge card balances in calculating your insurance needs.

How often should I review my insurance coverage?

Financial planners generally advise you to review your life insurance needs when you buy any new policy as well as on a regular basis throughout your life. Depending on your changing circumstances, you may not have all the coverage you need at some point in your life, while you may be grossly overinsured at other times. Their recommendations include:

- Schedule a routine insurance checkup with your financial planners and insurance providers once a year,

- Take the time to shop and compare identical products and services, since rates can vary widely from company to company,

- Read your policies carefully and be sure you understand them.

The best move is to make sure you shop around and match the best coverage for you and your family with the appropriate types of policies and levels of coverage. Insurance experts note that consumers can save hundreds or even thousands of dollars just by taking these simple steps.

For example, if you are interested only in providing financial protection for a young family, then you need to reexamine your needs and coverage when your children are grown. On the other hand, if you plan to leave assets for your family, to pay estate taxes, have your own business or want to leave money to benefit a charity or other organization, you want to make life insurance a bigger part of your overall financial plan.

How do I claim benefits from a missing policy?

If a relative or anyone else dies and you think you are the beneficiary of a current, or even old, insurance policy, you can still collect, but you have to do your homework. The good news is that even if you do not identify the policy until years later, insurers will honor the policy. The bad news is that if payments have lapsed, the benefits you receive could be severely reduced.

Your first step is to check with the deceased's estate, late and former attorneys, accountants or other financial professionals that might have been involved, as well as checking safety deposit boxes, personal files or even canceled checks to see if payments were being made on any policies. You also can check with former employers to see if the insured person had a group policy through his or her workplace.

Once you have identified the policy, the first question is whether it was term or permanent life. If it was term, you need to see whether the policy was expired or was still in effect at the time of death. If it was in effect, you simply file a claim and collect the death benefit. If it expired, you receive no payment at all.

If you find that any coverage was under a permanent life policy, you need to find out the status of the policy. If it was fully paid at the time of death, then it is still in force and a full death benefit will be paid, along with interest if the death occurred some time ago.

If the premiums were not up to date, then the policy has lapsed. When that happens, insurers may convert the policy either to *extended term* insurance or to *reduced paid up* status. Under extended term, the insurers take the cash value of the policy and use it to purchase short-term life insurance to replace the lapsed policy. Under reduced paid up status, the insurer typically keeps the policy in force, but with a lowered final death benefit.

If the policy has lapsed and the extended term period ends before the insured dies, the policy ends and the insurer pays nothing. If the insured person dies during the extended term period, the death benefit is paid. In cases where the policy lapses because the insured person died and stopped making payments, the full death benefit is paid, whether or not the term is extended.

What happens if no one comes forward to claim my insurance death benefit?

Insurance companies usually send letters trying to contact you if you stop making payments, and if they do not get any response, your policy lapses. If no beneficiary ever comes forward to collect, after several years any cash value is transferred to the state where the insurance policy was purchased.

If your insurer knows you died but cannot locate one of your beneficiaries, the death benefit is turned over to the state where the policy was purchased, after three to five years, and it becomes part of the state's unclaimed property fund. Each state has its own database of unclaimed rent deposits, utility refunds, insurance benefits and other uncollected money owed to consumers. In general, however, very few policies are turned over to the individual states. Most companies have their own procedures for finding beneficiaries who have not made claims.

One final place to check on a missing insurance policy is with the Medical Information Bureau, which tracks insurers' requests for medical information within the past several years. Record searches can be requested through the Disclosure Office of the bureau.

How much life insurance do I really need?

There are a lot of old rules of thumb you might hear, and they are all wrong, according to financial advisors. Your best approach is a simple process that takes the time to look at your finances and project current and future needs of your family members, taking inflation and desired lifestyles into account.

First, make sure you do not fall for any of these old rules that are sure to leave you overinsured and wasting money or, worse, underinsured and risking your family's future:

- Multiply your annual salary by seven or eight. This simple formula ignores future obligations and individual needs,

- Cover your 'human life value': This means figuring how much money you will make between now and retirement and factoring in inflation and salary increases. This method also ignores your beneficiaries' needs and will probably cause you to overinsure yourself,

- Cover all your current debts: This means you purchase only enough life insurance to cover your mortgage balance, car loan, credit card debts and others, but does not provide any income for beneficiaries, such as for college costs for children.

Instead, insurance experts and financial planners say the best way to predict an accurate assessment of your life insurance needs is to add up your family's short-term and long-term needs and then subtract your resources to arrive at how much coverage you need to fill that gap. It is a simple formula that is very accurate, and which you can apply at any time during your life to gauge just how much life insurance you should be carrying at any one time.

The first part of the process is to total up your current short-term financial needs if you were to die tomorrow. This would include funeral and estate and probate expenses, along with any last medical and hospital bills, as well as outstanding debts and your cash reserve to cover medical or other financial emergencies. Of course, you have to estimate medical and hospital expenses based on your current state of health.

You then list your long-term debts, such as your mortgage. If you have children, or plan to have them, include the cost of a college education. A good estimate is the current average for state and private schools available from the College Board.

College costs have risen about five percent annually in recent years, so you can plug that inflation number into any one of a number of online calculators to determine the future cost for each year of school in the future.

The final step in calculating needs is to determine your family's annual household expenses, including utility bills, home maintenance, food, healthcare and other day-to-day spending. Using other online calculators, you can factor in the rate of inflation for however many years you determine you will have to cover family expenses. Adding up these three figures gives you a total of financial resources you want to leave behind.

Now it is time to determine what financial resources you have to put toward meeting those needs if something tragic should happen tomorrow. Total up all your available savings, stocks, bonds, mutual funds and other accounts, as well as any existing life insurance (such as group life through your employer). Also visit the Social Security Administration's website to estimate what benefits your family could claim.

Finally, add in your salary, figuring five percent compounded interest rate for each future year if you expect regular salary increases. For all of this you should include only current assets that are in cash or can be quickly converted, such as savings bonds, and not home equity or other assets that will be needed to support your family.

Subtracting the total of your current resources from your projected expenses gives you the amount of money you want life insurance to provide for your family at this point in your life. If it seems dauntingly high, do not give up. Rerun your assessment, looking at where you can budget less money or find other alternatives, such as assuming your children will take college loans or otherwise pay for some part of their own education.

What is involved with giving my life insurance to charity?

Whether it is for purely charitable reasons, to take advantage of tax deductions or a combination of those motives, the first step is to check that the charity is legally registered as a nonprofit organization and that its administration is interested in receiving a gift of life insurance, since not all groups are experienced or interested in accepting insurance as a donation. The next step, if you want to be able to declare this as a charitable donation, is to make the charity not only the beneficiary of the policy, but also the owner of the policy.

If you donate term insurance, you can claim the premiums as a tax deduction. Donating term insurance also raises the risk that the policy term will expire before any death benefit is paid out, leaving your designated charity with nothing.

If you donate a whole life policy, the charity can make use of the cash value as well as the death benefit, which is guaranteed in permanent life insurance policies as long as they are not allowed to lapse. In this case, you can take a tax deduction on both the cash value of the policy as well as the premiums you pay.

While most charitable groups would be happier receiving a donation now instead of waiting until you die, universities and other large charitable organizations do have financial managers who can make good use of a donated policy, usually by investing the money from your cash value policy immediately in higher-paying investments, rather than waiting to claim your death benefit. Of course, if you donate a term policy they just have to wait for the money, as well as finding out if you outlive the policy.

What about insurance for my children?

Before you buy insurance coverage for a child, think about why you are buying it. Aside from the devastating emotional turmoil, the loss of a child will not generally place a financial hardship on most families. On the positive side, insuring a child may guarantee insurability when they become an adult, which may be of value to some families.

In addition, insurance could cover any medical or funeral expenses if something tragic should occur to the youngster.

You should stop and look carefully at any special features of insurance for children, whether it is a special opportunity to add a child to your policy or a policy that gives your child an option to purchase more insurance on his or her own when they are older. In the first case, you should add insurance for a child only when it makes sense and to cover real, expected expenses, and only if you do not already have an emergency fund that will do the job. In the second, healthy young adults will not have any problem obtaining reasonably priced insurance on their own when they leave the nest.

What about insurance for my children at college?

As with younger kids, college age children probably are not going to need a lot of life insurance. They will not have many debts, dependents or estate issues, and any income they receive usually goes toward their own expenses and education rather than contributing to the family's cash flow.

Unlike younger children, those in college face a lot of other liabilities once they are on campus, from health insurance to auto coverage and more. College students do not only have higher auto accident rates than the general population, they also are heavily involved in campus sports activities and can be easy and often naive or careless targets for burglars and thieves. In addition, once your child turns eighteen, he or she probably is not eligible for coverage on your standard health insurance, unless enrolled as a full time student. So, as with any other significant change in your life, sending your kids off to college should prompt an insurance review, not only so you can adjust your coverage but also to assess their insurance needs to prevent their problems from becoming an expensive blow that drains their student checking accounts or puts a big hit on yours.

Auto insurance: Car insurance is the responsibility of the owner, so if the student is taking a family car to college (or at least one still registered in your name), you have already put your student on your auto policy as an additional driver. However, you will have to let the insurer know that the car is being taken away from home. In addition, if the college is out of state, you may have to adjust coverage to meet the new state's requirements.

If your child owns the car outright, then they probably already have their own policy and have to inform the insurance company that the car is going with them to State U and arrange any out-of-state requirements. If the car is new, you should decide what makes the most sense when it comes to register the vehicle. Your insurance will certainly be cheaper if your youngster is not listed as a driver, but your child is likely to pay higher rates as a young driver. You have to decide not only what is less expensive, but also how much responsibility you want your young driver to shoulder for their own vehicle at school.

Note: if your child does not take a car to college but moves more than one hundred miles away, let your auto insurer know. It may lower your premium, since your son or daughter is less likely to be driving any of the family cars.

Health insurance: Your health insurance may cover your kids at college, provided they are full-time students and have not reached any age limit specified in your policy. Sometimes the limit is as young as eighteen years old, although many health plans place the cutoff at age twenty-three. Whatever the limit, once children reach that age the policy will not cover them. For youngsters who are not attending school full-time, the cutoff age is likely to be eighteen. Be sure to check with your benefits administrator, insurance agent or insurance company to see what the rules are for each of your children's individual situations.

If your child is not going to be covered by your own health policy, you have several options, including paying to continue their coverage or enrolling your student in a college or university health plan.

If your child loses eligibility to stay on your plan, they are eligible for limited COBRA benefits, just as you would be if you left your job. Under federal law, your child can purchase thirty-six more months of insurance coverage through COBRA. It may be expensive, but can be worth it if your child has an existing serious medical condition. It continues the same standard of coverage and can help the child get insurance later under the federal Health Insurance Portability and Accountability Act, which can keep them from being excluded from obtaining insurance because of pre-existing medical conditions.

Besides age eligibility, make sure your college student will be within any geographical limits placed on coverage, which is often included in HMO and other managed care plans, and that your child will be able to find doctors and other medical providers approved by the plan near their school.

If your student does not continue on your plan, check into health insurance offered by the college or university, which usually includes basic but affordable coverage. You also should see whether any new or existing policy requires supplement coverage if your child plays athletics or takes part in other risky activities that might not be covered under a general policy, such as skiing or hang gliding. Finally, students who spend time abroad should consider traveler's health insurance or make sure they have policies that will cover them while overseas.

What other kinds of insurance issues should I consider when my child goes to college?

Besides health and auto concerns, check your general homeowner's policy to see how it will cover any property your student takes to college, such as electronic or photography equipment, computers, jewelry and other personal property. You can purchase riders of varying amounts or individual policies that will replace a lost, stolen or damaged computer, for example.

Whether your student lives in an off-campus apartment or a dorm, look into renter's insurance to cover personal property and liability. Such policies are not that expensive and some can be shared between roommates. Otherwise, insist that renter's insurance be part of any roommate's responsibility. Document personal belongings with an insurance inventory.

What about other types of insurance coverage?

Beyond life insurance, determining insurance coverage for your home, auto, health and other personal property is a somewhat easier proposition. You are not worried about providing income for loved ones, managing estate taxes, providing benefits to charities or looking for policies with cash value features. Instead, this insurance simply acts to protect you from a sudden loss if you have to replace or repair damaged property, such as a car that is wrecked or a home that is hit by a windstorm.

Nonetheless, homeowner's and other insurance policies can be complicated, and if you make a mistake in purchasing coverage you usually will not find out until after any accident or disaster, when you go to file a claim. Pay attention to coverage limits, replacement cost rules and other aspects of your policies, as well as cost. Comparison shop and get a good understanding of what you are buying to help save you money on policies now and disappointment later.

What do I need to know about purchasing homeowner's insurance?

You have many options in purchasing homeowner's coverage, ranging from simple dwelling policies that cover only the basic structure of your home to policies that combine several types of coverage.

Dwelling: This aspect of your policy pays for damage to your house and any outbuildings, such as detached garages and storage sheds,

Personal property: This coverage reimburses you when household items such as furniture, clothing and appliances are damaged, stolen or destroyed,

Liability: This protects you against being sued for someone else's injury or property damage. A typical homeowner's policy automatically provides some level of coverage, but can be extended for an extra premium. Liability coverage prevents you from having to take cash from bank accounts, investments or to liquidate other assets if you have to pay a legal claim,

Medical payments: This covers medical bills for people hurt while on your property, and may cover some injuries that happen away from your home, such as your dog biting someone. Again, most policies start with a basic amount that can be extended for an additional premium,

Loss of use: This part of the policy covers living expenses if your home is too damaged to live in during repairs. Typical policies pay up to twenty percent of the amount for which your house is insured.

What kinds of problems do most policies cover?

Typically, there are several types of general policies that are sold in each state, with the requirements varying according to where you live. In most cases, you will find that basic homeowner's policies will cover damage and losses resulting from:

- Fire and lightning,

- Damage from aircraft and vehicles,

- Vandalism and malicious mischief,

- Theft,

- Explosion,

- Riot and civil commotion,

- Smoke,

- Windstorm, hurricane, and hail, or

- Sudden and accidental water damage.

That covers a lot, but not everything. For instance, in recent years mold problems have become a big point of contention, and many policies do not specifically cover mold remediation beyond repairing water damage. Other losses that most policies do not cover include:

- Flood,

- Earthquakes,

- Damage from termites,

- Damage from insects, rats or mice,

- Freezing pipes while your house is unoccupied (except in some cases),

- Wind or hail damage to trees and shrubs,

- Losses if your house is vacant for sixty days or more,

- Wear and tear or maintenance, or

- Water damage resulting from continuous and repeated seepage.

You need to be very specific and ask detailed questions when buying your policy. For example, if you live in a coastal area, your home may be covered for hurricane and windstorm damage, but not for any flooding that will follow the increased rainfall that comes with the storm. In fact, for any kind of rising water damage you need to purchase a separate flood insurance policy, sold by most agents under a program maintained by the federal government.

Another example comes from the Texas Department of Insurance, which notes that in parts of that state with its history of hail storms, some insurers limit policies to 'actual cash value coverage' for roofs instead of full replacement cost. Rather than replacing a damaged roof, you would receive a payment covering the damage minus depreciation on the roof, depending on its age and condition, leaving you to make up the rest of the replacement cost.

What is the difference between policies offering 'guaranteed replacement' and those that offer 'extended replacement' for my home?

This is a recent twist in homeowner's insurance that you should be sure to understand. Guaranteed replacement is designed, as the name implies, to pay the replacement cost of rebuilding your home should it be destroyed, no matter what the final expense and how much it differs from the original assessment of your property and the value listed on your policy. Since the late 1990s, though, many insurers have offered the similar-sounding 'extended replacement' coverage, which pays only the amount listed on your policy plus some additional amount, typically twenty to twenty-five percent more. Extended policies offer cheaper premiums, but could leave you under insured after a disaster, especially if building prices in your area have risen substantially. You also should check the value set on your home in your policy. A lower value keeps your premiums lower, but leaves you unable to completely rebuild if the home is destroyed.

As part of buying any new homeowner's policy and during your regular insurance checkup, you should double-check the replacement value of your home and the terms of the policy. According to several insurance experts, nearly two-thirds of the homes in the US are under insured by more than twenty-five percent, and many are insured for less than half of their replacement cost today.

Besides guaranteed and replacement cost, some policies offer replacement cost only up to a dollar limit specified in your coverage. Other policies offer only actual cash value coverage, which is the replacement cost of your home minus depreciation. In a case where your home was destroyed, actual cash value coverage might leave you unable to completely rebuild it.

In the case of a partial loss to your property, check your state's rules on coverage. In some cases, you must insure your home for a certain percentage of its replacement cost to collect full payment for other types of damage, such as a tree falling on your roof. Otherwise, your insurer covers only part of the damage.

To determine your current coverage, check the Declarations Page on the front of your policy, which should state how much coverage you have, and discuss any questions or changes with your insurance agent or company representative. Again, check on the specific rules in your state. For example, in Texas, if your home is completely destroyed in a fire, state law requires the insurance company to pay the full amount of the policy, even if that is more than the replacement cost of the house.

What about the contents of my home?

A typical policy automatically covers most of your household contents, such as furniture, clothes, appliances and other personal belongings, up to a set percentage of the amount for which your house is insured. You can opt to buy higher coverage for more money, or you may want to purchase specific additional riders to extend coverage on jewelry, computers, hobby equipment or other items. Generally, this kind of automatic coverage pays only the actual cash value (the item's replacement cost, minus depreciation) of damaged, stolen or destroyed household goods. Again, you should be able to buy replacement cost coverage that will pay for a new item by upping your premium. In some cases, the insurer can offer to replace the items instead of paying you cash, but usually that choice is yours.

How do I prove what personal property I own?

Although many homeowners fail to do this, you should compile and then regularly update at least a basic inventory of your home's contents for insurance property. Besides a written list, with several copies filed in safe places, including at least one in a safety deposit box or some other location outside the home, you can document your home's contents with still photographs or even a narrated video or recorded DVD.

Insurance experts recommend that your household inventory lists each item, its value and serial number. Go through each room of your home, including closets and drawers, and do not forget your garage and any storage sheds or other outbuildings. Keep receipts for major items in a fireproof place, along with your inventory.

What if I live in something besides a regular single-family home?

You will find you can get coverage for just about any type of property, but the specifics will change from category to category. Here are the major types of residential insurance:

Renter's insurance: Your landlord's insurance will not cover your personal property. Instead, renter's insurance covers your belongings, gives you liability protection and can pay extra living expenses if a fire or other disaster forces you to move temporarily from your rented home.

Condominiums: Condominium insurance is similar in coverage to renter's insurance, but also adds coverage to repair damage to improvements, additions and alterations to the condominium unit.

Townhouses: Townhouses may be insured by either an individual homeowner's policy or an association master policy. If a townhouse is owner-occupied and the townhouse association does not have a master policy on the building, you can purchase a homeowner's policy on your individual unit. If the association has a master policy, you should get a separate policy to insure your personal property.

Mobile homes: Mobile homes without wheels and resting on blocks or a permanent foundation qualify for a homeowner's policy in some states and under certain conditions. At other times, mobile homes are insured by some type of auto coverage for mobile homes used as residences.

Farm and ranch owners: In some states, farm and ranch owner's policies cover homes outside city limits or in agricultural areas on land used for farming and raising livestock. You can pay extra and get coverage for certain farm equipment and outbuildings.

How should I go about shopping for homeowner's insurance?

You will find that rates for different policies vary widely among companies, so it pays to shop around. Insurance regulators recommend these steps to make sure you get your money's worth when buying insurance:

- Decide before shopping what are the specific types and amounts of coverage you need,

- Buy a policy with the highest deductible you can afford. Even though you have to pay more out of your own pocket if you file a claim, a higher deductible lowers your premium,

- Check with several companies and different agents for price quotes. When looking at rates, make sure you compare apples to apples by getting similar policies with the same coverage. Individual states' insurance commissioners or local consumer affairs offices often publish rate guides and lists of annual premiums to help you shop,

- Do not lie or mislead the agent when getting a price quote or applying for insurance. Incorrect information could lead you to be underinsured, or provoke a denial or cancellation of coverage,

- Other than price, consider the insurer's financial rating and complaint record. Purchase insurance only from licensed companies and agents. You can check out companies and agents with your state insurance office,

- Remember to ask if there are any discounts that might apply to your situation. Some discounts are required by certain individual states, while others are optional with companies. For example, installing smoke alarms and detectors, fire extinguishers and other safety equipment can often get you a discount.

What do I have to do to file a claim?

Filing a claim with your insurance company on anything ranging from a small accident to a major disaster can be a lengthy, stressful and sometimes difficult process. The following checklist from the Foundation for Taxpayer and Consumer Rights explains how you can protect your rights under your homeowner's insurance if a fire, earthquake or other natural disaster causes you a loss. While this applies to the worst cases, much of this applies just as readily to collecting after an automobile fender-bender as much as after a major tragedy.

Be prepared: If you have the advantage of knowing that a threatening condition is looming, such as an approaching wildfire or hurricane watch, follow suggestions or orders from local public safety officials to evacuate your home.

Take your insurance records: If a disaster strikes and you must leave your home, take these files with you. This will help you fill out a complete claim and make it easier to document what you own and the condition of your property. If your safety is at immediate risk, do not worry about your possessions or anything else on this checklist. Protect your family and pets and get out. Let your insurance policy take care of the things you can replace.

After a disaster strikes: Read your insurance policy and know your rights. Insurance policies are very complicated, but try to understand as much as you can about what it covers, what is excluded and to what you are entitled. If possible contact your state insurance commissioner for any help or advice and to find out your exact rights under your state laws to a fair claim settlement, such as what specific regulations insurers must follow when handling your claim.

Contact your insurance company to make a claim: Don't delay, even if you have not figured out exactly what your damage or property loss will total. Inform your insurer, authorized agent or broker in writing immediately that you have sustained a loss. If you have lost your insurance documents, request a replacement copy. Ask your insurance agent or company for a copy of your policy and Declarations Page.

Take a video or pictures of all damaged property: Document your losses as much as possible.

Take detailed notes: Every time you call, write or speak to anybody affiliated with an insurance company, get their name and phone number. Write down the date and time of the communication, what you said and what they said. Do not assume you will remember a conversation or that they will.

Keep a copy of all paperwork: The general rule is that you must get everything in writing and put everything you request or information you provide in writing – *everything*. Then make a copy of everything you sign and/or send (e-mail, regular mail, etc.).

Keep a receipt of every penny you must spend as a result of the disaster: For example, if you are forced to evacuate, keep records of purchases of food, lodging, clothing, etc.

Try to protect your remaining property to prevent further damage: Do what you can, without jeopardizing your safety, to prevent further damage or losses. For example, contact utilities to shut off water and gas mains. Your insurance company might not cover post-disaster damage that you could have reasonably prevented.

Make a detailed list of every item damaged: Do not leave anything out. File a claim for every item. You will not get compensation for anything for which you do not submit a claim. Contact your credit card companies and retailers to help reconstruct purchases and identify costs for replacing lost items. Family members, friends and neighbors can help you create a full description of your losses.

Estimate the value of your damaged or destroyed property: Estimate what it would cost to replace and what it was worth before it was damaged. Why the two different numbers? Insurance policies offer different kinds of coverage. Contractors can provide you with an estimate, and the insurance company will appoint an adjustor to handle your claim. The adjustor is paid by the insurance company and works for the company, not for you. Moreover, the adjustor is not an expert on your policy and may not know what it covers. If you think the adjustor is wrong, you may reject the estimates and demand reconsideration. You can also hire a 'public adjustor' to help you out.

Have your valuables appraised independently: For antiques, art and other valuable items, you should get your own appraisal to compare with the insurance company's assessment.

Get insurance company approval for repairs: Do not start repairing or replacing property or throw away damaged property without your insurance company adjustor's approval.

> The guarantees are backed by the claims paying ability of the issuing insurance company. There are no guarantees that this will keep pace with the rate of inflation.

Take your time: Do not be pressured into agreeing to low-ball estimates, repairs or rebuilding. Give yourself time to review the proposed claims settlement and determine whether it is fair and acceptable to you.

Do not sign releases or waivers until you know your rights: If you have an undisputed claim, you should not have to sign a release to settle. If you are asked to sign a release, find out why and be cautious about signing away your rights.

Always be firm but polite. Know your rights and insist that the insurance company meet its legal obligations to you. The calmer you remain the better off you will be, emotionally and financially, when it is all through.

If you have a dispute with your insurance company: Be prepared to fight for a fair settlement and get help if you need it. If your insurer is not offering a fair settlement, you can try to resolve the dispute yourself by working your way up the chain of command of the insurance company. Involve your insurance agent and broker on your behalf, but remember, they have a long financial relationship with the insurance company. If necessary, call the office of the president of the insurance company.

If the dispute is serious, or you are unable to resolve it to your satisfaction, contact a lawyer. Many lawyers work on a contingency basis: you pay the lawyer nothing unless and until he or she succeeds in obtaining what you are owed, and then the lawyer takes a cut. Insurers can be made to pay extra – *punitive damages* – if they deliberately deny payment to which you are entitled. Unfortunately, some unscrupulous insurers will not pay you in full unless they believe you will take legal action.

If you need a lawyer, public adjustor or contractor, shop around: Make sure they are properly licensed and check references. Interview several candidates before making a selection. Choose someone who has been personally recommended to you by someone you trust. State laws provide protection when you hire these professionals.

Keep it honest: Insurance fraud is a serious crime. Never attempt to make a claim for property you did not own, or falsify the value of a possession.

How do I go about choosing an insurance company or insurance agent?

What you are looking for is a relationship where you will receive appropriate types of coverage with values and limits that will protect your assets while not causing you to pay too much for your policies, along with a company that will respond quickly and fairly when you have a problem or need to file a claim.

The first step is to visit your state's department of insurance website or contact the department by phone. Many states publish *consumer complaint ratios* for all companies offering policies in that state. You want to check out this ratio, which tells you how many complaints an insurance company received per thousand claims filed. You can use the complaint ratios to screen insurers that will offer you good prices on your premium quotes versus the number of complaints they have received. If your state does not maintain a public list of complaint ratios, experts advise surveying the ratios from several other states. Do look at more than just one, since insurance offerings and regulations can vary widely from state to state.

Another step is to check out the annual ratings of insurers compiled and published by J.D. Power and Associates. This firm collects data from individual policyholders nationwide and rates them according to coverage options, price, claims handling, satisfaction with company representatives and the overall experience. You can view these results on the web at *www.jdpowers.com*. The firm publishes an annual survey of major auto and homeowner's insurers, as well as other consumer companies such as homebuilders and mortgage providers.

You also want to make sure your potential insurer is financially sound. You can check a firm's financial condition by looking at either the A.M. Best or Standard & Poor's ratings. Both companies publish financial strength ratings for all insurance companies that calculate the firm's financial ability to pay claims. While most large and well known insurers are financially sound, if you are using a small local or regional insurer it is a good idea to check up on them.

A.M. Best ratings are ranked as letter grades going from A++ (the highest) to D. Some companies may earn a rating of E (indicating regulatory action regarding the company's solvency), F (in liquidation) and S (suspended). Insurance experts advise that you limit your dealings to companies that have at least a B+ rating.

The Standard & Poor's ratings range from AAA (the highest) to CC, although some insurance companies receive ratings of R (under regulatory supervision) and NR, which means 'not rated.' The letter grades can be enhanced with a plus or minus mark. Experts advise that you choose companies that are rated BBB or better.

Should I use an insurance agent?

If you are just buying a simple auto policy or basic homeowner's coverage, you are equally well off buying either directly from a company or working through an insurance agent. If you want more than basic coverage, though, and need advice relating to tax matters, estate planning or other complicated issues, and want a professional who can work with other financial advisors, you may want to consider dealing with an insurance agent.

There are two kinds of agents. A so-called *captive agent* represents only one insurance company, usually a major insurer of whom you have heard. In fact, even if you purchase insurance directly from some big firm websites, you are still assigned to a local agent. There also are independent insurance agents, or brokers, who represent several insurance companies. These agents may have a wider variety of policies and types of coverage they can discuss with you, and they are not tied to any one particular company. While many insurance agents are paid by commission for selling policies, some independent agents charge fees for their advisory services. Most qualified agents are typically certified by Independent Insurance Agents of America or Professional Insurance Agents (PIA).

What are some independent sources for information about insurance?

Besides your state or local office of consumer affairs and your state insurance commissioner's office, there are two well known groups offering information about insurance and purchasing policies. Consult the Insurance Consumer Advocate Network (I-CAN) on the web at *www.ican2000.com*, where you can subscribe to print or online newsletters and mailings, or the Foundation for Taxpayer & Consumer Rights, a California-based consumer advocacy group on the web at *www.consumerwatchdog.org* or by phone, 310-392-0522.

ANNUITIES

What do I need to know about annuities?

An annuity is a kind of investment insurance hybrid where you pay in money either in a lump sum or over time and receive a stream of payments over time. This kind of contract is useful for retirement planning, tax planning and as a way to promote savings for investors who might otherwise be undisciplined about setting retirement money aside.

There are two phases in an annuity's existence: Accumulation and distribution. During the accumulation phase, you invest either payments over time or a lump sum, with your money earning a rate of return. Later, you move into the distribution phase, where you begin to receive a regular stream of income from the contract, which is called annuitization.

Alternatively, you can simply withdraw interest and possibly principal from the contract periodically. In this case, you would lose tax advantages and guarantees that would be available from annuitization. With fixed annuities, the death benefit will equal your principal and accumulated interest. With a variable annuity the death benefit is generally the greater of your account value or the premiums you have paid. As contracts and death benefits vary greatly, please carefully read your contract documents and consult with your financial advisor. For example, some annuity contracts impose surrender charges at the death of the beneficiary, while some do not.

If you have annuitized your contract, the death benefit is generally a continuation of the annuity payments as annuitized to the beneficiary. However, a life only annuity payment ceases at the death of the annuitant, and no further payments will go to the beneficiary. For this reason, life only annuities are generally limited to very specific estate planning purposes. Again, check with your advisor.

What about taxes and annuities?

Although the money in an annuity grows tax-deferred, you do have to pay taxes on the payments you receive at your ordinary income tax rate. Like an IRA, this offers the advantage of having the money that would go toward taxes compound over many years in your account, especially during your peak earning years when you will be in the highest tax rate. Then, at retirement, when you have less income and may be in a lower tax bracket, you are taxed only on the money actually paid out, leaving the rest of your annuity investment to continue growing to provide some inflation protection.

If you die before you start receiving annuity payments, the death benefit goes directly to your beneficiary rather than passing through your estate. The beneficiary then has to pay tax on the proceeds at his or her ordinary income tax rate.

When should I consider an annuity?

In general, before you go shopping for an annuity you should already be maxing out contributions to other retirement plans, such as Individual Retirement Accounts (IRA)s, employer sponsored 401(k) and 401(b) accounts, Keoghs and others. These other plans share many of the same tax-deferral benefits of an annuity and are less expensive, or even free, to set up. Younger investors also tend to avoid annuities because of the ten percent penalty tax if you withdraw money from your annuity before age 59 ½ for reasons other than death or disability.

Financial planners say the best time to consider an annuity is around age fifty-five. At this time you are in the last phase of retirement planning, although many retirees who need income right away opt for purchasing an immediate annuity, which starts making payments as soon as you invest in the contract. This can be especially useful if you have received a lump-sum distribution from a pension or other retirement plan.

Are there different types of annuities?

Like any kind of investment product there are multiple options, but in general there are three kinds of annuities:

Fixed annuity: You invest money that earns a guaranteed, fixed rate during the first phase of the annuity, giving you fixed payments when you start to collect. This gives you little risk, but means you sacrifice potential gains if stocks or other investment vehicles perform better than expected.

Variable annuity: You invest money in one or more subaccounts, which function much like mutual funds. Like a fund, each subaccount will have its own risk profile, running the gamut from aggressive growth stock funds to stable bond funds. Variable annuities offer you the chance to realize investment gains rather than guaranteed returns, but you also face the risk that the investments do poorly and that you will lose money. You also may have to pay to move money between subaccounts. When you start receiving payments from a variable annuity, they will fluctuate along with the performance of your investments unless you purchase an annuity with *fixed annuitization*, in which you receive fixed payments. The insurance or investment company recalculates your payments each year based on the performance of your investments.

Equity-indexed annuity: This is a lot like buying an index mutual fund. In an equity-indexed annuity, your money goes into a fixed account where you earn additional interest based on the performance of a particular stock index, such as the Standard & Poor's 500 Index, the Dow Jones Industrial Average or others. This gives you the guarantee of a fixed annuity with the upside potential of a variable contract. The gains, however, are smaller than in a variable annuity, and depend on the particular indexing method used in your annuity. Payments you receive from an equity-indexed annuity are fixed.

What kind of indexing methods are used in equity-indexed annuities?

These kinds of annuities are fairly recent, having been introduced in the last ten years, and many investors may not be totally familiar with them. There are many ways insurance companies calculate your index-linked returns. According to the experts at the Insure.com website, these are the most widely used methods you will run acrossss:

The European, or point-to-point, method: This method's name comes from European stock markets, where options can be exercised only on their expiration date. This indexing approach divides the index on the maturity date by the index on the issue date and subtracts one from the result; other indexing methods use this same formula, with different data points. This ignores all the fluctuations between start and finish, making this method the simplest both to understand and to calculate.

The Asianing method: With its name originating from Asian stock markets, this approach involves averaging several points of the index to establish the beginning and/or ending index. This method can help shield consumers from the risk of a market decline on the maturity date. Some companies take an average of the twelve monthly indices to establish the policy's maturity index level.

The look-back or high-water-mark method: Another popular approach is where the company notes the index level on each policy anniversary. The highest of these is then taken and figured as the index level on the maturity date.

The low-water-mark method: This uses the lowest of the indices on each of the policy anniversaries before maturity as the level of the index at issue. This method tends to lessen the risk of market decline.

The annual reset, cliquet or ratchet method: This is among the most complicated indexing approach. The increase in the index is calculated each policy year by comparing the indices on the beginning and ending anniversaries. Any resulting decreases are ignored. Appreciation is figured by adding or compounding the increases for each policy year.

I know an annuity is a long-term contract, but what if I need to get out?

Most financial planners strongly advise against getting out of your contract, or surrendering your annuity. Annuities really are for the long term, and the earlier you try to end the contract the more it will cost you. Most companies charge a surrender fee if you quit your annuity within the first seven to eight years of owning it, which is called a surrender period.

Some insurers allow you to access some of your annuity money without surrendering your contract. Typically, they charge some percentage of your investment, about ten to fifteen percent, under certain circumstances, such as serious illness or disabily. When the surrender period ends you can withdraw any amount of money from your annuity, subject to taxes and the ten percent penalty for withdrawals before you are age 59 ½.

What about waivers?

If you are disabled, need to go to a nursing home or become hospitalized, a growing number of annuities offer waivers that allow you to access money in your annuity without triggering the usual surrender fees.

The conditions of these waivers vary from company to company, with differing limits and thresholds. For instance, one insurer might require a ninety day nursing home confinement before your benefits are activated, while another might call for sixty days. In addition, one company may consider you disabled if you are unable to work in any occupation, while another may require only that you are unable to work in your current occupation.

The most commonly found waiver in annuities sold today is the death benefit waiver. As discussed earlier, this allows the beneficiary to receive your annuity if you die during the accumulation phase, before you begin receiving payments. Some annuities also offer waivers if you need to enter a nursing home and remain there for several months, or under certain circumstances if you become terminally ill. Under both waivers, the insurer will want proof from your doctor. Other waivers include those that allow for disabilities, and some that apply if you become unemployed.

A policyholder must understand that replacement can include . . .

- New sales loads
- New company rights to challenge a death claim during contestability and suicide periods
- Changes in age or health that increase the risk
- Changes in policy loan rates
- Less favorable non-forfeiture values and guarantees
- Loss of grandfathered rights
- Gain in policy values for income tax purposes
- Potential surrender charges for replacing the policy

In other words, taken together, whatever financial gains might be anticipated by the replacement of one policy for another may also involve significant trade-offs. The loss of these may outweigh the potential gains.

In most annuities, these waivers are built into the contract and there is no extra charge for them; however, there can be tax consequences that apply to the withdrawals, depending on your age and the circumstances.

Can I move my money from one annuity to another?

Yes, and if you do it the right way, under Section 1035 of the federal tax code you won't have to pay taxes on any gains from the first annuity. Under a so-called 1035 exchange, you can exchange both annuities and life insurance policies for a new contract or policy, and you can also swap a life insurance policy for an annuity.

When it comes to trading an annuity for a life insurance policy, though, you would have to pay taxes on any investment gains.

What do I look for when buying an annuity?

If you decide to shop for an annuity, the editors of the website *www.Insure.com* have shopping tips for you to consider:

Decide how much you need: Figure out how much you have accumulated in other tax-deferred savings plans or pensions. Determine if there is a possibility that you could outlive your retirement assets.

Determine what kind of annuity you want: Do you want your investment to be steady and guaranteed? Then you may want to consider a fixed annuity. Are you willing to ride out the highs and lows of the stock market in the hopes of making more money? Then you may want to opt for a variable annuity.

Estimate how long you plan to have your money in the contract: As noted earlier, on most annuities you pay hefty surrender fees during the first seven to eight years on your contract. You also must have your money in the contract for a long time in order to have the tax deferral justify the high fees. It may take as long as fifteen years of tax-deferral to justify owning a variable annuity instead of a mutual fund.

Consider the financial strength of the provider: Most, though not all, states protect you from the insolvency of an annuity provider through *guarantee associations* or *guarantee funds*, but there are limits to that protection. In most states the limit is $100,000 for the current value of the annuity or $300,000 in total lifetime benefits. This means that if the annuity provider fails, you are no longer assured an income for the rest of your life. Check your insurer's financial strength.

Examine the *mortality and expense* fees: Fees vary by company and by contract, so make sure you are getting good value for what you are spending.

Other features to consider: Some annuities have features and riders that can meet a future need. For example, some variable annuities have long-term care riders that pay for nursing home costs. Others give you a bonus of one to five percent of your investment when you open an annuity.

How do the fees work in annuities? Are they really that expensive?

Fees on annuities are structured in a more complicated manner than for setting up an IRA or other type of investment account. You face three different types of annuity fees: the mortality and expense (or M&E) fee, the subaccount fee and the annual charge for contract maintenance.

M&E fee: This covers your insurance expenses, including the death benefit, and helps the insurer cover its risk in promising to pay you a lifetime income stream. This expense also covers commissions paid to the broker who sold you the annuity.

Sub account fee: This is the management charge for overseeing the investment accounts for your annuity.

Maintenance fee: Expect to see an annual contract maintenance charge of about $30 a year, with the average fee for a variable annuity costing about 2.12 percent, according to experts.

Note that on fixed and equity-indexed annuities the charges are similar to a no-load mutual fund. That is, there are no up-front charges for these contacts. Instead, the insurance company makes money on these by subtracting the amount of money it is required to pay on these by investing the assets in the annuities.

What is involved in opening an immediate annuity?

If at some point just before or after you have retired you find yourself with a sum of money, such as from a lump-sum pension plan, retirement savings or some other source, you may want to consider opening an immediate annuity, which gives you a steady stream of income right away with the distribution phase of a standard annuity contract.

With an immediate annuity, you purchase the annuity with a lump sum and immediately start receiving your monthly payments. Your payments can be fixed or variable. With fixed payments, the amounts are guaranteed for the period of the annuity. With variable annuities, those payments vary with the performance of your investments, although some immediate variable annuities guarantee a floor for your monthly payment.

When deciding on a fixed or variable annuity, you have to decide whether to trade off the comfort of a fixed, regular payment with the option to make more money if your investments produce healthy returns. Do not forget to factor in the cost of inflation, which will surely erode the value of fixed payments, while an immediate variable annuity provides income but also can gain or lose value in the stock or bond market.

Immediate annuities are generally recommended to retirees who are concerned about outliving their money. They are specifically not recommended for younger investors, who because of age take advantage of lower-cost IRAs and 401(k) plans.

How much can I realistically get out of an annuity?

That depends on what kind of annuity you buy and how it is structured. The factors affecting a lifetime annuity are going to be your age, gender and health, along with the expected return the insurance company believes it will make off your contributions to the contact. If you outlive the insurer's bet on your life expectancy, the company still pays you at its own loss.

Choosing between receiving lifetime income or payment over a certain period (ten years certain, twenty years certain) changes your payment amount. The longer the guaranteed period of payments, the lower each payment will be. Other than that, your age, gender and health are the biggest factors in the calculations that the insurance company's actuarial will use in figuring your life expectancy and how long the firm will be paying you.

Another factor is if you opt for what is called a *survivorship annuity payout*, which means that your retirement payments continue going to your spouse after you die. Again, this lengthens the amount of time the insurance company will be making payments, and so tends to lower the amount of each payment.

What exactly are the advantages and disadvantages of buying an annuity?

Annuities are a good choice if you are worried about 'outliving your money' since you get regularly scheduled income payments as long as you live. An annuity can be a good safety net as part of a retirement plan, although you should consider other investments, such as equities, to offset the effects of inflation and rising health care costs, as well as always maintaining an adequate emergency fund. Here are the advantages and disadvantages of annuities:

Advantages

- Payments come on a regular basis, and can even be for set amounts,

- Payments can be extended over a surviving spouse's lifetime,

- There is the security of having steady income with no new investment decisions to make,

- Investments grow tax-deferred until payments are received,

- Death benefits of pre-annuitized contracts go directly to beneficiaries, not to your estate,

- There is no limit on how much you can contribute,

- There are no income restrictions.

Disadvantages

- Fixed annuities carry significant inflation risk, lowering your buying power over time,

- Variable annuities may produce better results, but have up and down periods and won't generate a predictable regular payment,

- Taxes are due as you receive payments, with no option to defer payments if you have other income that year and end up in a higher bracket,

- You depend on the financial stability of the company backing the annuity for a long period of time.

Choosing an Advisor

How do I choose a professional to help me with my financial planning, insurance or estate planning?

There are many times when you will want some kind of professional advice. Often you can get answers to simple questions from your bankers, retirement account administrators or through some basic financial planning books or websites. At other times, you will want to work with a trained, experienced professional who will take a good look at your specific situation and make recommendations based on what is specifically best for you and your family.

In all cases, whether you are selecting a planner, attorney or other advisor, you want to cover a few basics.

- How much experience does the individual have with your specific type of issues?

- What is his or her professional training?

- What professional groups and accrediting bodies does he or she belong to?

- Are there any complaints registered with the governing authorities?

- What current or former clients can you contact for references?

In addition, you want to make sure you work out and understand the fee structure, as well as determining exactly how much time, help and guidance the advisor will provide, along with questions such as who files the paperwork, prepares taxes and deals with court filings.

What should I consider in choosing a financial planner?

Financial planners come from a variety of backgrounds. They often specialize in one area or another, such as investing or insurance, and can be unlicensed, licensed or a member of one or more financial planning organizations. The services offered can range from simple budgeting and retirement planning to investment options, insurance and estate planning. The various designations for financial planners are:

Certified Financial Planner (CFP): This designation means the planner has passed exams accredited by the Certified Financial Planner Board of Standards, a regulatory body that sets standards for CFPs throughout the country. The tests focus on the advisor's knowledge and ability to work with clients' estates, insurance investments and tax affairs.

Chartered Financial Consultant (ChFC): This designation is handled by the American College in Bryn Mawr, Pennsylvania, and is given to financial planners with several years of experience who also must complete ten courses and twenty hours of examinations in the areas of economics insurance, taxation, economics, estate planning and more.

Chartered Financial Analyst (CFA): This designation is awarded by the Institute of Chartered Financial Analysts. The CFA focuses heavily on portfolio management and securities analysis, but also addresses economics, financial accounting, portfolio management and professional standards.

Registered investment advisor: This designation means the advisor has been approved by the Securities and Exchange Commission to give financial advice to clients for a fee.

Registered representative: This is the official designation for a stockbroker or brokerage account executive and means the broker has passed the licensing exams administered by the National Association of Securities Dealers. In some states, brokers also have to complete local testing, as well.

How do I decide whether a planner is a good match for my needs?

Just as in choosing any other professional, you may want to start by asking friends and co-workers who they recommend. This can help you get a good idea of how the planner works with individual clients in areas such as simply handling investments, getting deeply involved in estate planning or preparing for a child's college education.

You should talk to several candidates, asking about their experience, training and other aspects of their professional background, including whether they have ever been disciplined for any reason. If so, get a full explanation and check it out if you are considering working with the advisor. Also ask your list of planners if they have experience working with clients in situations such as yours, and have them describe what they do and how they make their financial recommendations. You should also request a sample of their work to see a concrete example of whether their financial advice will be suited to your needs.

Finally, be sure to get referrals to clients your planners have worked with, and avoid anyone who refuses on the basis of confidentiality or other excuses. Reputable professionals should be willing and able to let you contact their other clients.

When it comes to money, don't be shy. Make sure you understand whether the planner is being paid by you (usually by the hour) for advice, as a fee-only planner or whether the planner receives commissions for selling you certain financial products. In general, fee-only planners are recommended, since commissioned planners may tend to focus on investments that pay them best.

What other questions should I make sure to ask?

Other important questions to ask include whether the planner will work with you directly or if you will be working with assistants and others in the office. Be sure to get the names and check out the backgrounds of any other professionals (such as attorneys, insurance agents or tax specialists) the planner will involve in your affairs.

In addition to determining how the planner is paid, find out how much the typical charge is for your kind of situation. An experienced planner should be able to give a reasonable estimate of costs. Also ask planners to give you a description of any of their conflicts of interest in writing if, for example, they sell insurance policies, securities or mutual funds and have business dealings with the providers of those financial products and receive referral fees or other types of compensation.

Lastly, be sure that any planner you choose gives you a written agreement that spells out the services you will receive, and file it for reference.

How can I check up on the background of a planner I'm considering?

Depending on the individual's background, training and expertise, you can start with his or her professional accrediting organization, or any licensing agencies such as those listed later in this chapter. You also can check with:

Certified Financial Planner Board of Standards, Inc.
Phone: 888-237-6275 - Website: www.CFP.net/search

North American Securities Administrators Association
Phone: 202-737-0900 - Website: www.nasaa.org

National Association of Insurance Commissioners
Phone: 816-842-3600 - Website: www.naic.org

Financial Industry Regulatory Authority (FINRA)
Phone: 301-590-6500 - Website: www.finra.org

National Fraud Exchange (fee involved)
Phone: 800-822-0416

Securities and Exchange Commission
Phone: 202-942-7040 - Website: www.sec.gov

Where can I find additional information and ways to evaluate and identify qualified financial planners?

A good starting place is with the various educational and accrediting bodies for financial planners. The list includes:

The National Association of Personal Financial Advisors
Phone: 800-366-2732. Website: www.napfa.org

The Certified Financial Planner Board of Standards
Phone: 888-237-6275. Website: www.cfp.net

The American College
Phone: 888-AMERCOL (263-7265). Website: www.theamericancollege.edu

CFA Institute (Chartered Financial Analysts)
Phone: 800-247-8132. Website: www.cfainstitute.org

What should I ask when choosing an insurance agent?

You can follow pretty much the same procedure for choosing an insurance agent or other professional advisor, gathering referrals and finding agents who specialize in your particular matters of concern. After that point, there are a few additional questions you should ask.

Is the agent properly licensed? Each state requires agents to be licensed to sell life insurance. Agents who sell variable products also must register with the National Association of Securities Dealers and may have to have additional licenses from the individual state office of securities.

Which companies does the agent represent? You should be familiar with the companies the agent represents, including their current financial condition, reputation and areas of expertise.

Does the agent have any professional affiliations or designations? Professional designations include Chartered Life Underwriter (CLU) and Life Underwriting Training Council Fellow (LUTCF). In addition, agents who also work as financial planners may have earned one of the financial planner designations discussed earlier.

Is the agent enrolled in a professional association? The major professional insurance association is The National Association of Life Underwriters (NALU), which provides local educational seminars that helps agents stay up to date.

What will the agent do for you? Rather than just selling policies, an agent should be able to advise you and explain various types of policies, insurance coverage and other matters, and be able to help you put together a comprehensive insurance plan with a clear picture of when you need to update, change or review your coverage.

How do I go about finding an attorney?

A good place to start, after referrals from friends and co-workers, is with your state and local bar associations, which generally compile referral lists by legal specialty. However, a referral is not the same as a recommendation. Some bar associations charge lawyers and firms to be included on the referral list or keep their lists open to any association member. You may want to pay attention to lawyers who serve on bar committees that offer training or handle public service work in specialized areas. When using a referral service, ask how attorneys qualify to be listed.

Other resources for finding an attorney include the *Martindale Hubbell Law Directory*, usually available at your local library, which lists 600,000 American and Canadian lawyers alphabetically by state and by categories, with a biography and other information, as well as a rating based on information supplied by fellow lawyers. You also can consult the *Who's Who in American Law* directory, which lists about 24,000 lawyers and their biographies. In addition, your community may operate its own lawyer referral service.

What kinds of questions should I ask?

After compiling a list of lawyers you want to consider, you can start with a preliminary telephone conversation before committing yourself to a personal interview. Some questions to ask include:

- Will you provide a free consultation?

- How long have you been in practice, overall and in this area?

- How many of your cases are similar to mine?

- Can you provide references, including other attorneys and clients?

- Do you represent any other clients that could create a conflict of interest in handling my case?

- What's your fee arrangement, and are your fees negotiable?

- What information do you need for the initial consultation?

Follow up with two or more personal interviews, concentrating on whether the attorney has the experience you need and is interested and available to take your case, as well as determining the fee arrangement and, most importantly, if you will be comfortable working with the attorney. Besides the questions from your phone interviews, you should determine how long each attorney has handled cases such as yours and what they expect the likely outcome to be for your situation.

You also should determine who you will work with, such as assistants, paralegals or outside professionals, as well as any additional fees you may have to pay and how they are billed, such as filing fees, copying, messenger services and more. You should get a written fee agreement (for instance, are you billed in six-minute or fifteen-minute intervals), as well as determining how often you will be billed and whether you need to pay a retainer. You also should discuss a schedule of work and a timeframe for consultations, meetings and completing specific work, such as compiling a will or establishing a trust.

What should I consider when choosing a tax accountant or CPA?

By now, you have a pretty good idea of what it takes to find and select a competent, qualified and experienced professional to help with your finances. In addition to the tips above, consider the following when hiring a tax accountant or CPA:

What kind of advice and service do you need? Depending on where you are in your financial life, you can choose between tax preparers, accountants and Certified Public Accountants (CPAs). The higher up the list you go, the more training, education and experience the professional will have, which will be reflected in their fees. CPAs, for example, must pass a rigorous, multi-day licensing test in most states and maintain their skills by taking courses that keep them up-to-date on changes in tax laws, rules and regulations.

How much will it cost? Most accountants and tax professionals either charge by the hour or a fixed amount agreed upon in advance, so make sure you determine how to structure your work up front. You should request a letter of agreement that outlines the amount of work, the schedule and any extra costs for additional services, as well as your's and the accountant's responsibilities for specific matters.

Questions to ask in choosing an accountant: You should determine how many clients the individual accountant is responsible for and if your situation is typical for the type of work the firm performs. Also clarify whether the accountant or someone else in the firm will be your main contact, and if any outside professionals (such as tax preparers, attorneys or others) will be involved with your work. Also review the accountant's educational background and recent professional courses, and ask for several references, ideally clients in similar situations to yours.

What do I do if I have questions about or problems with a financial professional?

There are a number of federal, state and local agencies you can contact, depending on what kind of financial advisor or professional you are consulting. Banks and financial institutions can be chartered at the federal and state level, for example, while insurance is regulated at the state level, with laws varying widely from state to state. There also are state and local consumer laws that cover other types of advisors, such as financial advisors, attorneys and others.

What are the various federal agencies that can help me obtain information about financial services and planning, government benefits programs and other consumer issues?

There are a number of federal agencies that oversee consumer financial affairs and government benefits programs, from commodities exchanges to federally chartered banks. For a complete list, visit *www.consumeraction.gov.*

Glossary

Adjusted Gross Income (AGI)
An interim calculation in the computation of income tax liability. It is computed by subtracting certain allowable adjustments from gross income

Administrator
A person appointed by the court to settle an estate when there is no will.

After-Tax Return
The return from an investment after the effects of taxes have been taken into account.

Aggressive Growth Fund
A mutual fund whose primary investment objective is substantial capital gains.

Alternative Minimum Tax
A method of calculating income tax that disallows certain deductions, credits, and exclusions. This was intended to ensure that individuals, trusts, and estates that benefit from tax preferences do not escape all federal income tax liability. People must calculate their taxes both ways and pay the greater of the two.

Annuity
An insurance-based contract that provides future payments at regular intervals in exchange for current premiums. Annuity contracts are usually purchased from banks,credit unions, brokerage firms, or insurance companies.

Asset
Anything owned that has monetary value.

Asset Allocation
The process of repositioning assets within a portfolio to maximize return for a given level of risk. This process is usually done using the historical performance of the asset classes within sophisticated mathematical models.

Asset Class
A category of investments with similar characteristics.

Audit
The examination of the accounting and financial documents of a firm by an objective professional. The audit is done to determine the records' accuracy, consistency, and conformity to legal and accounting principles.

Balanced Mutual Fund
A mutual fund whose objective is a balance of stocks and bonds. Such funds tend to be less volatile than stock-only funds.

Bear Market
When the stock market appears to be declining overall, it is said to be a bear market.

Beneficiary
A person named in a life insurance policy, annuity, will, trust, or other agreement to receive a financial benefit upon the death of the owner. A beneficiary can be an individual, company, organization, and so on.

Blue Chip Stock
The common stock of a company with a long histoiy of profitability and consistent dividend payments.

Bond
A bond is evidence of a debt in which the issuer promises to pay the bondholders a specified amount of interest and to repay the principal at maturity. Bonds are usually issued in multiples of $1,000.

Book Value

The net value of a company's assets, less its liabilities and the liquidation price of its preferred issues. The net asset value divided by the number of shares of common stock outstanding equals the book value per share, which may be higher or lower than the stock's market value.

Bull Market

When the stock market appears to be advancing overall, it is said to be a bull market.

Buy-Sell Agreement

A buy-sell agreement is an arrangement between two or more parties that obligates one party to buy the business and another party to sell the business upon the death, disability, or retirement of one of the owners.

Capital Gain or Loss

The difference between the sales price and the purchase price of a capital asset. When that difference is positive, the difference is referred to as a capital gain. When the difference is negative, it is a capital loss.

Cash Equivalents

Short-term investments, such as U.S. Treasury securities, certificates of deposit, and money market fund shares, that can be readily converted into cash.

Cash Surrender Value

The amount that an insurance policyholder is entitled to receive when he or she discontinues coverage. Policyholders are usually able to borrow against the surrender value of a policy from the insurance company. Loans that are not repaid will reduce the policy's death benefit.

CERTIFIED FINANCIAL PLANNER® Practitioner

A credential granted by the Certified Financial Planner Board of Standards, Inc. (Denver, CO) to individuals who complete a comprehensive curriculum in financial planning and ethics. CFP®, CERTIFIED FINANCIAL PLANNER® and federally registered CFP (with flame logo)® are certification marks owned by the Certified Financial Planner Board of Standards. These marks are awarded to individuals who successfully complete the CFP Board's initial and ongoing certification.

Certified Public Accountant (CPA)

A professional license granted by a state board of accountancy to an individual who has passed the Uniform CPA Examination (administered by the American Institute of Certified Public Accountants) and has fulfilled that state's educational and professional experience requirements for certification.

Charitable Lead Trust

A trust established for the benefit of a charitable organization under which the charitable organization receives income from an asset for a set number of years or for the trustor's lifetime. Upon the termination of the trust, the asset reverts to the trustor or to his or her designated heirs. This type of trust can reduce estate taxes and allows the trustor's heirs to retain control of the assets.

Charitable Remainder Trust

A trust established for the benefit of a charitable organization under which the trustor receives income from an asset for a set number of years or for the trustor's lifetime. Upon the termination of the trust, the asset reverts to the charitable organization. The trustor receives a charitable contribution deduction in the year in which the trust is established, and the assets placed in the trust are exempt from capital gains tax.

Chartered Financial Consultant (ChFC)

A professional financial planning designation granted by The American College (Bryn Mawr, PA) to individuals who complete a comprehensive curriculum in financial planning. Prerequisites include passing a series of written examinations, meeting specified experience requirements and maintaining ethical standards. The curriculum encompasses wealth accumulation, risk management, income taxation, planning for retirement needs, investments, estate and succession planning.

Chartered Life Underwriter (CLU)

A professional designation granted by The American College to individuals who complete a comprehensive curriculum focused primarily on risk management. Prerequisites include passing a series of written examinations, meeting specified experience requirements, and maintaining ethical standards. The curriculum encompasses insurance and financial planning, income taxation, individual life insurance, life insurance law, estate and succession planning, and planning for business owners and professionals.

COBRA

The Consolidated Omnibus Budget Reconciliation Act is a federal law requiring employers with more than 20 employees to offer terminated or retired employees the opportunity to continue their health insurance coverage for 18 months at the employee's expense. Coverage may be extended to the employee's dependents for 36 months in the case of divorce or death of the employee.

Coinsurance or Co-Payment

The amount an insured person must pay for a covered medical and/or dental expense if his or her insurance doesn't provide 100 percent coverage.

Commodities

The generic term for goods such as grains, foodstuffs, livestock, oils, and metals which are traded on national exchanges. These exchanges deal in both "spot" trading (for current delivery) and "futures" trading (for delivery in future months).

Common Stock

A unit of ownership in a corporation. Common stockholders participate in the corporation's profits or losses by receiving dividends and by capital gains or losses in the stock's share price.

Community Property

State laws vary, but generally all property acquired during a marriage - excluding property one spouse receives from a will, inheritance, or gift - is considered community property, and each partner is entitled to one half. This includes debt accumulated. There are currently nine community property states: Arizona, California, Idaho. Louisiana. Nevada, New Mexico, Texas, Washington, and Wisconsin.

Compound Interest

Interest that is computed on the principal and on the accrued interest.

Compound

interest may be computed continuously, daily, monthly, quarterly, semiannually, or annually.

Consumer Price Index

The U.S. Department of Labor's main indicator of inflation. The Consumer Price Index is calculated each month from the cost of some 400 retail items in urban areas throughout the United States.

Deduction
An amount that can be subtracted from gross income, from a gross estate, or from a gift, thereby lowering the amount on which tax is assessed.

Defined Benefit Plan
A qualified retirement plan under which a retiring employee will receive a guaranteed retirement fund, usually payable in installments. Annual contributions may be made to the plan by the employer at the level needed to fund the benefit. The annual contributions are limited to a specified amount, indexed for inflation.

Defined Contribution Plan
A retirement plan under which the annual contributions made by the employer or employee are generally stated as a fixed percentage of the employee's compensation or company profits. The amount of retirement benefits is not guaranteed; rather, it depends upon the investment performance of the employee's account.

Diversification
Investing in different companies, industries, or asset classes. Diversification may also mean the participation of a large coiporation in a wide range of business activities.

Dividend
A pro rata portion of earnings distributed in cash by a corporation to its stockholders. In preferred stock, dividends are usually fixed; with common shares, dividends may vary with the fortunes of the company.

Dollar Cost Averaging
A system of investing in which the investor buys a fixed dollar amount of securities at regular intervals. The investor thus buys more shares when the price is low and fewer shares when it rises, and the average cost per share is lower than the average price per share. This strategy does not protect against loss in declining markets and involves continuous investments, regardless of fluctuating price levels.

Efficient Frontier
A statistical result from the analysis of the risk and return for a given set of assets that indicates the balance of assets that may, under certain assumptions, achieve the best return for a given level of risk.

Employer-Sponsored Retirement Plan
A tax-favored retirement plan that is sponsored by an employer. Among the more common employer-sponsored retirement plans are 401(k) plans, 403(b) plans, simplified employee pension plans, and profit-sharing plans.

Equity
The value of a person's ownership in real property or securities; the market value of a property or business, less all claims and liens upon it.

ERISA
The Employee Retirement Income Security Act is a federal law covering all aspects of employee retirement plans. If employers provide plans, they must be adequately funded and provide for vesting, survivor's rights, and disclosures.

ESOP (employee stock ownership plan)
A defined contribution retirement plan in which company contributions must be invested primarily in qualifying employer securities. Estate Conservation Activities coordinated to provide for the orderly and cost-effective distribution of an individual's assets at the time of his or her death. Estate conservation often includes wills and trusts.

Estate Tax
Upon the death of a decedent, federal and state governments impose taxes on the value of the estate left to others (with limitations).

Executive Bonus Plan
The employer pays for a benefit that is owned by the executive. The bonus could take the form of cash, automobiles, life insurance, or other items of value to the executive.

Executor
A person named by the probate courts or the will to carry out the directions and requests of the decedent.

Fixed Income
Income from investments such as CDs, Social Security benefits, pension benefits, some annuities, or most bonds that is the same every month.

401(k)Plan
A defined contribution plan that may be established by a company for retirement. Employees may allocate a portion of their salaries into this plan, and contributions are excluded from their income for tax purposes (with limitations).

Contributions and earnings will compound tax deferred. Withdrawals from a 401(k) plan are taxed as ordinary income, and may be subject to an additional 10 percent federal tax penalty if withdrawn prior to age 59 !4.

403(b) Plan
A defined contribution plan that may be established by a nonprofit organization or school for retirement. Employees may allocate a portion of their salaries into this plan, and contributions are excluded from their income for tax purposes (with limitations). Contributions and earnings will compound tax deferred. Withdrawals from a 403(b) plan are taxed as ordinary income, and may be subject to an additional 10 percent federal tax penalty if withdrawn prior to age 59 Vz.

Fundamental Analysis
An approach to the stock market in which specific factors - such as the price-to-earnings ratio, yield, or return on equity - are used to determine what stock may be favorable for investment.

Gift Taxes
A federal tax levied on the transfer of property as a gift. This tax is paid by the donor. The first $12,000 a year from a donor to each recipient is exempt from tax. Most states also impose a gift tax. The gift tax exemption is indexed annually for inflation.

Holographic Will
A will entirely in the handwriting of the testator. Without witnesses, holographic wills are valid and enforceable only in some states.

Index
A calculation that uses a selection of stocks or bonds to gauge a certain market. The Dow Jones Industrial Average, for example, is an index of 30 large industrial companies on the New York Stock Exchange.

Individual Retirement Account (IRA)
Contributions to a traditional IRA are deductible from earned income in the calculation of federal and state income taxes if the taxpayer meets certain requirements. The earnings accumulate tax deferred until withdrawn, and then they are taxed as ordinary income. Individuals not eligible to make deductible

contributions may make nondeductible contributions, the earnings on which would be tax deferred.

Inflation

An increase in the price of products and services over time. The government's main measure of inflation is the Consumer Price Index.

Intestate

The condition of an estate left by a decedent without a valid will. State law then determines who inherits the property or serves as guardian for any minor children.

Investment Category

A broad class of assets with similar characteristics. The five investment categories include cash equivalents, fixed principal, equity, debt, and tangibles.

Irrevocable Trust

A trust that may not be modified or terminated by the trustor after its creation.

Joint and Survivor Annuity

Most pension plans must offer this form of pension plan payout that pays over the life of the retiree and his or her spouse after the retiree dies. The retiree and his or her spouse must specifically choose not to accept this payment form.

Joint Tenancy

Co-ownership of property by two or more people in which the survivor(s) automatically assumes ownership of a decedent's interest. Jointly Held Property Property owned by two or more persons under joint tenancy, tenancy in common, or, in some states, community property.

Keogh Plan

This retirement plan, named for Eugene Keogh, is designed for self-employed individuals. Up to $46,000 of self-employed income may be deducted from compensation and set aside into the plan.

Liability

Any claim against the assets of a person or corporation: accounts payable, wages, and salaries payable, dividends declared payable, accrued taxes payable, and fixed or long-term obligations such as mortgages, debentures, and bank loans.

Limited Partnership
Limited partnerships pool the money of investors to develop or purchase income-producing properties. When the partnership subsequently receives income from these properties, it distributes the income to its investors as dividend payments.

Liquidity
The ease with which an asset or security can be converted into cash without loss of principal.

Living Trust
A trust created by a person during his or her lifetime.

Lump-Sum Distribution
The disbursement of the entire value of a profit-sharing plan, pension plan, annuity, or similar account to the account owner or beneficiary. Lump-sum distributions may be rolled over into another tax-deferred account.

Marginal Tax Bracket
The range of taxable income that is taxable at a certain rate. Currently, there are six marginal tax brackets: 10 percent, 15 percent, 25 percent, 28 percent, 33 percent, and 35 percent.

Marital Deduction
A provision of the tax codes that allows all assets of a deceased spouse to pass to the surviving spouse free of estate taxes. This provision is also referred to as the unlimited marital deduction.

Money Market Fund
A mutual fund that specializes in investing in short-term securities and that tries to maintain a constant net asset value of $1.

Municipal Bond
A debt security issued by municipalities. The income from municipal bonds is usually exempt from federal income taxes. In many states, it is also exempt from state income taxes in the state in which the municipal bond is issued.

Municipal Bond Fund
A mutual fund that specializes in investing in municipal bonds. Mutual Fund A collection of stocks, bonds, or other securities purchased and managed by an investment company with funds from a group of investors.

Net Asset Value

The price at which a mutual fund sells or redeems its shares. The net asset value is calculated by dividing the net market value of the fund's assets by the number of outstanding shares.

Pooled Income Fund

A trust created by a charitable organization that combines the contributions of several donors and distributes income to those donors based on the earnings of the trust. The trust is managed by the charitable organization, and contributions are partially deductible for income tax purposes.

Portfolio

All the investments held by an individual or a mutual fund.

Preferred Stock

A class of stock with claim to a company's earnings, before payment can be made on the common stock, and that is usually entitled to priority over common stock if the company liquidates. Generally, preferred stocks pay dividends at a fixed rate.

Prenuptial Agreement

A legal agreement arranged before marriage stating who owns property acquired before marriage and during marriage and how property will be divided in the event of divorce. ERISA benefits are not affected by prenuptial agreements.

Price/Earnings Ratio (P/E Ratio)

The market price of a stock divided by the company's annual earnings per share. Because the P/E ratio is a widely regarded yardstick for investors, it often appears with stock price quotations.

Principal

In a security, the principal is the amount of money that is invested, excluding earnings. In a debt instrument such as a bond, it is the face amount.

Probate

The court-supervised process in which a decedent's estate is settled and distributed.

Profit-Sharing Plan

An agreement under which employees share in the profits of their employer. The company makes annual contributions to the employees' accounts. These funds usually accumulate tax deferred until the employee retires or leaves the company.

Prospectus
A document provided by mutual fund companies to prospective investors. The prospectus gives infomiation needed by investors to make informed decisions prior to investing in a specific mutual fund. The prospectus includes information on the minimum investment amount, the fund's objectives, past performance, risk level, sales charges, management fees, and any other expense information about the fund, as well as a description of the services provided to investors in the fund.

Qualified Domestic Relations Order (QDRO)
At the time of divorce, this order would be issued by a state domestic relations court and would require that an employee's ERISA retirement plan accrued benefits be divided between the employee and the spouse.

Qualified Retirement Plan
A pension, profit-sharing, or qualified savings plan that is established by an employer for the benefit of the employees. These plans must be established in conformity with IRS rules. Contributions accumulate tax deferred until withdrawn and are deductible to the employer as a current business expense.

Revocable Trust
A trust in which the creator reserves the right to modify or terminate the trust.

Risk
The chance that an investor will lose all or part of an investment.

Risk-Averse
Refers to the assumption that rational investors will choose the security with the least risk if they can maintain the same return. As the level of risk goes up, so must the expected return on the investment.

Rollover
A method by which an individual can transfer the assets from one retirement program to another without the recognition of income for tax purposes. The requirements for a rollover depend on the type of program from which the distribution is made and the type of program receiving the distribution.

Roth IRA
A nondeductible IRA that allows tax-free withdrawals when certain conditions are met. Income and contribution limits apply.

Security
Evidence of an investment, either in direct ownership (as with stocks), creditorship (as with bonds), or indirect ownership (as with options).

Simplified Employee Pension Plan (SEP)
A type of plan under which the employer contributes to an employee's IRA. Contributions may be made up to a certain limit and are immediately vested.

Single-Life Annuity
An insurance-based contract that provides future payments at regular intervals in exchange for current premiums. Generally used as a supplement to retirement income and pays over the life of one individual, usually the retiree, with no rights of payment to any survivor.

Split-Dollar Plan
An arrangement under which two parties (usually a corporation and employee) share the cost of a life insurance policy and split the proceeds.

Spousal IRA
An IRA designed for a spouse with no earned income. Between a spousal IRA and a regular IRA, the maximum combined contribution that a couple can make is $10,000 in 2008 ($11,000 if one spouse is age 50 or older or $12,000 if both are age 50 or older) or 100 percent of earned income, whichever is less. This total may be split between the two IRAs as the couple wishes, provided the contribution to either IRA does not exceed $5,000 ($6,000 for those aged 50 or older).

Tax Bracket
The range of taxable income that is taxed at a certain rate. Brackets are expressed by their marginal rate.

Tax Credit
Tax credits, the most appealing type of tax deductions, are subtracted directly, dollar for dollar, from your income tax bill.

Tax Deferred
Interest, dividends, or capital gains that grow untaxed in certain accounts or plans until they are withdrawn.

Tax-Exempt Bonds

Under certain conditions, the interest from bonds issued by states, cities, and certain other government agencies is exempt from federal income taxes. In many states, the interest from tax-exempt bonds will also be exempt from state and local income taxes.

Taxable Income

The amount of income used to compute tax liability. It is determined by subtracting adjustments, itemized deductions or the standard deduction, and personal exemptions from gross income.

Technical Analysis

An approach to investing in stocks in which a stock's past performance is mapped onto charts. These charts are examined to find familiar patterns to use as an indicator of the stock's future performance.

Tenancy in Common

A form of co-ownership. Upon the death of a co-owner, his or her interest passes to his or her chosen beneficiaries and not to the surviving owner or owners.

Term Insurance

Term life insurance provides a death benefit if the insured dies. Term insurance does not accumulate cash value and ends after a certain number of years or at a certain age.

Testamentary Trust

A trust established by a will that takes effect upon death.

Testator

One who has made a will or who dies having left a will.

Total Return

The total of all earnings from a given investment, including dividends, interest, and any capital gain.

Trust

A legal entity created by an individual in which one person or institution holds the right to manage property or assets for the benefit of someone else. Types of trusts include:

- *Testamentary Trust* - A trust established by a will that takes effect upon death;
- *Living Trust* - A trust created by a person during his or her lifetime;

- *Revocable Trust* - A trust in which the creator reserves the right to modify or terminate the trust;
- *Irrevocable Trust* - A trust that may not be modified or terminated by the trustor after its creation.

Trustee
An individual or institution appointed to administer a trust for its beneficiaries.

Trustee-to-Trustee Transfer
A method of transferring retirement plan assets from one employer's plan to another employer plan or to an IRA. One benefit of this method is that no federal income tax will be withheld by the trustee of the first plan.

Universal Life Insurance
A type of life insurance that combines a death benefit with a savings element which accumulates tax deferred at current interest rates. Under a universal life insurance policy, the policyholder can increase or decrease his or her coverage, with limitations, without purchasing a new policy.

Variable Universal Life Insurance
A type of life insurance that combines a death benefit with a savings element that accumulates tax deferred. Under a variable universal life insurance policy, the cash value in the policy can be placed in a variety of subaccounts with different investment objectives. The policyholder can transfer funds among the subaccounts as he or she wishes. Fees are charged after a certain number of transfers.

Volatility
The range of price swings of a security or market over time.

Welfare Benefit Plan
An employee benefit plan that provides such benefits as medical, sickness, accident, disability, death, or unemployment benefits.

Whole Life Insurance
A type of life insurance that offers a death benefit and also accumulates cash value, tax deferred at fixed interest rates. Whole life insurance policies generally have a fixed annual premium that does not rise over the duration of the policy. Whole life insurance is also referred to as "ordinary" or "straight" life insurance.

Will

A legal document that declares a person's wishes concerning the disposition of property, the guardianship of his or her children, and the administration of the estate after his or her death.

Yield

In general, the yield is the amount of current income provided by an investment. For stocks, the yield is calculated by dividing the total of the annual dividends by the current price. For bonds, the yield is calculated by dividing the annual interest by the current price. The yield is distinguished from the return, which includes price appreciation or depreciation.

Zero-Coupon Bond

This type of bond makes no periodic interest payments but instead is sold at a steep discount from its face value. Bondholders receive the face value of their bonds when they mature.

Index

Symbols

401(k) account 69
401(k) plans 110, 148, 151

A

A.M. Best 297
abusive trusts 142
academic awards 146
accumulation 271, 302
Adjusted Gross Income (AGI) 138
adjustments 85, 152, 153, 165, 173
airlines 93, 102
Albert Einstein 73
alimony 136, 156
alimony payments 156
alternative Minimum Tax 84, 172
American Council of Life Insurance 275
American Depository Receipts 104
American Savings Education Council 226
American Stock Exchange 90, 103
Amex 90
AMT 172, 173, 174
analysts 85, 90, 92, 95, 96, 113
annual percentage yield (APY) 76
annuities 69, 136, 148
annuitization 300
annuity 148, 236, 244, 247, 275, 298-306
antiques 72
art 72

Asianing method 301
asset allocation 71
auction 80
automobiles 72
awards 126-129, 137, 140, 145, 146

B

baby bonds 86
baby Boomers 114, 216, 230, 257
Bankrate.com 76
bankruptcy 72, 85
bearer bond 86
betting against a stock 100
blackout period 244, 245
blue chip 92
Boeing 247
bond-pricing model 88
bond call 88
bond Funds 106
bondholder 79, 80
bonds 71-89, 96, 105-124
book value 96
broker 80, 86, 93, 96, 98-105, 111
brokers 77, 80, 92, 98, 113, 297
bull markets 104
bunching 164

C

'cliff' formula 246

calculators 73, 74
capital gains 93, 107
captive agent 297
cash 69, 71-75, 80, 82, 91, 93, 95-96,
        101, 106, 109, 124
cash balance pensions 247
cash equivalents 71, 95
cash value 275-285, 288, 290- 291
casualty and theft losses 157
casualty losses 162
CDs 75-76, 107
certificates of deposit 71
certified financial planner 220, 226
certified public accountants 165-166
charitable deductions 157
charitable gifts and contributions 161
checking accounts 74
child and dependent care credit 151
child support 137, 149
closed-end fund 109
COBRA benefits 287
coins 72
college education 116-120, 133
commodities 72
common shares 91
common stock split 94
compound interest 73
Congress 126, 141-142, 173
consumer complaint ratios 296
Consumer Price Index 82
Convertible Bonds 85
convertible bonds 89
corporate bond 78, 85
Corporate bonds 85
Country Funds 113
coupon rate 77, 86
courtesy discounts 145
credit card accounts 69
Credit for the elderly or disabled: 151
credit life insurance 280
credits 125-127, 143, 149-169, 171,
        254, 255, 256, 264
current expenses 120, 223
Cyclical stocks 93

D

damages 149
day order 99
day trading 99
debentures 85
deep-discount brokers 98
defined benefit pension 234, 245, 247
Department of Labor 223, 226, 240,
        249
dependent care assistance 145
deposit insurance 74
discount 79, 80, 83, 86, 94, 95
discount brokerage 80
discount brokers 98
discrimination 149
dividend 72, 91, 95, 96, 106
dividend re-investment program 93
dividend yield 96
dividend yields 95
Dow Jones Industrial Average 92, 102,
        300
downgraded firm 88

E

'extended replacement' 290
earnings per share 97
Education IRA 122, 231, 233
electrical utilities 93
eligible educational institution 154
employee benefits 144
employee business expenses 163
employer-sponsored retirement plan 69
employer educational assistance payments
        145
Enrolled Agents 165
EPS 97
equity investments 71
estate 70, 72, 116, 124, 135, 137, 145,
        157, 161
estate planning 135
estate tax 124, 137
excludable Income 144
exercise price 89
expected family contribution 120, 128

extended term 282
extension 133, 143, 159, 172
extension deadline 172

F

face value 77, 79, 80, 82-84, 86, 88
fallen angel 87
FDIC 76
federal government 77
federal income tax 141, 147
Federal Reserve bank 80
filing status 138, 158-159, 170-171
financial advisor 69, 74
financial analysts 92, 95
financial institutions 80, 81, 83, 90,
        124, 133
financial stability 87
fixed-income instruments 72
fixed-income securities 71
fixed annuitization 300
fixed annuity 300
flexible benefits 145
floats 81, 84
focused fund 108
Ford 247
foreign bonds 72
foreign taxes 161
Free File Alliance 168
fund family 109
fund fees 111
fund manager 107, 108

G

'guaranteed replacement' 290
gains 82, 137, 150
General Electric 102
General Motors 247
general obligation 84
gifting 124
gifts 137, 164
global funds 113
gold 72, 108
Government Accounting Office 157
Government Pension Offset 268

grain 72
gross Income 138, 152
gross income adjustments 152
group legal services 145
growth stocks 93
guarantee associations 303
guaranteed returns 71, 78
guaranteed scholarships 130
guarantee funds 303

H

health insurance 152, 154-55, 156
health insurance credit 152
health savings account 154
hedging 110
high-water-mark method 301
high rate bonds 72
Hope tax credit 125
hospitalization premiums 144
hotels 93

I

IBM 247
immediate annuity 299, 304
income funds 107
income stocks 93
income taxes 160
independent insurance agents 297
independent insurance agents of
        America 297
individual development accounts 124
individual retirement account 69
inflation 73-74, 78, 79, 81-83, 108,
        114, 116-118, 120, 152, 154,
        173, 215, 220-222, 225, 227,
        231, 256, 265
inheritances 116, 117, 137, 146
initial public offering 89
institutional investors 81, 94
insurance 74, 84, 103, 114, 133, 137,
        140, 144-145, 149, 152, 154-
        156, 160, 163, 215, 223, 225,
        228-229, 236, 248, 253-254,
        261, 271-298, 300, 302-305

insured municipal bond 84
Interest 81, 82, 83, 133, 136-137,
       149, 154, 155, 161
interest rates 75, 78, 79, 80, 84, 86,
       88, 93, 108, 131, 132
International Funds 112
international funds 112, 113
international stocks 72
Internet 70, 98, 105
investment-grade bonds 87
investment banks 77, 89, 90
investment goals 69, 98, 107, 109
investments 69, 70, 71, 72, 73, 75,
       78, 83, 87, 90, 93, 94, 96, 98,
       99, 106, 108-110, 112-114,
       117-119, 123-124
investor 71-72, 77-81, 85-87, 93, 95,
       101-103, 109, 111
Investor deductions 158
IPO 89
IRAs 110, 121-122
itemized deductions 138, 143, 158-
       159, 164, 174

J

J.D. Power and Associates 296
John Sladek 113, 215
joint account 74
junk bonds 72, 79, 87, 106

K

Keogh 156

L

laddering 75
large-capitalization stocks 72
large caps 92
life expectancy 115, 148, 216, 221,
       235
life insurance 133, 145, 228, 271-
       285, 287, 302-303
life only annuity 298
lifetime learning credit 126
limit order 99

loads 111-112
loans 131-133
local tax preparation outlets 165
long-term care insurance 155, 160
low-water-mark 301
lump sum 75, 176, 243, 247

M

M&E fee 304
machinery 95
market-neutral funds 109
market cap 92
market capitalization 92
market conditions 87
market indexes 102
market orders 98
market timing 99
maturity value 77
maximum benefit 265
medical deductions 157
medical expenses 160
medicare 140, 144, 147, 155, 225,
       254, 257, 261, 268
medicare 'hospital insurance' 254
metal funds 108
mid-caps 92
minimum withdrawals 235
miscellaneous costs 156
miscellaneous deductions 157
miscellaneous employee deductions
       157
missing money 250
money market accounts 71, 74, 76
money market funds 106
Moody's Investors Service 86
Morningstar Inc. 111
mortality expense 278, 279
mortgage lenders 93
moving average 103
muni bonds 84
municipal bond 84
municipal bonds 77-78, 84-85, 106-
       107, 137, 146
mutual fund 75, 105, 106, 109-113

mutual funds 69, 105-106, 109-110, 111, 117, 120-121

N

Nasdaq 90, 94, 103
Nasdaq Composite Index 103
National Association of Securities Dealers 90
National Association of Unclaimed Property Administrators 224, 250
national debt 81
National Merit Scholarships 130
net asset value 110
newspaper 70
no-load funds 112
non-guaranteed term 273
non-guaranteed term life 273
non-refundable tax credits 151
NYSE Composite Index 103

O

OASDI ('old-age, survivor and disability insurance') 254
Offer in Compromise 176
offshore accounts 142
oil futures 70
Online Brokerages 98
on margin 101
Optional Cash Purchase Plans (OCPs) 93
oranges 72
Ordinary Permanent Life 274

P

Paper 85, 88
parking lots 75
par value 77, 78
patents 95
Patriot Bond 83
payout ratio 97
payroll savings plans 82
Penalties on early withdrawal 156
penalty 75, 79, 82, 119, 121-123

Pension Benefit Guaranty Corporation 248, 249, 250
pension plan document 251
Pension Rights Center 250
percent yield 96
Perkins Loans 132
permanent policies 276
personal property taxes 161
Phantom taxes 86
plants 85, 95
point-to-point, method 300
pork 70, 72
pork bellies 70, 72
precious metals 70, 72
predicted growth 95
preferred stock 91
premium 78, 79, 80
prepaid plan 118, 119
price/earning ratios 95
price/earnings ratio 95
principal 72, 77-84, 86, 119
principal of securities 81
private activity bonds 84
private insurance 84
prizes 146
professional money managers 100
projected revenue 95
projected revenues 87
property 71-74, 125
property taxes 161
prospectus 89, 113
proxy 105
public assistance 147

Q

qualified retirement plan 156
Quant Funds 108
quick issue 277

R

range 71, 97, 103, 107, 109, 116-118, 121
ratchet method 301
rate of return 73, 74, 82, 118

real estate 70, 72, 157, 161, 221, 225,
      237
redemption payments 83
reduced paid up 282
refundable tax credits 149, 150-151,
      171
registered bond 86
Renter's insurance 292
retired couple 272
retirees 75, 78, 93
retirement benefits 115, 148
retirement home 71
retirement plan 69, 113, 136, 156, 169,
      215, 219, 222-224, 230, 231,
      236, 241, 246, 249
return on equity 97
revenue bonds 84, 85
reverse stock split 94
risk factors 71, 74, 116
Roth IRA 230, 232-234, 236
Roth IRAs 110, 121
Russell 2000 103

S

sales charges 112
Sarbanes-Oxley Act 245
savings account 69, 74, 75
savings bonds 78, 81, 82
scholarships 117-119, 125-130
secondary buyer 79, 80
secondary market 78, 79, 81, 83-84,
      86-87, 90, 109
secondary offering 89
second home 69
section 1035 302
sector funds 108
Securities and Exchange Commission
      89, 104, 113
self-employed 140, 143, 155-156, 175
self-employed retirement plans 156
self-employment taxes 155
separate trading of registered interest 81
SEP IRAs 121
series EE 81-83

series EE/E 82
series EE Bonds 81, 82
series HH Bonds 81, 82
series I 82
series I Bonds 82
short-term bonds 71, 77
short-term Treasury bills 71
short selling 100
silver 72, 108
simplified issue 277
Social Security Administration 141,
      147
Social Security benefits 115, 137,
      138, 147-148, 216, 229, 246,
      254-258, 262, 263-269
Social Security payments 114, 147
Social Security taxes 142, 150, 155
special account 120
Standard & Poor's 86
Standard & Poor's ratings 297
standard deduction 138, 144, 153,
      157, 159
stock funds 106
Stock indexes 102
stock options 89
stock ownership 72, 105
stocks 69, 70, 71, 72, 75, 88, 90, 91,
      92, 93, 94, 95, 96, 98, 99, 100,
      101-124
stop price 99
strike price 89
strippable 84
STRIPS 81, 83-84, 121
student loan 127, 133, 138, 154
summary annual report 248-249
summary plan description 248-249
super gift 123
Supreme Court 142
surrender period 301
survivorship annuity payout 305

T

'the long bond' 84
tangibles 71, 72

tax-free 78, 106-108, 110, 118, 121, 122, 126-127, 137, 155
taxable Income 138
tax attorney 166
tax bracket 143, 144, 146, 149, 171
tax credits 125, 126
taxes 73, 74, 81, 82, 84, 86, 87, 106, 110, 118, 121-127, 135-136, 138-175
Tax Freedom Day 141
taxpayer ID number 142
tax preparer 140, 148, 164, 166, 168
tax refund 126, 139, 143, 150
tax scams 142
tax software 158, 166, 167, 168
tax table 171
term insurance 275-277, 282, 284
term life insurance 273, 276
  Non-Guaranteed Term Life 273
the appeals process 269
the big board 90
the windfall elimination provision 268
thrifts 76
time horizon 70
TIPS 81, 83, 121
total return 96
traditional IRA 231
travel agencies 93
Treasury 71, 77-84, 87, 109, 121, 132
Treasury bills 71, 77, 80, 109
Treasury Inflation-Protected Securities 81
Treasury issues 79, 81, 87
triple A 87
tuition 71, 117-120, 122-127, 128, 134

U

underwriters 89
universal life 274
unsecured debt 69
US Treasury bills 77, 80, 109
US Treasury bonds 77

V

'vested' 246
variable annuity 300, 303-304
variable life 275
venture capital 70
volatile investments 71
volatile stocks 71, 99
volatility 70, 97
volume 96

W

W-2 reports 257
waivers 118, 128, 295, 302
Wal-Mart 217
Wall Street 90
warrant 101
welfare payments 147
widows' and widowers' benefit statement 251
wine 72
withholding tax 139
worker's compensation 137, 145

Y

yield 70, 72, 76, 79-80, 87-88, 96, 106, 110
yield to maturity 88

Z

zero-coupon government bonds 81
zero coupon bonds 78
zeroes 86